T5-BYY-558

Maryland and the Empire, 1773

MARYLAND BICENTENNIAL STUDIES

Sponsored by the Maryland Bicentennial Commission

Monographs

A Spirit of Dissension: Economics, Politics, and the Revolution in Maryland, by Ronald Hoffman

Documentary Editions

Maryland and the Empire, 1773: The Antilon-First Citizen Letters, by Peter S. Onuf

Maryland and the Empire, 1773

THE ANTILON–FIRST CITIZEN LETTERS

EDITED AND WITH AN INTRODUCTION BY PETER S. ONUF

THE JOHNS HOPKINS UNIVERSITY PRESS   BALTIMORE AND LONDON

Publication of this volume was assisted by the
Maryland Bicentennial Commission.

Copyright © 1974 by The Johns Hopkins University Press
All rights reserved. No part of this book may be
reproduced or transmitted in any form or by any means,
electronic or mechanical, including photocopying,
recording, xerography, or any information storage and
retrieval system, without permission in writing
from the publisher.

The Johns Hopkins University Press, Baltimore, Maryland 21218
The Johns Hopkins University Press Ltd., London

Library of Congress Catalog Card Number 73-8128
ISBN 0-8018-1547-9

Library of Congress Cataloging in Publication data
will be found on the last printed page of this book.

dedicated to:

Kristin K. Onuf

Rachel K. Onuf

Jack P. Greene

George Wilkins

Peter and Josie Coy

Todd Rundgren

Brian Wilson and the Beach Boys

my parents, Bronis and Barbara Onuf

Contents

Preface

Daniel Dulany, Jr., was the great lawyer and intellect of colonial Maryland. Charles Carroll of Carrollton, although only fifteen years younger, was a leading figure in independent Maryland's Revolutionary generation. Their careers, and importance, were made in different eras. Dulany is best remembered as author of the *Considerations*, one of the ablest protests against British taxation; Carroll was a signer of the Declaration of Independence. During the first few months of 1773, however, their careers crossed. The results of that confrontation, Dulany's "Antilon" letters and Carroll's "First Citizen" replies in the *Maryland Gazette*, are published in this volume.

The exchange was prompted by the continuing controversy over the constitutionality of Governor Robert Eden's 1770 proclamation establishing officers' fees in the colony. Eden's proclamation followed the failure of the assembly to provide legislation for that purpose. It was defended by Dulany as necessary to good government, and attacked by Carroll as the usurpation of the legislature's function by arbitrary prerogative. The issue was peculiarly local; its implications, however, were as large as the first British Empire, and central to the constitutional crisis that destroyed it in the American Revolution.

Despite the local, provincial context of the fee controversy, it is extremely revealing of American political and constitutional theory before the Revolution. Marylanders faced the same questions all Americans faced in the years before independence. The dilemma of the Revolutionary generation was not born new in 1776: its possibilities had already been explored and developed. In Maryland, the tension between parliamentary supremacy and local autonomy was reflected in the fee controversy; Dulany and Carroll described the problem and promise to the people of Maryland. When their debate was done, it was clear that Dulany and the colonial era were passing; and it was just as clear that the era of revolution was arriving.

A previous edition of these letters was published in 1902 by Elihu S. Riley.[1] Aside from a brief narrative of events and a discussion of Annapolis society, the texts were not supported by annotation or explanation. A critical framework is essential if these documents are to have any place in the literature of the Revolution; a modern editorial apparatus is necessary if they are to be intelligible. It is hoped that this edition will satisfy these requirements and enable the letters to receive the attention they deserve. The correspondence is taken from the *Maryland Gazette* and all peculiarities in spelling and punctuation are preserved, with the exception of a few obvious typographical errors. Bracketed numbers in the text refer to pagination in the *Gazette*. The editor's footnotes are referred to by Arabic numerals, the footnotes in the original documents by letters and symbols.

My teacher, Jack P. Greene, and my wife Kristin have read the introduction carefully and offered many valuable suggestions. Kristin was also extremely helpful in discovering the original source of many citations. I am indebted to Mrs. D. J. Mistri, of the Classics Department at the University of Virginia, for her invaluable assistance in locating and translating many of the Latin quotations.

[1] Elihu S. Riley, ed., *Correspondence of "First Citizen"—Charles Carroll of Carrollton—and "Antilon"—Daniel Dulany, Jr., 1773, with a History of Governor Eden's Administration in Maryland, 1769–1776* (Baltimore, 1902).

Maryland and the Empire, 1773

Introduction

THE CONSTITUTIONAL BACKGROUND

There was a period of apparent peace and quiet in the American colonies from the collapse of nonimportation in 1770 to the Boston Tea Party in late 1773. The *Gaspée* incident in March 1772 was one of the few exceptions to the new rule of order, and provided a link between the earlier and later periods of unrest. But the first British Empire and its supposedly perfect constitutional order were as surely crumbling in this period as when the issue of taxation first challenged it, or when the advent of hostilities later destroyed it. The absence of great events merely disguised the continuing presence of great, unresolved constitutional questions.

The pre-1764 empire, and the old constitution, thrived on their inconsistencies and on the "benign neglect" of imperial authorities.[1] The cautious policy of Lord North and the ministry after 1770 might be mistaken for more "neglect," for a return to those good old days before questions were asked and doubts expressed. Any similarity, however, between the empire before 1764 and after 1770 was only apparent. North hoped that the absence of grievances would isolate colonial radicals; the ministry could then reorganize the empire along more rational lines. But colonial sensitivity

---

[1] John C. Miller, *Origins of the American Revolution* (Boston: Little, Brown & Co., 1943), p. 325.

about local rights and liberties continued to grow. English "neglect" on the eve of the Revolution was merely tactical; without formal, articulated, and institutionalized guarantees for American rights, there was nothing in this neglect to dispel constitutional anxieties. Neglect could not undo the damage already done to the constitution, or revive Americans' old, unquestioning faith in its perfection.

A simple succession of events—an escalation of provocation and protest—cannot explain the timing of the Revolution. There are enough discontinuities in the narrative, including the 1770–1773 hiatus, to demand a broader ideological explanation, a definition of the intellectual context which shaped American perceptions of events at home and abroad, and of the American "mind" which recalled old oppressions and projected new ones. That the Revolution was caused by ideas, as well as events, is an ancient and familiar truism. John Adams wrote Thomas Jefferson in 1815, "the Revolution was in the minds of the people, and this was effected, from 1760 to 1775." Building on Adams's insight, Bernard Bailyn has illuminated many of the hitherto obscure connections between ideas and incidents in his *Ideological Origins of the American Revolution*.[2]

But if we have begun to overcome the old reliance on narrative as explanation, we are still influenced by an interpretation closely tied to unfolding events. Bailyn has gone beyond those older historians who unsympathetically saw American constitutional arguments as mere expedients that masked a long-standing urge to escape the imperial connection. But he has oversimplified the problem by sympathetically considering the Revolution as the reluctant recognition of the issue of sovereignty; that is, he argued that the tortured constitutional meandering of patriot leaders could be reduced to this irreducible core, which remained after independence. The criterion of relevancy for either argument is the relation of ideas—or events—to the unmasking—or realization—of sovereign pretensions. A corollary test is the connection of local debates on these issues with the national movement toward independence: to what extent did a local issue or event contribute to the intercolonial cause?

[2] Cambridge: Harvard University Press, Belknap Press, 1967. The Adams letter is cited on p. 1.

We are thus victims of two basic and misleading simplifications. First, by organizing our inquiries around the sovereignty concept, we undervalue and misinterpret the intrinsic importance of much American constitutional theory and practice before and after independence. Patriots and revolutionaries, as well as constitution-makers, sought to *avoid* the issue of sovereignty and develop a political theory in which the ultimate power was not located within government. The significance of colonial constitutional thought transcends the simple renunciation of English sovereignty; it was part of the new nation's efforts to avoid another institutional sovereign on the British model. Second, by considering the Revolution a national movement, intracolonial developments are slighted. We are led to underestimate the role of colonies and states in early American constitutional history.

The concern with locating sovereignty and the interpretation of the Revolution as a national movement are mutually supporting, and misleading. Because earlier efforts at intercolonial union and cooperation were failures, we are surprised to discover a surge of national feeling during the Revolution. Knowing the attachment of Americans to colony and state governments, we are amazed at the ease with which the founding fathers instituted a sovereign, national government. Both developments are seen as sudden and dramatic breaks with the past. But the "miracles" of Revolution and constitution are modern inventions; the era had its own logic and continuity. The quest for constitutionally limited government, not sovereignty, was its motif. Because states never aspired to what we call sovereignty, there was no necessary tension between them and a suprastate government with superintending authority. It was possible in 1787 to consider the new constitution the ultimate and perfected instrumentality of interstate cooperation.

In another sense, sovereignty may still be considered the ultimate question of the Revolutionary era.[3] It was not a question,

---

[3] "Sovereignty was the single most important abstraction of politics in the entire revolutionary era," according to Gordon Wood, in his *Creation of the American Republic, 1776–1787* (Chapel Hill: University of North Carolina Press, 1969), p. 345. The concept was "absolutely crucial. . . . It was over this issue that the Revolution was fought," Bailyn writes in *Ideological Origins*, p. 198; but goes on to show that Americans believed sovereignty "in some

however, of who had it or where it was located. Constitutional developments of this period reflected, instead, American efforts to resist sovereignty in its institutional form of king-in-parliament; and after independence, to reduce—or elevate—it to an abstraction which would no longer threaten their constitutions.

The doctrine of the "absolute sovereignty of the crown-in-parliament" was already "the dominant and central working assumption in British politics" by mideighteenth century.[4] The assumption was not, nonetheless, unchallenged. Opposition theorists of the right and left saw parliament and its authority in narrow, institutional terms. The coalescence of the branches of government and of various interests in the state which, in orthodox theory, justified parliament's pretensions to sovereignty, was to the opposition evidence of parliament's "corruption." The sovereignty concept proposed that parliament be considered the state itself. But the opposition believed the Whig ascendancy left important state interests unrepresented. Parliament was not the state, only a faction within it. It might, in pursuit of its own ends, endanger true national interests and liberties.[5]

---

sense divisible." Though they were eventually forced to accept parliamentary sovereignty—to the extent of declaring independence of it—constitutionalism remained alive in America, "preparing the way for a new departure in the organization of power." *Ibid.*, pp. 198–229. Bailyn notes an indebtedness to Andrew C. McLaughlin's "The Background of American Federalism," *American Political Science Review* 12 (1918), 215–40, and his argument "that the essential qualities of American federal organization were largely the product of the practices of the old British Empire as it existed before 1764." By applying this constitutional experience, "realistic and pragmatic" Americans sought to avoid the either-or, all-or-nothing implications of sovereignty. That unlimited parliamentary power would precipitate revolution, as the last defense of local rights, was demonstrated in the exchange between Governor Thomas Hutchinson and the Massachusetts Assembly in 1773, in *The Speeches of His Excellency Governor Hutchinson* (Boston, 1773). Sovereignty may thus be accorded a central place in precipitating American constitutional thought, but it is a mistake to infer that it was ever more than an "abstraction," or that the concept is of any analytical value in discussing the actual organization of authority in the American constitutions.

[4] F. H. Hinsley, *Sovereignty* (London: Watts, 1966), p. 152.

[5] For a good discussion of opposition theory, see Isaac Kramnick, *Bolingbroke and His Circle* (Cambridge: Harvard University Press, 1968), pp. 148–59. According to Bolingbroke, the party out of power was the guardian of national liberty. He considered "Walpole's government . . . factious . . . and his own Opposition the true national power." He no longer relied on "the functional differentiation of branches of government" to defend liberty, but instead on "an opposition party whose avowed principle was the transcendence of party."

While orthodox English doctrine anticipated modern sovereignty theory in many ways, it differed in one important respect. The English concept was tied to particular institutions and, whatever its claims to universality, to the community in which those institutions existed. It was one thing to say that there must be a final authority in every community, but another to say that a particular parliament was that authority; or that parliament was the state itself, or the entire empire. Americans knew what to do with sovereignty-as-abstraction, but neither they nor the first British Empire could cope with the institutional sovereignty of the British parliament.[6]

Americans developed two successive defenses against parliamentary sovereignty. First, they adopted the English opposition position that parliament's power was not unlimited within the

---

[6] Modern sovereignty theory avoids the identification of sovereignty with a particular branch of government, or even with the government as a whole. Sovereignty, according to Hinsley's *Sovereignty*, is the principle of association in a polity, the mutuality of state (the government) and community. "So long as the relations between the community and state continue to require regulation—there will be need for the concept of sovereignty, which authorizes and justifies the regulating authority" (p. 235). Hinsley stops short of making the community itself sovereign, an abstraction which Americans found harmless and useful. But this abstraction, as much as the older idea of a sovereign king or government, could be dangerous to constitutional government. Bertrand de Jouvenel, in his *On Power* (Boston: Beacon Paperback, 1969), argues that sovereignty only makes sense when applied to one extreme or the other: they are, in fact, identical. "Theories like those of divine right [or omnipotent parliament] and popular sovereignty, which pass for opposites, stem in reality from the same trunk, the idea of sovereignty—the idea, that is, that somewhere there is a right to which all other rights must yield" (p. 27). In a "purely nominalist conception of society," the sovereignty notion may be "intelligible." "Society consists only of associated men, whose disassociation is always possible" (p. 45). Power may be absolute in society, when there is absolute freedom to remove from society. De Jouvenel's answer to sovereignty is very similar to Hinsley's definition of sovereignty: while for Hinsley sovereignty is the principle which restrains both government and community, De Jouvenel calls for a constitutionalist solution. "The advances in law and liberty for which democracy gets the credit were in fact the fruit of complex governmental machinery in which no human will, whether single or collective, was sovereign" (p. 253). Hinsley's definition is mystifying in anything but a constitutional government. Where else is there a "regulating authority"? It is perhaps more helpful to adopt De Jouvenel's distinction between sovereignty and constitutionalism, than Hinsley's identification, or confusion, of the two concepts. Americans, however, were accustomed to believe that sovereignty or absolute authority was only dangerous when exercised by government, and that it could be integrated into their constitutions if attributed to the people or community.

English constitution and community. Second, when forced to concede that it was, Americans argued that their colonies were distinct communities, not under the British constitution at all. Both responses were constitutionally plausible, if not strictly "legal."[7]

The English constitution had not yet become the exclusive preserve of king-in-parliament, Blackstone and the Whig establishment notwithstanding. Even while claiming omnipotence for parliament, the *Commentaries* paid their respects to natural law, thus recognizing an indigenous constitutional tradition.[8] That tradition had been

[7] The most significant trend in Revolutionary thought was the gradual emergence of the concept of colonies as distinct communities. Professor Charles Howard McIlwain in his *The American Revolution: A Constitutional Interpretation* (Ithaca, N.Y.: Cornell University Press Paperback, 1966) thought he had discovered a legal warrant for the Revolution in the alleged distinction between realm and dominions, "that acts of the Parliament bind not dominions of the king elsewhere" (p. 20). This view had been exploded by R. L. Schuyler in *Parliament and the British Empire* (New York: Columbia University Press, 1929), who showed that "the jurisdiction of parliament was never confined to the realm of England [and] from the earliest time [was] . . . imperial in the scope of . . . authority" (p. 33). See also A. Berriedale Keith, *Constitutional History of the First British Empire* (Oxford: Clarendon Press, 1930), pp. 374–83, for an exhaustive attack on McIlwain's position. McIlwain was certainly on shaky legal grounds, and his use of William Molyneux's arguments in *The Case of Ireland* (London, 1770; originally published in 1698) was anachronistic; but there was considerable authority for the distinction between English and colonial jurisdictions, even if the colonies were not legally autonomous. Sir William Blackstone asserted in the *Commentaries on the Laws of England* (London, 1821), 1:112, that the colonies were "no part of the mother country, but distinct, though dependent dominions." This contention was somewhat at odds with the English doctrine that colonies were "mere corporations," since, as such, they would have been part of the mother country. And, if parliament were sovereign in English constitutional theory because it was the political embodiment of the English community, the nature of its authority *outside* that community was radically different. In the colonies, it was not the community ruling itself. There were practical benefits for imperial government in considering the colonies separate communities: namely, that the colonies thereby had no claim to the common law and there were thus no limits to royal or parliamentary authority there. But the distinction also encouraged Americans to picture their community interests as opposed to, rather than as identified with, parliamentary sovereignty. Ultimately, English constitutional tradition, English history, and natural law doctrine authorized the community to defend its own interests. The argument that King George III was "King of Massachusetts-Bay" and that that colony was not "subject to the King as the Head . . . of another people, in whose Legislative they have no voice or interest" (*Speeches of Hutchinson*, pp. 112–13), was an attempt to reconcile community interests and English authority. The combination of parliamentary omnipotence and multiple statuses and jurisdictions in the empire was, finally, a contradiction in terms, whose dialectical resolution destroyed the empire.

[8] Blackstone, *Commentaries*, 1:94, "if the parliament will positively enact a thing to be done which is unreasonable, I know of no power in the ordinary

carried on, in various guises, from the era of the Glorious Revolution, through Tory and Commonwealth Whig attacks on Walpolean hegemony to midcentury radicalism.[9]

During the pre-Revolutionary debate, Americans gradually came to believe they alone remained uncorrupted and capable of defending the last vestiges of English liberty. Ideologically, the debate was between advocates of orthodox and opposition theories of the constitution: in fact, the debate was the inevitable result of the failure to extend parliamentary sovereignty to America. How could it be anything but disastrous to reduce the confusion of jurisdictions and legal systems in the empire to the absolute and unlimited authority of the insular legislature? Parliament might pretend to be England; it was even less convincing in the role of British empire incarnate.[10]

Americans first sought salvation in slavish imitation of the British original, which led the assemblies dangerously toward similar pretensions of legislative supremacy.[11] With a last unconsciously

---

forms of the Constitution, that is vested with the authority to controul it." But, 1:44, "Upon these two foundations, the law of nature and the law of revelation, depend all human laws; that is to say *no human laws should be suffered to contradict these*" (emphasis added). According to Sir William Holdsworth in *A History of English Law* (6th ed., London: Methuen & Co., 1938), "Blackstone's training as a lawyer, his sympathy with the Whig doctrine which had triumphed at the Revolution, and consequently with the theory that men had natural rights given them by a divinely ordained law of nature, made him susceptible to both the legal and political influences which induced an hesitation to accept all the consequences of the theory of sovereignty," 10:529.

[9] Caroline Robbins, *The Eighteenth Century Commonwealthman* (Cambridge: Harvard University Press, 1959); Kramnick, *Bolingbroke*; Bailyn, *Ideological Origins*, and *The Origins of American Politics* (New York: Knopf, 1968).

[10] See Richard Koebner, *Empire* (Cambridge: Cambridge University Press, 1961). The use of the expression "British empire" "was formally authorized by the foundation of the Imperial Crown and by the union" of England and Scotland (p. 84). Empire meant different things in Britain and America, however, and the Stamp Act helped precipitate the distinction. Was the imperial relationship to be one of subordination or coordination? "Obedience could be made the main issue in the name of imperial authority, or the objections of the colonists could be admitted in the interests of the unity of the Empire" (p. 153).

[11] Professor Jack P. Greene used the term "mimesis" in his "Political Mimesis: A Consideration of the Historical Roots of Legislative Behavior in the British Colonies in the Eighteenth Century," *American Historical Review* 75 (1969), 337–60. The dangers of too powerful assemblies are detailed in Wood, *Creation of the Republic*, pp. 403–9.

ironic bow to the constitution-as-ultimate-institution, Americans finally embraced the sovereignty concept, fully convinced the only limitation on power was independence of it. America's legendary caution in approaching independence, that is sovereignty, resulted from an unwillingness to see the constitution reduced to nothing more than the will of parliament.

With independence, a painful decade of constitutional reconstruction began. Sovereignty, so easy to define in the negative as independence, was much harder to integrate into actual government. In fact, it was only manageable, and appropriate, in foreign policy.[12] In other respects, early American constitutional history, often seen as the emergence of a sovereign federal government, may be read as an evasion of, and retreat from, the sovereignty concept. Popular sovereignty, however impressive in the abstract, merely enabled Americans to avoid the institutional question of ultimate authority. If sovereign authority were outside government, government might consist of balanced, coordinate branches.[13]

Parliamentary sovereignty eventually left "mixed" and "balanced" government far behind; it had already destroyed the empire. Though independent Americans were obliged to deal with sovereignty—after all, it had launched their republican careers—they were determined not to be destroyed by it. The extent of their success is revealed in the perennial debate over its location. Those unseemly anomalies, concurrent and coordinate sovereign-

---

[12] The concept of sovereignty is an essential convention in international law and theory. If all the American states were "sovereign" in relation to each other, there could by definition be no authority to settle disputes among them; and, according to the mechanism of the international balance of power, they would—if not united—be easily overwhelmed by European powers. The clear impact of the sovereignty concept on the organization of American states for foreign policy—that there must be a single, ultimate authority—is misleading when applied to constitutional developments within and among the states. Unity in foreign policy and coordination of the states were designed to preserve, not supplant, the multiplicity of jurisdictions and authorities. For an excellent discussion of foreign policy in the constitutional era, see Felix Gilbert, *To the Farewell Address* (Princeton, N.J.: Princeton University Press, 1961).

[13] This theme is developed persuasively in Wood, *Creation of the Republic*, pp. 532–36. "Relocating sovereignty in the people by making them 'the fountain of all power' seemed to make sense of the entire [Federal] system. . . . By attempting to confront and retard the thrust of the Revolution with the rhetoric of the Revolution, the Federalists fixed the forms for the future discussion of American politics" (p. 562).

ties, which so offend modern scholars, marked the victory of limited, constitutional government over an institutional sovereign on the British model. By making the people, or even the constitution itself, sovereign, Americans saved their resurrected constitutions from the corruption and encroachment of another institutional sovereignty.

Sovereignty, in this negative sense, was the central problem of American constitutionalism. In order to support and not jeopardize the constitution, it had to be isolated from government, to be abstract, not institutional. There was only one sense in which revolutionary sovereignty was institutional, and that was in independence from English institutions. As such, it was only a hiatus in a constitutional continuum.

The reconstitution of American governments was the main business of American politics in the years after independence. Much effort was expended in compensating for the vacuum left by the overthrow of English authority and for the absence of English conditions in the new states. There were no satisfactory existing models. The imperial crisis demonstrated to Americans the gap between British government and its constitutional principles. The old colony governments, left to the lower houses with shadowy executives and upper houses, were incomplete. And simultaneously with the constitutional crises within the states, Americans had to find a substitute for the superintending imperial authority, to establish their system of states on a peaceful, equitable and permanent basis of coordination.[14]

---

[14] This coordination of the states was the clear mandate of "national" government after independence. Imperial authority in this area had never been challenged and it was assumed Congress would succeed to it. Since in modern international relations theory, a state which surrenders its foreign policy prerogative and international independence is no longer sovereign, it is considered that congressional conduct of foreign affairs, and the war, marked a transfer of sovereignty from the states. Yet it is more likely that Americans considered congressional authority to be complementary, rather than in opposition to, state "sovereignty." The case for the United States as an "international organization" by James Brown Scott (*The United States of America: A Study in International Organization*, New York: Oxford University Press, 1920) is anachronistic in a quite different way. Scott hoped to find a model for an effectual League of Nations in the federal constitution, a well-meaning but, according to modern ideas, absurd suggestion. The American states did seek to guarantee their "sovereign" existence under the constitution, but they had a considerably more modest concept of what this entailed than do modern

12 *Introduction*

American solutions to these constitutional problems marked a dramatic departure from the orthodox idea of the British constitution in the eighteenth century. They did not constitute a radical break with the Americans' experience, however, or with their idea of the constitution, as articulated during the protracted imperial crisis.

There was a continuity in American constitutional thinking throughout the years before and after independence. The clarification of this thinking, brought about by the imperial crisis, was a necessary prologue to the future of constitutional government in America. The Revolution was essentially a conflict between two different ideas of the eighteenth century constitution. It was a triumph for constitutionally limited—sovereignless—government over unlimited parliamentary sovereignty.

If we are to overcome our traditional obsession with the Great Events leading to national revolution and sovereignty, we must discover new and broader contexts for the American constitutional experience. Constitutional disputes within the different colonies must assume a new significance. There was no absence of such disputes in the early 1770s.[15] One of the most important of these was the fee proclamation controversy which immobilized Maryland government during the "quiet" years, 1770–1773. It is easy to dismiss the dispute, and the newspaper debate between Daniel Dulany, Jr., and Charles Carroll of Carrollton which accompanied it, because of its narrow, local focus. There seems to be an infinite gap between the question of Governor Robert Eden's prerogative

states. The special circumstances which made the American experiment possible are discussed in F. H. Hinsley, *Power and the Pursuit of Peace* (Cambridge: Cambridge University Press, 1963), pp. 312–13. The superintending role of imperial authority is sketched in Holdsworth, *History of English Law*, 11:98. Discussion of this authority in American pamphlet literature was usually favorable. See, for instance, Thomas Fitch, *Colonies Should Not Be Charged with Internal Taxes* (New Haven, 1764), pp. 17–20; John Randolph, *The Present State of Virginia* (Williamsburg, 1774), p. 11; Carter Braxton, *Address to the Convention of Virginia* (Williamsburg, 1776), pp. 23–24, and "Tullius," *Three Letters to the Public* (Philadelphia, 1783), pp. 8–9.

15 For instance, the Wilkes fund controversy in South Carolina. Jack P. Greene, *The Nature of Colony Constitutions* (Columbia: University of South Carolina Press, 1970), reprints pamphlets by Sir Egerton Leigh and Arthur Lee on that dispute.

rights and the later intercolonial movement for independence; the Dulany-Carroll exchange hardly figures in the "literature of revolution." But if we redefine our interests and consider the older and enduring question of the nature of constitutional government, it assumes a new and greater importance. Dulany and Carroll outlined the positions and possibilities which dominated American constitutional history during the next fifteen years.

THE HISTORICAL CONTEXT

On November 26, 1770, Maryland Governor Robert Eden issued a proclamation, establishing officers' fees on a scale confirmed by statute in 1763, but now lapsed through the failure of upper and lower houses to agree on a new tobacco inspection bill with a fee scale.[16] Eden claimed the proclamation was issued to prevent "oppressions and extortions" by the officers. The lower house, which had hoped for a radical diminution of fees, considered the proclamation an attempt to usurp by prerogative its constitutional role. The proclamation, it thought, was issued in the interest of the officers, some of whom—including Dulany—were members of the upper house and advisors of the governor. As long as the council declined to reform the fee scale, the old rates could be sustained by proclamation.

There was something old and something new in lower house opposition to the fee proclamation. The settlement of fees had

---

[16] The best study of Maryland politics in this period is Charles A. Barker, *Background of the Revolution in Maryland* (New Haven: Yale University Press, 1940). See also the previous edition of these letters, Elihu S. Riley, *Correspondence of "First Citizen"* . . . *and "Antilon"* . . . *with a History of Governor Eden's Administration in Maryland, 1769–1776* (Baltimore, 1902). Legislative developments may be followed in the upper and lower house journals and laws of Maryland, reprinted in *Maryland Archives* (Baltimore: Maryland Historical Society, 1883). For details, and more extensive citation, see the text of the letters and notes below. The fee proclamation, with another proclamation setting land office fees, are in *Archives* 63: 109–11. The fee controversy was one of three related disputes, the others involving clergy's revenue and land office fees. The clergy question was debated elsewhere. The land office issue was considered briefly in these letters, Carroll claiming that the arguments against both proclamations were identical.

always been a controversial issue in the colony. They were set by proclamation in 1733 and were the subject of bitter dispute until finally limited by statute in 1747. Because of this continuing controversy and the personal interest of leading members of the court party[17] in fees, they had become a perennial, almost symbolic, issue in the lower house crusade against proprietary prerogative power.

The legislative impasse over fees in 1770 was a tactical victory for the antiproprietary country party. Confident the governor would feel compelled to establish fees by proclamation—the delegates warned him against such a move—the country group was assured a dramatic "encroachment" on liberty with which to edify their fellows. And, because the fee scale was tied to the inspection act, the lower house had political leverage. All Marylanders agreed that the staple regulation was essential to the colony's economic life.

It was not difficult to dramatize prerogative power in Maryland. In no other colony did court power wield such influence, nor did crown or proprietor have such extensive authority.[18] Even when constitutional and legal precedent authorized the exercise of prerogative—as it probably did in the case of fees—that authority was an easy target for attacks based on English constitutional principles. The delegates successfully exploited this tension in the fee controversy.

The country party tried to identify fees with taxation, and so associate the continuing struggle against proprietary power with the recent intercolonial protests against parliamentary taxation. If they failed to make a strong connection in a strictly legal sense, proclamation opponents did show that fee settlement was as vital to community control of finances in Maryland as taxation was elsewhere. If the assembly lost control of fees, government would become financially independent.[19]

The legal and constitutional arguments over the proclamation were familiar long before Dulany and Carroll debated them in the

[17] The "court" party in colonial Maryland comprised groups supporting proprietary government. The "country" party was antiproprietary.
[18] Bailyn, *Origins of American Politics*, pp. 121–22.
[19] Barker, *Background of Revolution*, pp. 349–50.

Maryland Gazette. The opposing positions were developed in 1770 and 1771 in a series of messages by the two houses and Governor Eden, published and circulated by the publicity-conscious delegates.[20] Nor did the Dulany-Carroll exchange resolve the controversy. An inspection act was passed in 1773, without the fee scale. By agreeing to that regulation, the lower house lost its leverage on fees. Despite its stand on principle, the house was unable to prevent the effective operation of the proclamation.

The lower house may not have achieved its legislative objectives, but it did emerge victorious in the battle for popular support. This was the victory of "First Citizen," Charles Carroll of Carrollton, over "Antilon," Daniel Dulany Jr., the famous lawyer and pamphleteer. Carroll succeeded in portraying the proclamation as a threat to the constitution; Dulany was unable to dissociate himself from conflict-of-interest charges or to convince Maryland that the fee question was merely legal, and not to be judged by Carroll's constitutional abstractions.[21]

Dulany was the towering intellect of colonial Maryland and one of the finest lawyers in the colonies. He had gained a lasting reputation as a defender of liberty from his famous 1765 pamphlet, *Considerations on the Propriety of Imposing Taxes in the British Colonies.* In 1773 he was in his fiftieth year and, as provincial secretary and unofficial "minister of Maryland," at the peak of his power. When Dulany submitted the first Antilon letter for publication on January 7, 1773, he doubtless thought his dialogue between two citizens, defending the proclamation, would be the last words

[20] These include the lower house reports on officers' fees, October 3 and 12, *Maryland Archives*, 62: 218–19 and 232–33; lower house resolves of November 1, *ibid.*, pp. 300–301; lower house message of November 17, *ibid.*, pp. 411–15; upper house messages of November 10 and 20, *ibid.*, pp. 352–53 and 366–69, and Governor Eden's message and lower house reply of November 20, *ibid.*, pp. 421–26.

[21] The best biographical treatments of Dulany and Carroll are Aubrey C. Land, *The Dulanys of Maryland* (Balimore: Johns Hopkins Press, 1968), and Ellen Hart Smith, *Charles Carroll of Carrollton* (Cambridge: Harvard University Press, 1942). Land discusses the hostility between their families, ordinarily kept within the bounds of cordiality, in *Dulanys*, pp. 291–92. Dulany may have been the leading intellect in the colony, but he struck young Carroll as "imperious . . . & dogmatical" when the two met in London in 1762; Smith, *Carroll*, p. 102. The Dulanys were powerful in colony politics; the Carrolls were excluded from political life because of their Catholicism.

on the subject. He expected to undermine the pretenses of country party members in the newly elected assembly, and perhaps even induce a popular outcry for passage of the stalled inspection bill. When Carroll entered the lists against him in February, Dulany was surprised, and furious. It can fairly be said that he lost his composure.

Charles Carroll of Carrollton was the scion of a wealthy Maryland Catholic family, long on unfriendly terms with the Dulanys. He was educated at the best continental seminaries and commanded an intelligence and learning to rival the great Dulany's. Fifteen years his adversary's junior, Carroll was in 1773 still unknown in politics. With his First Citizen successes, however, he began a distinguished career in local and national affairs.

On a superficial reading of these letters, insult, innuendo, and recrimination seem to overwhelm the discussion. This personal bitterness, in combination with the conspicuous display of legal and classical knowledge, made the letters the sensation of the season in Annapolis; and they also contribute mightily to their inaccessibility and obscurity for the modern reader. But beneath the legal quibbling and the insults, two diametrically opposed and ultimately irreconcilable ideas of the constitution can be discovered. It is these ideas, what they reveal about opposing conceptions of the constitution, and what they can tell us about the sovereignty question during the era of the Revolution, that make this exchange of continuing interest to the historian.

THE ARGUMENTS

Nature of the Constitution

The Dulany-Carroll exchange in the *Maryland Gazette* is important not only for the light it sheds on Maryland politics in the late colonial period, but also for its articulation of those divergent constitutional theories which destroyed the empire within three short years.

Carroll championed the popular position as the defender of Maryland liberties against encroaching prerogative. His position has been identified, somewhat inaccurately, with the natural rights school.[22] The lone invocation of natural rights in his letters, "jura naturae sunt immutabilia," was unexceptionable in orthodox English theory; furthermore, it is found in apposition to a British constitutional maxim, that a man should not be "judge in his own cause."[23] Carroll did not believe the constitution had been built of lofty abstractions. It was, instead, both the product and the purpose of history. "The wisdom of ages, and the accumulated efforts of patriotism" had been required "to bring the constitution to its present point of perfection."[24] The constitution was the unique expression of the political experience of the English people. Constitutional principles and maxims—historical abstractions— gave meaning and direction to that experience. Patriotism, history taught, was not the exclusive prerogative of crown, courts, or parliament. It was the saving virtue of a vigilant people, always jealous of encroachments on its liberties.

Dulany was the defender of established government. He thought the chief danger to the political order was "the horrors of Anarchy," fomented by popular leaders. The constitution was, in effect, good government, and it was a "monstrous contradiction" to destroy its "every good effect" in the defense of empty abstractions.[25] His was a constitution whose perfection was achieved, not achieving. It was no more or less than government itself, administered by its officers, and the law, dispensed by its judges.

The characteristic attitudes toward the constitution which Carroll and Dulany represented reflected the country and court philosophies which dominated English politics in the eighteenth century. The Maryland court party was cemented by proprietary patronage and controlled the provincial council; the assembly was the preserve of independent country members.[26]

[22] Land in *Dulanys* wrote that "Dulany spoke the language of the constitutional lawyer, Carroll that of natural rights" (p. 303). Though Carroll said he would leave "refutation of *Antilon*'s legal reasoning" to the lawyers, he felt his opponent was most vulnerable to an attack based on English "constitutional principles" (see below, pp. 77–78). Their differences might be reduced to this question: did such "principles" exist and were they applicable?

[23] See below, p. 95.

[24] See below, p. 207.

[25] See below, pp. 46, 47.

[26] On patronage, see Donnell Owings, *His Lordship's Patronage: Offices of Profit in Colonial Maryland* (Baltimore: Maryland Historical Society, 1953).

The country or opposition philosophy, long considered little more than the out-party reflex of Whig radicals and Tory reactionaries, actually was built on a consistent perception of the nature of the constitution and British history. As Isaac Kramnick demonstrated in his study of Bolingbroke, the radical response to Walpole's Whig establishment included a large measure of nostalgia for old, prefinance-capital England; the Tory position, a significant element of aristocratic "populism."[27] The country party recognized the impact of the new money on the old constitutional balance. The court, through "corruption" of the representatives, was able to buy influence in commons. The cherished independence of that branch was, to Tory and Commonwealth Whig alike, the only guarantee of English liberty.[28]

"Our constitution is founded on jealousy," Carroll wrote.[29] In England, a corrupted parliament was no longer capable of preventing crown encroachments. The opposition saw itself filling a constitutional vacuum by its vigilance over government: it preserved, even provided, whatever balance survived under the new dispensation. In Maryland, the country position was still represented in the lower house of assembly. For one thing, it was difficult to pretend that the proprietor-in-assembly was Maryland, as king-in-parliament was England. For another, the lower house had insured its purity with a place-bill, preventing the extension of prerogative patronage in its ranks.[30]

"Jealousy" and "independence" were the leading axioms in the country philosophy. Independence was neither that complete mutual autonomy of the branches of government nor the identification

---

[27] Kramnick, *Bolingbroke*, pp. 2, 3, 60, 234.

[28] On corruption, see *ibid.*, pp. 165–66. Opposition thinkers were attracted to Machiavelli because "he was the major theorist of decline, preoccupied . . . with Roman and contemporary models of corrupt and declining society." Also see J. G. A. Pocock, in "Machiavelli, Harrington, and English Political Ideologies of the Eighteenth Century," *William and Mary Quarterly* 22 (October 1965), 549, who discusses the "barrenness of Country ideology" resulting from its "insistence on regarding Parliament as a collection of men who had no more to do with power than exercise a jealous suspicion of it." English sources and American applications of corruption theory are noted in Bailyn, *Origins of American Politics*, pp. 42–48, 145–46, 160.

[29] See below, p. 127.

[30] Bailyn, *Origins of American Politics*, pp. 121–22.

of each with a specific function—executive, legislative, or judicial —which has come down to us as the separation of powers. Indeed, inasmuch as "jealousy" was the essence of equilibrium, functions and influence necessarily overlapped. The king, or governor; lords, or council; and commons, or lower house, were all part of the legislature: they all had to concur in legislation. But no one branch was supposed to assume sovereign preeminence, nor control the other branches through corruption of their members. Institutional checks, not personal influence, protected the constitution. Independence was immunity from corruption, not constitutional constraint.

Following historian David Hume's suggestion, Carroll thought parliamentary control over finances gave birth to English liberty.[31] But the introduction of the money nexus into the constitution cut both ways.

> Political writers in England have complained bitterly of the vast increase of officers, placemen, and pensioners, and to that increase have principally ascribed an irresistible influence in the crown over those national councils.[32]

For, as Lord Bolingbroke warned, "by the *Corruption of Parliament*, and the absolute Influence of a King . . . we return into that State," from which parliament had delivered us.[33] The legislature had to protect the constitution by control over finances, and so restrain government. It had to resist attempts to turn that control on itself, through corruption.

Carroll was confident corruption could be avoided in Maryland; the colony's constitution was chiefly vulnerable in its control over finances. If the support of officers were established without the assembly's concurrence, government would become independent of the people.

> In this colony, government is almost independent of the people. It has nothing to ask but a provision for its officers: if it can settle their

---

[31] David Hume, *History of England* (London, 1767), 6: 142; see below, pp. 213–14.

[32] See below, p. 212.

[33] From the *Dissertation upon Parties* (London, 1754), p. 116; see below, p. 212.

fees without the interposition of the legislature, administration will disdain to owe even that obligation to the people. The delegates will soon lose their importance; government will every day gain some accession of strength; we have no intermediate state to check its progress: the upper house, the shadow of an aristocracy, being composed of officers dependent on the proprietary and removeable at pleasure, will, it is to be feared, be subservient to his pleasure and command.[34]

Dulany and the court apologists wondered why constitutional mistrust and jealousy could not be as well directed at the popular branch. If "all judges" were automatically "suspected of corruption," "all kings of tyranny," why not "all patriots of venality," asked Antilon.[35] But the country party was concerned with constitutional mechanics, not personalities.[36] Given its perception of the constitutional role of commons as the protector of liberty—the limiting agent in limited monarchy—it was absurd to suggest the lower house could ever endanger the constitution. There was never too much security for liberty or too much vigilance over an encroaching prerogative.

One of the chief tenets of country ideology was the distinction between institutions and individuals, offices and officers, the king and his ministers. In Carroll's words:

> I would not have you confound Government, with the Officers of Government. . . . Government was instituted for the general good, but officers intrusted with its powers, have most commonly perverted them to the selfish views of avarice and ambition; hence the Country and Court interests, which ought to be the same, have been too often opposite.[37]

This did not mean that "government and liberty" were incompatible: in fact, "I think they cannot subsist independent of each other." But if the delegates were to perform their constitutional mandate, they had to be able to check the encroachments of the other branches.

[34] See below, p. 214.
[35] See below, p. 121.
[36] Kramnick, *Bolingbroke*, p. 5.
[37] See below, p. 56.

The court apologists began with a different assumption, namely that the branches of government were all competing for power, the lower house not excepted. Government depended on a final, sovereign authority over the legislature in order to function. Constitutional balance was dangerous if it meant that the branches would cancel each other out, with no residual authority left in government. It was dangerous if it enabled the popular branch to assume this authority itself and leave government impotent. If sovereignty were really at stake, it was beside the point to talk about constitutional checks and balances.

There was apparent warrant for the court argument. If the constitution were considered to be the actual distribution of powers, and if the assemblies' "quest for power" were the quest for all power—for sovereignty—the emasculation of the council and executive in most colonies was conclusive evidence for that view. It is difficult today, imbued as we are with the sovereignty concept, to appreciate the opposite perspective. In fact, colonial ideologists of the country party regretted that their councils were not more powerful and independent: like the lower houses, guardians of liberty and the constitution.[38] They wished the governor corresponded more closely with the king.

Carroll found a Jamaican writer's analysis of his colony's constitution applicable to Maryland.

> The legislature of this province wants in its two first branches (from the dependent condition of the Governor and council) a good deal of that freedom, which is necessary to the legislature of a free country, and on this account, our constitution is defective in point of legislature, those two branches not preserving by any means, so near a resemblance to the parts of the *British* legislature, which they stand for here, as the assembly does.[39]

[38] On this subject, see Jack P. Greene, *The Quest for Power* (New York: W. W. Norton & Company, 1972), esp. pp. 440–41. "Unlike the peers in Britain, who held their seats in the House of Lords on a hereditary basis and could not be removed by the Crown, colonial councillors were entirely dependent upon the Crown and could be removed at pleasure. American leaders increasingly recognized that this arrangement was an important defect in the constitutions of the colonies."

[39] See below, p. 94.

The dependent nature of governor and council did not leave the lower house omnipotent by default: it meant, in fact, that the governor, failing to act in "loco regis" as King of Maryland, and the upper house, failing to act as Maryland nobility, were not performing their proper constitutional functions. They were mere tools in a conspiracy against liberty.

Pauline Maier has recently described the dialectic of blame and shown how the shifting focus of responsibility for English "oppression" was an essential prologue to revolution.[40] It may be suggested that early protests to English policy reflected the "anachronistic" country interpretation of the constitution; and that the English response to these protests achieved reluctant colonial acceptance of orthodox English constitutional theory. Americans sincerely believed the constitution to be self-correcting.[41] They trusted that the institutional balance in English government which had produced and sustained liberty would come again to its rescue. But Americans were ultimately disabused of these naive notions and came to accept the proposition that all the branches were one, that great indivisible English sovereignty, king-in-parliament. It had always been immaterial to orthodox English constitutional theory whether colonists held the king's ministers, parliament, or the king himself, responsible: they were the same, inseparable sovereign.

While there was still hope for the constitution, colonists saw the attack on power in the council as a holding action on the cancerous growth of prerogative. Despite their successes, prerogative was not weakened. Its assault on liberty was supported, if not sponsored, by the home government. "It is a common observation," Carroll wrote,

[40] *From Resistance to Revolution* (New York: Knopf, 1972), pp. 100, 105–6, 140, 200, 239, 269. The final step in this process, independence, was caused by the "failure of the English people to rise in the cause of liberty" and the ultimate attribution of "responsibility for the unconstitutional acts to the King, who embodied the state's authority."

[41] See, for instance, James Otis, *The Rights of the British Colonies Asserted and Proved* (Boston, 1764): "And 'Tis to be presumed the wisdom and justice of that august assembly will afford us relief by repealing such acts as through mistake or other human infirmities have been suffered to pass, if they can be convinced that their proceedings are not constitutional" (p. 40).

confirmed by general experience, that a claim in the colony-governments of an extraordinary power as incidental to, or part of the prerogative, is sure to meet with the encouragement and support of the ministry in Great-Britain.[42]

The colonial assemblies came to believe they were the last line of defense for local rights and liberties. The fact that the constitutional debate became empire-wide encouraged close identification with their communities. Because imperial authorities perceived issues in terms of the sovereignty concept, English sovereignty was inevitably pitted against colonial communities. The colonists thought the failure of governor and council to sustain their traditional roles, within the constitutional balances of colonial governments, of a piece with the collapse of balanced government in England. These developments eliminated *all the intermediary powers* between the colonies and sovereign parliament.

History

The rhetorical escalation in these letters, both personal and political, tends to overshadow their substance. There was a rare instance of honest and open disagreement over two questions of English history: the justification of the 1688 Glorious Revolution and the constitutionality of Charles I's assessment of ship-money. Elsewhere in the debate, constitutional points were parried with legal arguments, legal precedents were deemed exceptions to the constitutional rule and every other attempt at argumentation met with personal abuse and recrimination. But we are unequivocally faced with two different versions of history; and, not surprisingly, they best illuminate the two different concepts of the constitution at the heart of the fee controversy.

The discussion of these questions was historiographical in the broadest sense. Carroll and Dulany agreed, albeit reluctantly, on the facts.[43] Their interpretations differed on the connection between

---

[42] See below, p. 149.

[43] For instance, Carroll wrote, "*Antilon*'s account of the levy of ship-money, though not quite so impartial as he insinuates, I admit in the main to be true" (see below, p. 82).

historical and constitutional development. Was the constitution, in all its recently won perfection, now immune to historical process, as Dulany and the Whig establishment liked to believe? Or were the opposition views—reactionary or radical, that liberty must be preserved or promoted—correct in affirming the continued inter-relatedness of historical and constitutional process?[44]

The establishment and opposition interpretations made radically distinct demands on the past. If constitutional perfection was achieved, the 1688 revolution had to be the definitive and conclusive moment in a prior process, immemorial or modern. For the opposition, the continuing process reduced the epochal importance of any given event. The revolution settlement might be undone. It did not guarantee the liberties of the English people in perpetuity.

The Whig establishment's pieties concerning limited monarchy and the right to revolt belied its idea of history. Those doctrines made sense in 1688; they made none when Blackstone epitomized the orthodox position in his *Commentaries*. With king firmly entrenched in parliament, and parliament omnipotent, it was absurd to talk about limited monarchy.[45] But Carroll thought

[44] For background on British historiography in the eighteenth century, see David C. Douglas, *English Scholars, 1660–1730* (2nd ed., London: Eyre & Spottiswoode, 1951), and J. G. A. Pocock, *The Ancient Constitution and the Feudal Law* (Cambridge: Cambridge University Press, 1957). Both provide valuable insight into the establishment position. According to Douglas, "the quest for precedent became wearisome to those who found in the existing English constitution the best mechanism ever devised to satisfy the temporal needs of man" (*English Scholars*, p. 274). Pocock shows how "ideas of sovereignty undermined belief in an ancient custom binding on both king and community; the concept of custom itself had hardened into an obscurantist insistence that Parliament must not be known to have a beginning" (*Ancient Constitution*, p. 239). The opposition view of history has been sketched out by Kramnick in *Bolingbroke*. Bolingbroke and Walpole's publicists "refought the historiographic battles of the seventeenth century" (p. 26). "The Revolution, Bolingbroke claimed, did not alter the constitution but merely renewed it and restored it to the original principles of liberty, born in the Saxon past. The promise of the Revolution had never been fulfilled, however, and the perfection of the constitution never actually achieved" (p. 27). "Walpole's writers relied on the Tory histories of Brady and Dugdale, discounting the myth of the immemorial constitution" (p. 133). By mideighteenth century the debate over the ancient constitution was secondary to that over the perfection of the revolution settlement, and Tories "out-whigged" Whigs, and vice versa, in attacking or defending that perfection.

[45] On the gap between doctrine and political reality in Blackstone, see Sir Ernest Barker, *Essays on Government* (2nd ed., Oxford: Clarendon Press, 1951), p. 130. "If their unreality was known in England, the case was different in America."

Blackstone's sentiments still applicable. "The true liberty of the subject," he copied approvingly, "consists, not so much in the gracious behaviour, as in the limited power of the sovereign."[46] Three years after Carroll wrote, colonists invoked the resistance right, despite the Whig establishment's conviction that the Glorious Revolution was the revolution to end revolutions.

For Blackstone and the establishment, prerogative had been backed into a cul-de-sac of the common law:[47] the constitutional tension between prerogative and liberty was resolved in a sovereign parliament. This formulation may have been appropriate in England, even if the opposition doubted it. It was not appropriate in the colonies. The issues resolved in England in 1688 remained alive across the ocean. The coalescence of once distinct and opposed powers in sovereign parliament had not occurred in America. Lower houses continued to crusade for liberty, local rights, and political power. Governors and upper houses continued to rely on a kind of prerogative power now anachronistic in the mother country.

If colonists did not share the benefits of the Glorious Revolution, they were not sure they wanted to. Sovereign parliament, resulting from the permeation of crown influence through all branches, was, according to the country critique, as much problem as solution. "Since the revolution," Carroll claimed, "parliaments have relaxed much of their antient severity, and discipline."[48] The overt tyranny of the Stuarts had roused "the national indignation," but since their overthrow, liberty has been subjected to new, "more disguised, and concealed" attacks, "equally subversive" in their "consequences."[49]

The country view of history, in combination with actual colonial experience, heightened Carroll's sensitivity to "encroachments," however slight, and strengthened his growing conviction that local rights and English liberty were identical. Short of imitation and independence, however, there was no way the revolution settlement or any other suitable guarantee of liberty could be extended to America. The fusion of interests and powers in the

---

[46] From the *Commentaries*, 4:426; see below, p. 147.
[47] Sir David Keir, *The Constitutional History of Modern Britain* (5th ed., London: A. & C. Black, 1953), p. 271.
[48] See below, p. 211.
[49] See below, p. 82.

English parliament made colonial constitutions anomalous. It was the colonists' burden to preserve the constitutional multiplicity jeopardized by the settlement. They had to differentiate between principles and a glorified status quo, between fundamental and common law.

Carroll's position was precarious. To cast any doubt on the efficacy and finality of the Glorious Revolution was to condone other revolutions, in other contingencies. Was not the British constitution already perfect? Carroll said the fee proclamation "must not be endured"; those were "naughty words" to Dulany.[50] Did Carroll mean that popular leaders should produce a revolution every time they were displeased with government measures? Did they "hope, that the free people of Maryland will become a lawless mob at their instigation, and be the dupes of their infernal rage?"[51] Carroll's discomfort would only be allayed when, with the Massachusetts Assembly, his choice was narrowed to "slavery" or "liberty" and revolution was the last hope for the latter.

Contradictory interpretations of specific events were determined by the dialectical necessities of the larger debate. Carroll introduced the ship-money question in his first letter, by offering "a comparison between the *present ministers* of this province, and *those*, who influenced Charles the first, and brought him to the block."[52] He sought to demonstrate a similarity between the fee proclamation and ship-money, even though ship-money was a more obvious assault on liberty. The fee proclamation was more "dangerous" because it was more "disguised." Further, "there were some appearances" in Charles' favor when he levied ship-money, because the "boundaries between liberty and prerogative" were "far from being ascertained" at that time.[53] By moderating the oppressive reputation of ship-money, Carroll hoped to show the fee proclamation the less justified, because the continuing progress of the constitution had drawn a finer line between constitutional and unconstitutional acts; and the more dangerous because, if prerogative

[50] See below, p. 122.
[51] See below, p. 75.
[52] See below, p. 54.
[53] See below, pp. 82, 126, 129.

stepped over this fine line, the historical process, essential to perfecting the constitution, would be reversed.

Dulany thought comparison of the measures far fetched. "The boundary" between liberty and prerogative, he wrote, "could not have been more clearly marked out by the utmost precaution of jealous prudence or more outrageously transgressed by the most determined, and lawless tyranny" than in the case of ship-money.[54] Ship-money was an obvious violation of the constitution; whereas the fee proclamation was issued in the public interest, to prevent extortion by the officers. If there were anything *illegal* about it, this was to be determined in the "ordinary judicatories." "The rectitude, or impropriety of the measure," according to Dulany, could be shown "by its effects," not on Carroll's meaningless constitutional distinctions, but on the liberty and property of the people of Maryland.[55]

Without the concept of constitutional and historical process, Carroll's argument on the relative dangers of the two measures fell flat. But Dulany's position also depended on certain assumptions: that constitutional balance was immemorial; that only open, avowed, and obvious transgressions on liberty justified resistance; and that the revolutionary settlement of 1688 made that right to resistance anachronistic. To Carroll, the constitutional process illuminated events; to Dulany, the constitution was a constant in history. Dulany argued that violations of the constitution in one era were directly comparable with supposed violations in another: and so, the fee proclamation dwindled away into puny insignificance. Here was a fundamental difference in historiography, two different systems of evaluating events, resulting from Carroll's theory of the interrelatedness of the constitution and historical process, and Dulany's insistence that the constitution itself was outside history.

The question of the impact of the Glorious Revolution on English constitutional history informed the entire historiographical debate. Actual discussion of the revolution, however, focused on a specific issue which arose in 1688 and was the source of everlasting controversy: did King James II abdicate the crown on his own voli-

[54] See below, p. 102.
[55] See below, pp. 165, 166.

tion or was he driven to abdicate by the revolution? Carroll wrote that "the revolution . . . followed," and then corrected himself in midsentence, "or rather brought on James's abdication of the crown."[56] Dulany was gleeful at what he perceived to be a disastrous slip by his opponent: "the effect of the Citizen's suggestions," he gloated, "is, that the revolution was *rather* an act of *violence*, than of *justice*."[57] Dulany's position was orthodox dogma. The enervation of the right to resistance was complete when the revolution was said not simply to follow the oppression of James, but awaited his actual abdication. According to this curious inversion, revolutions could only be held at the discretion of prerogative. But whatever its peculiarities, the theory of abdication was an important prop to that more important article of faith, that there would be no more revolutions.

Carroll, as well as Dulany, reflected orthodox assumptions in his discussion of the revolution. There was a real difference in nuance, however, in their two versions. Carroll's revolution was more the people's prerogative, less passive reflex.

> Should a King, deaf to the repeated remonstrances of his people, forgetful of his coronation oath, and unwilling to submit to the legal limitations of his prerogative, endeavour to subvert that constitution in church and state, which he swore to maintain, resistance would then *not only* be *excusable, but praiseworthy*, and deposition, and imprisonment, or exile, might be the only means left, of securing civil liberty, and national independence. Thus James . . . justly deserved to be deposed and banished.[58]

Dulany thought "the abdication of James was, *the wrong done by him*."[59] To contradict this was "the very defence of jacobitism."[60] Carroll declined to pursue the question and make the choice, to embrace or reject the revolution, or right to resistance, entirely. But he did not retreat from his central idea that the community itself was the ultimate judge of constitutional questions.[61]

---

[56] See below, p. 88.

[57] See below, p. 103.

[58] See below, p. 88, emphasis added.

[59] See below, p. 103.

[60] See below, p. 187.

[61] "General discontent among the people" of Maryland was a "sure proof" that the fee proclamation was unconstitutional. See below, p. 205.

The historiographical debate was inconclusive. Dulany's main rhetorical strength was in pushing Carroll to unacceptable extreme positions, such as open advocacy of revolution. But there were liabilities in the simplification of issues which this strategy required. Dulany might succeed in forcing a "yes" or "no" answer to the question of parliamentary sovereignty, and his views of the constitution and history. Yet when that answer was forthcoming three years later, it was not the expected "yes," but that resounding "no," heard round the world.

The Carroll-Dulany differences on the constitution and history were also reflected in their discussion of the specific applicability of precedents to the fee controversy. Though this discussion was less well focused and forthright than the historiographical debate, it sheds considerable light on the underlying tension between Carroll's constitutionalism and Dulany's sovereignty.

Precedents[62]

Carroll and Dulany both sought to exploit precedents. They differed, however, on the criteria of acceptability, and on the generality of application. The distinctions they groped for were subtle enough to convince each the other had fallen into fatal error and self-contradiction.

The role of precedents is, in any interpretation, central to

---

[62] Jack P. Greene argued in *The Nature of Colony Constitutions*, p. 53, that the imperial court position reflected "the original and fundamental principles of the British constitution" in constitutional controversies like that over the Wilkes Fund in South Carolina. The colonial country opposition was "forced to justify the often idiosyncratic 'privileges' they had developed as a defense against exaggerated claims of the governors by an appeal to local usage and custom." Superficially, the positions appear reversed in the Maryland fee controversy: Carroll argued from principles, Dulany from usage. Yet Carroll discovered a role for precedents in his theory: the "principles" he advocated were not of uniform and universal application, by a single authority. They described instead the ideal toward which the various governments in the empire should aspire. The diversity of governments, each with its "idiosyncrasies" was central to the larger constitution of the empire as a whole. Thus, the defense of idiosyncrasies was the defense of constitutional multiplicity, the autonomy and integrity of colony governments. The universal application of *English* constitutional usage might destroy the constitutional multiplicity of the empire and impose what colonials thought to be corruptions rather than principles of the constitution in the colonies. In such a way, precedent and principle were not opposed but aligned in Carroll's argument.

British constitutional theory. The British constitution is "unwritten"; its principles must therefore be gathered from history, much as is the common law. History, as we have seen, is susceptible to contrary interpretations. Because the authority of the common law, and ultimately of constitutional law, is immemorial usage, its source—the will of the king or of the community—is unknowable.[63] For the same reason, there is another fundamental question: does the king or community retain the residuum of authority outside of law; which is the ultimate source of authority? Beginning with this central ambiguity, precedents might be variously construed as evidence for the emergence of a fundamental law, or be accepted, without discrimination or reference to any ideal, as the constitution itself.

Dulany's central argument for the fee proclamation was that fees had been settled separately, and on the independent authority of "the House of Lords, the House of Commons, the Courts of Law and Equity in Westminster Hall" and "the Upper and Lower Houses of Assembly."[64] These precedents could not conflict, by definition, with whatever general principles or maxims might be adduced from the constitution. Precedents were the source and evidence for principles. So Dulany, noting that "legal maxims have been understood to be rather unpliant,"[65] thought he had won the day when he juxtaposed the legal maxim that only the legislature as a whole can "lay a tax" with the precedents of parliamentary usage.

There was no qualitative difference in Dulany's argument between principles and the precedents from which they were drawn. If there were a difference, principles or maxims could be used to discriminate between good and bad precedents. The principle of *stare decisis*, the supersession of former by more recent decisions, might assume this function in common law; but there was considerable controversy over the anterior question of the original basis of decision, and whether or not "is" and "ought" were identical. In these letters, Dulany tended to make that identification. He was consequently led to view legal maxims as simplifications rather than ideal tests of the law.

[63] Pocock, *Ancient Constitution*, pp. 233–34.
[64] See below, p. 69.
[65] See below, p. 114.

Carroll argued that the "usage" of parliament in settling fees
did not have legal force as precedent for the exercise of such authority elsewhere. "The two houses of parliament," he wrote, "have
separately settled fees . . . by the usage, custom, and law of parliament, which is part of the law of the land."[66] The distinction
between usage, establishing particular rights, and precedents, evi-
dencing fundamental principles, was essential to Carroll's argument. Dulany rejected the distinction, or rather, pretended not to
see it. He charged Carroll with denying precedents on the one
hand, when they would have established the independent authority of the several branches of government to set fees, but invoking
them to explain that authority away.

> It is, indeed, strange that they, who object to the argument from
> precedents, should rely altogether upon them in support of a doc-
> trine so extraordinary, as that the legality of even taxes, not laid by
> the legislature, may be maintained by the precedents of their having
> been paid, and received![67]

The qualitative distinction between usage and precedent was as
difficult for Dulany to accept in 1773 as that between "is" and
"ought," or between common and fundamental law. If separate
branches of the legislature set fees, and these were taxes, that was
precedent for general exercise of the taxing power: it was obvi-
ously unthinkable for commons, lords, or crown to levy taxes inde-
pendently of the other branches. But to Carroll, anomalies like
these fee precedents did not invalidate constitutional principles.
"A partial deviation from a clear and fundamental maxim of the
constitution," he insisted, "cannot invalidate that maxim."[68] In this
case,

> the particular usage of parliament . . . must be deemed an exception
> to the general law, and ought, as all exceptions, to be sparingly
> exercised, and in such cases, and in such manner only, as the usage
> will strictly warrant.[69]

[66] See below, p. 131.
[67] See below, p. 158.
[68] See below, p. 196.
[69] See below, p. 195.

The central country position, that the settlement of 1688 had not fixed the constitution forever and that the constitution was still threatened—now by corruption—required a complex conceptualization to account for the remaining imperfections in the constitution. Just as legal maxims articulated the ideal constitution and were a compass with which the actual constitution might correct itself, Carroll's concept of usage explained exceptions to the rules. Much of the historical discussion which dominates his last letter is designed to show how difficult it was for guardians of liberty to detect, and extinguish, all vestiges of arbitrary prerogative and unconstitutional authority.

Officers were originally paid out of the king's own revenues, Carroll wrote, thus the ancient and "constitutional" authority to settle fees.[70] Because officers were now paid by the public, he argued, the public controlled their fees in many cases, and ought to in all. His analysis, borrowed from Lord Coke's discussion of the statute *de tallagio non concedendo*, emphasized the ambiguous character of fees: old, immemorial, unaltered fees could still be levied on the original, prerogative authority. New fees, however, had to be considered like taxes, as should new fees attached to old offices.

Throughout his letters, Carroll tried to explain the constitution in its full complexity. By showing that vestiges of old, unconstitutional authority coexisted with the modern "perfection" of the constitution, he illuminated the central dynamic of process and change, the result of enduring constitutional tensions and contradictions.

If the distinction between anomalous usage and precedent as principle were not recognized, Carroll thought, the indiscriminate use of precedents would lead to despotism. "Millions entertain no other idea of the legality of power," he quoted John Dickinson, "than that it is founded on the exercise of power."[71] Carroll noted that

> Precedents . . . have been brought to shew, that the power hath been exercised; so have many other unconstitutional powers; the

[70] See below, p. 133.

[71] From *Letters From a Farmer in Pennsylvania to the Inhabitants of the British Colonies* (Philadelphia, 1769), letter 11: 88; see below, p. 223.

exercise doth not prove the right, it proves nothing more, than a deviation from the principles of the constitution in those instances, in which the power hath been illegally exercised.[72]

Or, as Carroll delighted in quoting Dulany himself, "the question of right doth not depend upon precedents, but on the principles of the constitution."[73]

Dulany insisted that the fee question was legal, "determinable in the ordinary judicatories," not constitutional. To dismiss precedents so recklessly would, he thought, undermine the common law and the constitution itself. In line with his other simplifications, he chose to defend the efficacy of precedents in general, on the basis of their role in common law.

> The common law results from general customs, precedents are the evidences of these customs, judicial determinations and decisions the most certain proofs of them, and the arguments therefore from precedents, the practice of the courts, the decisions of judges respectable for their knowledge, and probity, and from the convenience of uniformity, are of great weight.[74]

Carroll, of course, did not reject all precedents. Not only did he distinguish anomalous usage, but also argued that some precedents—prior protests to fee proclamations, for instance—actually applied. There was a certain circularity, naturally, in Carroll's distinctions: precedents were anomalous if they contradicted the constitution; they were applicable if they supported it. The distinctions were defensible only insofar as "is" remained distinct from "ought"; they collapsed if they were identical.

The fundamental question, whether "is" was the same as "ought," remained submerged throughout the debate. Dulany was not prepared to say there was no "constitution" separable from the law as it then obtained, that there was no defense for Maryland liberties if parliament should curtail them *by law*. He had

---

[72] See below, p. 135.

[73] From *Considerations on the Propriety of Imposing Taxes in the British Colonies* (Annapolis, 1765), pp. 41–42; see below, pp. 135–36.

[74] See below, p. 176.

found himself on the other side of the question in 1765 and was hesitant to complete the about-face. Nor was Carroll ready to proclaim that the lower house and the colony of Maryland were entitled to pass on the constitutionality of all exercises of prerogative or British authority. But this was, inevitably, the logic of their positions.

One Constitution or Many

Dulany's argument was built on the identification of common with constitutional law and the legal with the political system. Insofar as the constitution was anything more than existing custom, it was those general principles to which jurists resorted in deciding ambiguous questions. Who but judges could have drawn those often subtle distinctions between the constitutional and unconstitutional exercise of power? Thus the fee proclamation was only effective against the people—requiring them to pay—after it had received the imprimatur of "legality" from the courts. "This effect," Dulany wrote, "flows . . . from the same principles, that the general protection, and security of men's rights are derived."[75]

Carroll took exception. Just because the *"legality . . . is* determinable in the ordinary judicatories; does it follow therefore, that the measure is *constitutional?"*[76] Here was the crucial question. The courts had passed on the constitutionality of ship-money in Hampden's trial "and it was actually determined to be legal by . . . the judges." What kind of security was this for English liberties? Yet if questions like this were not determinable in law, who would determine them? Dulany charged that the delegates thought their sole protests should have this effect, but wasn't this also an encroachment on liberty? Were mere resolutions of a single house of the legislature now to have the effect of law?

Carroll did not suggest that the lower house should be considered the ultimate authority. His attack on Dulany's contention that the question was a legal one notwithstanding, he believed the legal

[75] See below, p. 104.
[76] See below, pp. 138–39.

system did provide recourse in "the trial by jury."[77] The importance of this suggestion is not in its legal persuasiveness—at best tenuous—but in its anticipation of community sovereignty as a solution to constitutional deadlocks. Despite the failure of fee legislation, there was no need for a proclamation, which subverted this constitutional remedy.

> If a contest should arise between the officer and the person for whom the service is done about the quantum of recompence, the former must have recourse to . . . trial by jury . . . *the best security against the encroachments of power*, and consequently the firmest support of liberty.[78]

Carroll was perhaps on weak legal grounds in this argument—Maryland juries never had set fees—but he was on strong constitutional grounds. He recognized the inevitable predominance of the "prerogative"—governor and council—and imbalance of the constitution, if the proclamation stood. Dulany's suggestion that the governor might as easily have sided with the lower house in breaking the deadlock was ridiculous; as was his argument for the independence of the judges: "they rather confer a favour upon, than receive any from, government."[79] In fact, the governor could, through his control over the council, sustain the legislative deadlock, and so make the settlement of fees by proclamation perpetual. If the governor and council could have their way so easily, there was no incentive to compromise. Had not "the authority of the supreme magistrate interposed," Carroll thought, "and took the decision of this important question, from the other branches of the legislature to itself . . . time, and necessity would have softened dissention, and have reconciled jarring opinions, and clashing interests."[80] The judges, who were in some cases councillors—the governor was chancellor—should not be allowed to break the deadlock. Significantly, Dulany made no effort to differentiate the residual authority he claimed for judges to set fees, in the absence

[77] See below, p. 202.
[78] See below, p. 202, emphasis added.
[79] See below, p. 169.
[80] See below, pp. 93–94.

of legislation, from the power of the governor to set them by proclamation. With considerable irony, Carroll wrote:

> the question, though of the most momentous concern, might perhaps be safely left to their decision; but our judges are removeable at pleasure, some of them might be interested in the cause, and if suffered to establish their *own* fees would become both judge and party — a Governor . . . decreeing as chancellor fees to be paid upon the authority of his *own* Proclamation, would fall under that predicament.[81]

Carroll argued that constitutional balance had to be maintained at all costs. The temporary deadlock of the branches encouraged compromise. In the event the impasse could not be resolved, appeal should be made, beyond the legislature, to that residual authority of the people, through juries, to settle fees. Because the first interest of the people was to preserve liberty, there was no danger of encroachment in this recourse.

Dulany ridiculed Carroll's attempts to discover or maintain a balance in the Maryland constitution. Carroll ignored the larger imperial context, in which there was always appeal to England. The residual authority to settle fees, in case of deadlock, was not in the people's juries, but in the judges, in their "ordinary obligation . . . to discharge their duty."[82] The governor's proclamation was predicated on this authority; its "legality" might be challenged, and sustained, all the way to king-in-council. Dulany maintained that

> the chancellor, though he exercises a judicial power, and is vested with the executive, as governor, cannot commit the violence, and oppression dreaded, because there is an appeal to a superior provincial jurisdiction, and his decrees may be reformed, or reversed, and an *ultimate appeal too is provided to the king in council*.[83]

Any anomalies in Maryland government were either correctable from above or irrelevant, because of the possibility of appeal.

[81] See below, p. 91.
[82] See below, p. 171.
[83] See below, pp. 111-12, emphasis added.

The appeal to higher English authority, however, was not likely to quiet country party anxieties. What tenderness for local rights and privileges could be expected from the king-in-council? The whole concept of "local rights" depended on their independence from sovereign discretion. Imperial authority was as likely to support as check encroachments on local liberty. Intimations of a sovereign parliament, standing behind the initiatives of the Maryland court party and contempt for the Maryland "constitution," which the country party imagined to impose limits on government, were more apt to raise new and ominous questions and doubts, than to put an end to the fee controversy.

Here then were the vital differences between Carroll and Dulany. There was the question of context: was it, finally, the empire or the local community? Where, in the absence of legislation, was the residuum of authority: in government or community, judge or jury? Was there only one constitution, or many?

Dulany, in effect, denied the existence of a provincial constitution. Did not the crown *"lawfully* settle the fees of constitutional officers in the royal governments" and wasn't this "power conferred on the proprietor of Maryland by the charter, under which we derive the power of making laws for our good government?"[84] According to Dulany's view, the so-called liberties and rights of the colonists were mere concessions of prerogative. The freedom to make laws was all that separated the people of Maryland from proprietary power. But what if the law-making process became stalled? What if assemblies were repeatedly prorogued, as in South Carolina, or threatened with dissolution, as in New York, or suspended, as would happen in Massachusetts? This all might be legal. Anything might be legal to a sovereign parliament. It might, as well, destroy the empire.

IMPLICATIONS

We discover in these letters radically different, indeed ultimately irreconcilable, theories on the nature of the British constitution. That Carroll and Dulany were reluctant to develop their

[84] See below, p. 118.

logic to its full implication was not surprising in 1773. There was a recognition that the constitutional distinctions of one could not be reconciled with the legal logic of the other without disastrous results. The dialectic of history continued the argument, and its ramifications dominated American constitutional developments during the ensuing decades.

The fee proclamation controversy was a classic example of governmental breakdown through an excess of checks and balances. It was one of those unfortunate situations in which appeal had to be made beyond the constitution for restoration and revival. Only through manipulation of the electorate, in votes of confidence, have modern constitutional governments been able to integrate that appeal into their constitutions. In the eighteenth century, there was no such happy solution to constitutional deadlocks. According to orthodox theory, deadlocks could then only be broken by appealing to one branch, or jurisdiction, over the other; and, distasteful as that might have been, the location of that authority—sovereignty—necessarily precipitated revolutionary innovation. The people were not yet considered the authority behind all authorities; they were but a part, the popular branch, of a well-mixed government. Still, just as constitutional exigencies—the overwhelming urge to avoid further conflict between the branches —had led to the blurring of old lines in the single, institutionalized sovereignty of king-in-parliament, opposition theorists had begun to insist on the separability of the community and its government. Interestingly, opposition theory, which gradually came to be articulated in terms of "sovereignty," was devoted to generalizing, not centralizing, authority; to providing a new underpinning to the division of powers, formerly premised on the anachronistic sociology of medieval orders. If there had to be a last resort in the constitution because the government branches were no longer able to check each other, or checked each other to the point of immobility, it should be the community-at-large.

The emergence of the political community itself as the locus of legitimate authority is the central theme of American constitutionalism in the revolutionary period. It is a misleading simplification to identify this development entirely with the aspirations of the assemblies. Not just assembly privileges, but also other local rights issues, such as territorial integrity, provided fulcrums for revolutionary action in the various colonies. While independence was accompanied by the formal inversion of "sovereignty" above —in the king-in-parliament—to below—in the community at large —the relation of assembly to community was not essentially altered. The assemblies continued to defend and guarantee local rights, as dramatically demonstrated in the constitutional struggles over western lands, but their and their states' "sovereignty" did not extend beyond those rights—however extensive they may seem to us today—and, what is most significant, this "sovereignty" *never precluded the institution of a vigorous federal government.* Thus assemblies were accustomed prior to independence to picture themselves as defenders of local rights and privileges; these became identified, notwithstanding contemporary British and modern theory, with sovereignty, and this essentially passive, constitutionally limited and limiting state sovereignty was carried over into the American constitutional era.

The Letters

Let us, my countrymen, profit by the
errors and vices of the mother country;
let us shun the rock, on which there is
reason to fear, her constitution will be split.

CHARLES CARROLL OF CARROLLTON, JULY 1, 1773

Antilon's First Letter

Annapolis, January 7.
TO THE PRINTER

You will be pleased to give a place in your *Gazette* to the following dialogue, which was set down by a gentleman who overheard it, after a small recollection, perfectly in substance and nearly in words, as it fell from the speakers. The unhappy and prevailing aversion to *read* performances of elegance as well as moment to the publick seems to bode that this so deficient in the first point will not find a multitude of readers—But if I am not grossly mistaken, those few who will not be frightened by its length from travelling through it will receive both entertainment and instruction to requite them, in some degree, for their pains.

A DIALOGUE BETWEEN TWO CITIZENS

1st Cit. What, my old friend! still deaf to the voice of Reason? will fair argument make no impression on you? Consider well the irreparable mischief the part you are going to act, may do to the Cause of Freedom: Your Steadiness, your Integrity, your Independence made us set you down, as a sure Enemy to Government, and one too, whose force would be felt.

2d Cit. Let me repeat to you my caution, against this strain of compliment; it suits not with your professions of OPPOSITION, and is in truth, somewhat too courtly for my palate: But of this however you may rest assured, that no man is more open to conviction, than MYSELF. The publication of the opinionist, which you, with much zeal and devotion, would set up as the only rule of faith, has let in no new light upon my mind. I worship not the GOLDEN CALF; but cleave to the religious rights and ceremonies established by my forefathers; and in this, I think, I am both conscientious and politick. It was for the same despicable idolatry and falling off as yours that the unhappy and misguided king *Jeroboam* and his people were afflicted with those mighty evils, which are recorded in holy writ. 1 Kings, xii. 2 Chron. xiii.[1] I have impartially examined every thing you suggested in our last conversation, but, cannot discover therein, the least semblance either of reason, or argument; and until you press me with some more weighty objections, I shall still continue a cordial, and determined friend to Government, and, under favour, to Liberty too: But, in the name of Common Sense, no more fruitless experiments on my passions; a truce to your threadbare topicks of Arbitrary Princes, Proclamations, and your Forty per poll![2] You pretend at least, to be so haunted with these terrors, that I verily believe in my heart, if it were in my power, to produce the opinions of the greatest Counsel in England, upon a full and fair state of the case, point blank in favor both of the Proclamation and Forty per poll, you would swear that they were forgeries; or if you allowed them to be genuine, that their authors were barefaced knavish Lawyers, who would at any time, sell opinions contrary to their consciences, to serve a present turn, to get an office on this side the water, for some importunate dependent, or relation in the fourth or fifth degree; or that they would do it to support power, and very likely, that they were downright blunderbusses: And this, too, would be all *fair argument.*

---

[1] The citations are correct.

[2] The "forty per poll" law setting clergy's dues was debated extensively in the *Maryland Gazette* during late 1772. The leading argument against the revival of that 1702 law was made by William Paca on September 10, who argued that the assembly was illegally in session when the act passed, due to the death of King William.

1st Cit. I say nothing upon that matter for the present, but let such opinions appear when they will, there shall be those which shall confront them, though they come subscribed with the name of CAMDEN,[3] if that could possibly be.* But you declare yourself a determined friend both to Government, and Liberty. Monstrous contradiction! If this, however, be your final resolve, I am really sorry for it; Government has but too many, and too powerful friends already; the current sets so fatally strong that way, as to give us serious cause to dread, that we shall be overborn in all our struggles to resist it; the friends of the Constitution, with whatever cheerfulness they may affect to gild their countenances, wear a certain sadness about their hearts; they see the strongest symptoms of the sickness of their cause, even unto death; Court-influence, and Corruption, rear their glittering crests.

2d Cit. Court-influence and Corruption! But, my flowery antagonist, is every man who thinks differently from you on public

---

* *Here it is difficult to determine the speaker's meaning. He may either intend that Lord Camden, after having been a judge and otherwise dignified, can no longer give opinions as a practicing lawyer; or that if he could, he cannot possibly differ from our own great lawyers. And in this latter presumption he may think himself warranted by his Lordship's sentiments, which are cited in that fine monument of reasoning and literature, the Address of the Lower House; which may be seen in the Votes and Proceedings of 1771, page 66; which citation it is well worth reviewing and comparing with another of the sentiments of the same light and ornament of the present age, page 86.[4]*

---

[3] Charles Pratt, first Earl Camden (1714–1794), lord chancellor.

[4] The address is printed in *Maryland Archives* (Baltimore: Maryland Historical Society, 1883–), 63:192–200. It was read to the house November 22, 1771, and adopted by that body by a vote of 31–3. The lower house referred to the words of a "light and ornament of the present age" (Camden) to the effect that "taxation and representation are inseparable. This position is founded in the Laws of Nature . . . whatever is a Man's own, is absolutely his own; No Man hath a Right to take it from him without his consent, either expressed by himself or his representative" (p. 199). The second reference is to Governor Eden's reply of November 30, 1771, *ibid.*, pp. 218–33. Eden noted that "on another subject," Camden asserted that the "Constitutions of the two Assemblies," Maryland's and Great Britain's, "differ fundamentally in many respects. Our House of Commons stands upon its own Laws; whereas Assemblies in the colonies are regulated by their respective Charters, Usages, and the common law of England, and will never be allowed to assume all these Privileges" of Commons. "I am satisfied, neither the Crown nor Parliament will ever suffer the Assemblies to erect themselves into the power of the British House of Commons" (p. 232).

measures, influenced and corrupted? Now, I must confess you give me no reason to complain of your over-complaisance. Is the majority of your fellow-citizens, which you seem to apprehend will be against you, thus all over blotched and tainted?

1st Cit. God forbid it should BE THE CASE OF EVERY INDIVIDUAL! but alas! it is so of too many. Your conduct, and the conduct of such as you, we rather incline to impute to the irresistible bias of personal attachment, or to a certain unaccountable infatuation, which will sometimes overtake the wisest, and the best.

2d Cit. Your insinuation is too gross and injurious to be qualified, or atoned for, by this apology of yours; it will not pass upon one of MY STEADINESS *you know*. You would brand every man with the odious appellations of Court-hireling and Sycophant, who dares to exercise his own judgement, in opposition to yours, and that of your party. Is it not the most criminal, and unpardonable arrogance, thus to strike at the public reputation? I know not what, or whom you mean, by *We* and *the friends of the Constitution*; but, whilst you are thus wrongheaded, and breath so imperious and tyranical a spirit withal, you will be the constant object of derision, or hatred; you may upbraid with the epithets of Tool, or Courtier (than which nothing can be more foul, or reproachful), you will still be regarded with the scorn, or pity of every man of sense or spirit; the blessings of Order, will be preferred to the horrors of Anarchy; for to such must the principles of those men inevitably lead, who are fixed in their purpose, of opposing Government at all adventures, and preposterously contend, that such a system is neither interest, nor faction, but genuine patriotism. Alas Sir! Ill must it fare with the popular interests, when the Leading Representatives, and Great Speakers, instead of making amends to their Country, by some master stroke of wise policy, for having rejected a regulation offered upon such advantageous terms, as the most sanguine, and staunch friend of the people, never dreamed of; still rush on in their destructive career, laying their trains at each outset of public business, to blow up everything into a combustion, in order, that the rage and delusion of the present, may support and sanctify the mischiefs of the preceding Session; whilst the publick Debt, without purchasing any benefits, is swelling to an enormous size, on the Journals; our staple falling into disgrace in foreign markets; and every man's property in a degree, decreasing and mouldering away. Friends to the Constitution, whilst they are stretching every sinew to confound all the public counsels, and thereby, destroy every good effect of that Constitution. Gracious powers! *is not this a monstrous contradiction?*

Take a liberal and impartial review of your adversaries, in every point of light: Have they not as deep a stake in the safety of the Constitution as you, or your friends? What can possibly tempt them to join in the demolition of that bulwark, which alone shelters them in the enjoyment of their fortunes, and of every comfort that can plead to the reason, and interest the heart of man? If they are Tools and Hirelings for this purpose, then are they a kind of lunatick wretches, that no language can describe. Will the general behavior of none of them authorize you to entertain more honorable sentiments of their spirit, than you express? Would they not, think you, spurn at an attempt to frighten, or bribe them, with indignation equal to that which would fire the breasts of those, who are eternally crying out as if the enemy were in the gate, and scattering distraction and distrust through the community? Who are forever reviling others, and bepraising their own integrity, wisdom, and I know not what? Lay this truth sadly to heart, Sir, the Politician who stuns you with harangues on his own angelical purity, is as certainly an arrant imposter, as the woman who unceasingly prates of her own chastity, is no better than she should be; or the soldier who is always the hero of his own boisterous tale, is at bottom but a rank coward. Are there among them no substantial merchants, who are much likelier to be gainers by sticking close to their own business, than by watching the smiles or frowns of a Court? These are men, whom I should hardly expect to find in a plot against Liberty; since Commerce is ever engrafted on the stock of Liberty, and must feel every wound that is given to it, for when Liberty is struck to the heart, Commerce can then put forth her golden fruit no more, but, must per force droop and die. Do you conceive, that such men can possibly be hired, unless they be overtaken by the *infatuation* you talked of, to engage in pulling down a fair and stately and useful edifice, with the ruins of which, as soon as it is levelled to the ground, they and their families are to be stoned to death? For, they are not entitled, by their mercantile education, to keep a constant eye upon the great and gainful publick offices, or to expect that any of them will fall to their share, as those of some other professions are. In all growing cities, and communities at large, they are especial useful and able members, when acting in concert with the Commons, but, put them into the other scale, and they will instant lose all their weight. I fancy you will hear many of my brother-mechanicks raising their voices against you, who scarce know the meaning of your Court-influence, and Corruption, who will stand on the side of him, whom they think, from an unprejudiced observation of his manners, the likeliest to shield them from oppression; or may it be, the encrease of whose business, as it is closely connected with the prosperity of the city, bids the fairest to enlarge the sphere of action, and importance, not only of every tradesman, but, of every inhabitant who lives by his labour, and the sweat of his brow.

1st Cit. To these questions I do not choose to give an answer. But, thus much I will venture to assert, that a thousand arguments may be brought to prove, that our LEADERS cannot be either mistaken, or dishonest. I will only mention two, which are abundantly sufficient. First, the clear and undeniable consistency of their publick conduct; and secondly, their noble and uniform abhorrence of being seen at Court, or in the infectious company of Courtiers.

2d Cit. Consistency, according to your meaning of it, may be now and then the sign of a good heart, but it never is of a good head. It is evident to a man of *my* plain understanding, that a wise politician, if he cannot steer due on to his point, will shape his course a different way, and win upon it by degrees, and yet be both firm and consistent. He will never scruple to give up trifles; to gain solid advantages. But, the possession even of this consistency, when it is appealed to as a merit, must undergo a severe scrutiny. I am somewhat advanced in life, you know; and easiness to believe, is a plant of slow growth, in an aged bosom. A man must not pretend to reconcile his conduct with consistency, by deceitful refinements; it will not serve his turn to tell me, that he acts in two different characters, when I find him declaring one thing to day, and another to morrow, on some publick and important question; or, when I hear him pronouncing, that certain bodies of men have peculiar and indubitable rights, at the very time he is moving heaven and earth to destroy the only Law, which is the foundation of those rights. Neither must this uniform abhorrence of Courts; this excessive delicacy in the choice of company, be received on the mere assertion of the party. When a Candidate, or his friends, warn me of the danger of trusting a man who associates with such and such particular persons, whom they are pleased to traduce as Courtiers and Place-hunters; or who happen to dine at Court, now and then, I am not pained, or difficulted to ask them, whether, they cannot recollect the time, when they themselves were guilty of this very crime? or when they were even the common objects of ridicule, for being *hand and glove at Court*, as it were, *all of a sudden?* Whether, they have not been so bit, so intoxicated, as to forget the old proverb, that *walls have ears*, and to break out into boasts and raptures at their brightening and unexpected hopes of preferment? If I can catch them tripping, or prevaricating upon this trial, they cannot be angry with me upon the matter, if I conclude, that their patriotism is all a cheat, and that in fact, disappointment is rankling in their hearts, nay that, notwithstanding their old sores, if the bait were again thrown out to them, they would be such gudgeons as to swallow it with the utmost greediness.

1st Cit. However this feigned trial of yours might turn out, I cannot see how my friends would be affected by it; as it is notorious to the whole city, as well as to the whole province, that no part of their conduct can possibly fall within the description.

2d Cit. GOD FORBID IT SHOULD BE THE CASE OF EVERY INDIVIDUAL! or indeed of any of them. But to pursue my train: If I can tell them with truth, that I have not only been one of those, who have stared with astonishment at their childish and unguarded Court familiarities even in the publick streets, but that I can recount to them their courtly voyages by water, and journeys by land, their carousings, their illuminations, their costly and exquisite treats, to gorge the high-seasoned appetite of Government; if I can name the very appointments they have laid their fingers upon, and assure them, that I have been well informed of their eager impatience for the removal of every impediment, which stood in the way of their exaltation, with many other glorious and patriotick particulars; if—

1st Cit. For Heaven's sake, to what purpose is all this idle talk, You well know, it does not touch us, we are not galled, and therefore cannot wince.

2d Cit. I shall push it no further then. I only meant to shew you the rules I lay down to myself, for judging on these occasions; and in this, no creature can accuse me, either of ill nature, or foul play; for, I would by no means confine the man of my choice to any particular set of acquaintance. If he has a relish for society, I like him the better for it; since it proves he has a generous heart. I think he may spend his hours of relaxation in the company of sensible persons, though they chance to differ with him in their political creed, and yet return to his own parlour, the same hearty and unshaken friend to his old publick opinions as ever. I never tremble on this account. Indeed, if I be rightly informed, the conversation of these kind of people, seldom turns upon the politics of their own country, in mixt circles; they are willing enough to leave behind them, when they go abroad, what is sufficiently vexatious and troublesome, when they are obliged to apply their thoughts that way. I have often lamented, that *Electioneering*, as it is called, should be so ruinous to private attachments and good fellowship, and should generate such black blood in society as it does; and those who administer to this cruel distemper, whether they lurk in secret, or act openly, have (in my humble opinion) much to answer for. We frequently see the bonds of nature rudely torn asunder; and I believe there may be instances produced from story, of confederated bands of Politicians hacknied in their trade, who have availed themselves, without remorse, of the avowed rawness, simplicity, and vanity of youth, to accomplish their purposes, though they have divided a house against itself, and kindled the inextinguishable flames of hatred and animosity, even in the hearts of brothers.

1st Cit. Wormwood! Wormwood![5]

2d Cit. This indeed must turn the milkiest nature into bitterness. Had I been trained up in the schools of those orators who were heretofore the subjects of your glowing panegyrick, I should dress my thoughts in such language, as well might justify your exclama- [2]tion. These shocking convulsions have often tempted me to think, that I should not break my heart if a Law were expressly provided against this darling privilege of canvassing; that the suffrages of the people might be permitted to take their free course on

---

[5] Anything bitter or grievous; bitterness. The first definition is, "a European woody herb," one species of which is used in making absinthe.

the day of election.[6] As to what you whispered to me yesterday, about the resolution of some of your patriotick friends, not to serve, unless those whose principles chime in with their own were chosen along with them; I must take the liberty to reply, that I look upon such a threat as a mere raw-head and bloody bones, which will not in the end advantage their cause; but, be that as it may, to speak in the language of the good old song of Chevy-Chace,

> I trust we have within the Realm,
> Five hundred men as good as they.[7]

Farewel, Sir, I shall torture your patience no longer with my tiresome and homely discourse; but learn, for the future, to be charitable to those who differ from you in opinion; and *judge not lest ye be judged.*

[6] Because of the recent death of the proprietor, a new assembly was to be chosen. The election was considered a referendum on the fee proclamation and related issues by the country party.

[7] The Chevy-Chase ballad may be found as an appendix to Corymbaeus, *Barnaby's Journal* (London, 1774). The lines quoted are 239–40, with slight variations.

First Citizen's First Letter

FEBRUARY 4, 1773

The FIRST CITIZEN to the editor of the Dialogue between TWO CITIZENS

SIR,

The intention of this address is not to entice you to throw off a fictitious, and to assume a real character: for I am not one of those who have puzzled themselves with endless conjectures about your mysterious personage; a secret too deep for me to pry into, and if known, not of much moment; of as little is it in my opinion whether your complexion be olive or fair, your eyes black or gray, your person strait or *incurvated*, your deportment easy and natural, insolent, or affected; you have therefore my consent to remain concealed under a borrowed name, as long as you may think proper, I see no great detriment that will thereby accrue to the publick; *you* will be the greatest! nay! the only sufferer; your fellow citizens, ignorant to whom they stand indebted for such excellent lucubrations, will not know at what shrine to offer up their incense, and tribute of praise; to you this sacrifice of glory will be the less painful, as *you are not actuated by vanity or a lust of fame*, and in obscurity you will have this consolation still left, the enjoyment of conscious merit, and of self-applause. Modest men of real worth are subject to a certain diffidence, called by the French *la mauvaise honte*,[a] which frequently prevents their rising in the world; you are not likely, I must

[a] *An awkward bashfulness.*

own, to be guilty of their fault; *in vitium ducit culpae fuga;*[b] you seem rather to have fallen into the other extreme, and to be fully sensible of the wisdom of the French maxim, *il fault se faire valoir,*[c] which for the benefit of my English readers, I will venture to translate thus — *"A man ought to set a high value on his own talents."* This saying is somewhat analogous to that of Horace — *sume superbiam quaesitam meritis.*[d,1] As your manner of writing discovers vast erudition, and extensive reading, I make no doubt you are thoroughly acquainted with the Latin and French languages, and therefore a citation or two from each may not be unpalatable.

Having paid these compliments to your literary merit, I wish it were in my power to say as much in favor of your candor and sincerity. The editor of the dialogue between two Citizens, it seems, is the same person, who *overheard and committed to writing the conversation.* I was willing to suppose the editor had his relation at *second hand,* for I could not otherwise account for the lame, mutilated, and imperfect part of the conversation attributed to me, without ascribing the publication to downright malice, and wilfull misrepresentation. Where I can, I am always willing to give the mildest construction to a dubious action. — The editor has now put it out of my power of judging thus favorably of him, and as I have not the least room to trust to his impartiality a second time, I find myself under the necessity of making a direct application to the press, to vindicate my intellectual faculties, which, no doubt, have suffered much in the opinion of the publick (notwithstanding its great good nature) from the publication of the abovementioned dialogue.

The sentiments of the first Citizen are so miserably mangled and disfigured, that he scarce can trace the smallest likeness between those, which really fell from him in the course of that conversation, and what have been put into his mouth.

[b] *The avoiding one fault is apt to lead us into another.*

[c] *In the text these words have received a liberal translation; they mean strictly —That a person should assume a proper consequence.*

[d] *May be translated—Assume a pride to merit justly due.*

---

[1] Horace, *Carmina* 3, 30, 15.

The first Citizen has not the vanity to think his thoughts communicated to a fellow citizen in private, of sufficient importance to be made publick, nor would he have had the presumption to trouble that awful tribunal with his crude and indigested notions of politics, had they not already been egregiously misrepresented in print. Whether they appear to more advantage in their present dress, others must determine; the newness of the fashion gives them quite a different air and appearance; let the decision be what it will, since much depends on the manner of relating facts, the first Citizen thinks he ought to be permitted to relate them his own way.

1st Cit. I am sorry that party attachments and connexions have induced you to abandon old principles; there was a time, Sir, when you had not so favourable an opinion of the integrity and good intentions of Government, as you now seem to have. Your conduct on this occasion makes me suspect that formerly *some men, not measures*, were disagreeable to you. Have we reason to place a greater confidence in our *present rulers*, than in those to whom I allude? Some of the present set (it is true) were then in power, others indeed were not yet provided for, and therefore a push was to be made to thrust them into office, that all power might centre in *one family*. Is all your patriotism come to this?

2d Cit. I do not like such home expostulations, convince me that I act wrong in supporting Government and I will alter my conduct, no man is more open to conviction than myself — (Vide Dialogue to the words, "Would be all fair argument")

1st Cit. I am not surprised that the threadbare topics of arbitrary princes, and proclamations, should give you uneasiness; you have insinuated that the repetition of them is tiresome, but I suspect that the true cause of your aversion proceeds from another quarter. You are afraid of a comparison between the *present ministers* of this province, and *those*, who influenced Charles the first, and brought him to the block; the resemblance I assure you would be striking. You insinuate that "*The opinons of the greatest Counsel in England*" are come to hand, in favor of the proclamation, and 40 per poll, and you seem to lay great stress on those opinions. A little reflection, and acquaintance with history will teach you, that the opinions of *Court Lawyers* are not always to be relied on; remember the issue of *Hambden's* trial:[2] "*The prejudiced or prostituted judges*" (*four* "*excepted*") (says Hume) "*gave sentence in favour of the Crown.*"[3] The opinion even of a Camden, will have no weight with me, should it contradict a settled point of constitutional doctrine. On this occasion I cannot forbear citing a sentence or two from the justly admired author of the Considerations, which have made a deep impression on my memory: "*In a question*" (says that writer) "*of publick concernment, the opinion of no Court Lawyer, however respectable for his candor and abilities, ought to weigh more than the reasons adduced in support of it.*"[4] He then gives his reasons for this assertion; to avoid prolixity I must refer you to the pamphlet; if I am not mistaken you will find them in page 12. Speaking shortly after of the opinions of Court Lawyers upon "*American affairs,*" he makes this pertinent remark — "*They*" (*Court Lawyers opinions*), "*have been all strongly marked with the same character: they have been generally very sententious, and the same observation may be applied to them all, they have de-clared* THAT *to be* LEGAL *which the minister for the time being has deemed to be* EXPEDIENT." Will you admit *this to be fair argument?*

2d Cit. I confess it carries some weight with it; I cannot with propriety dispute the authority, on which it is founded: make there-fore the most of my concession; should I admit your reasoning on this head to be just, does it follow, that the Court and Country interests are incompatible; that Government and Liberty are irrec-oncilable? Is every man, who thinks differently from you on publick measures, influenced or corrupted?

1st Cit. "*God forbid it should be the case of every individual.*" I have already hinted at the cause of your attachment to Government; it proceeds, I fear, more from personal considerations, than from a

---

[2] John Hampden (1594-1643) was tried in exchequer court in 1638 for his refusal to pay ship-money. Ship-money was levied on coastal towns and counties in 1634 and extended to inland jurisdictions in 1635. Writs for ship-money were issued by Charles I because of the alleged danger from pirates and in order to strengthen naval defenses. Judgement against Hampden was given on June 12, 1638. Five judges, two on technical grounds, decided for Hampden, but seven supported the Crown. Ship-money was levied for the last time in 1639 and was declared illegal by the Long Parliament in 1641.

[3] David Hume, *History of England* (London, 1767), 6:317.

[4] Daniel Dulany, Jr., *Considerations on the Propriety of Imposing Taxes in the British Colonies* (Annapolis, 1765), pp. 12–13.

persuasion of the rectitude of our Court measures; but I would not have you confound Government, with the Officers of Government; they are things really distinct, and yet in your idea they seem to be one and the same.

Government was instituted for the general good, but Officers instructed with its powers, have most commonly perverted them to the selfish views of avarice and ambition; hence the Country and Court interests, which ought to be the same, have been too often opposite, as must be acknowledged and lamented by every true friend to Liberty. You ask me, are Government and Liberty incompatible? Your question arises from an abuse of words, and confusion of ideas, I answer, that so far from being incompatible, I think they cannot subsist independent of each other. A few great and good princes have found the means of reconciling them even in despotic states; Tacitus says of Nerva, "*Res olim dissociables miscuit, principatum, ac libertatem,*"*[5] a wicked minister has endeavored, and is now endeavoring in this *free government*, to set the power of the supreme magistrate above the laws: in our mother country such ministers have been punished for the attempt with infamy, death, or exile: I am surprised, that he who imitates *their* example, should not dread *their* fate.

2d Cit. This is not coming to the point, you talk at random of dangers threatening liberty, and of infringements of the constitution, which exist only in your imagination. Prove, I say, *our ministers* to have advised unconstitutional measures, and I am ready to abandon them and their cause; but upon your *ipse dixit*, I shall not admit those measures to be unconstitutional, which you are pleased to call so, nor can I allow all those to be Court hirelings, whom you think proper to stigmatise with that opprobrious appellation, and for

---

* (*Thus translated by Gordon.*) *Nerva blended together two things, once found irreconcilable—Publick Liberty and Sovereign Power.*

---

[5] Tacitus, *Agricolam* 3, 3. Nerva was Marcus Cocceius, Roman emperor A.D. 96–98. After Domitian's assassination, he was regarded the best representative of the Senate's ideas and received imperial powers from that body. His short reign, in which he shared power with Trajan, was considered an exemplary one. *The Works of Tacitus* (London, 1728–1731) were translated by Thomas Gordon.

no other reason, but that they dare exercise their *own judgement in opposition to yours* — (Read the 2d Citizen's harangue from the last words (opposition to yours) to the following inclusively, *sweat of his brow*)

1st Cit. What a flow of words! how pregnant with thought and deep reason! if you expect an answer to all the points, on which you have spoken, you must excuse my prolixity, and impute it to the variety of matter laid before me; I shall endeavour to be concise, and if possible, avoid obscurity — you say — *I know not what or whom I mean by we, and the friends of the constitution* — I will tell you, Sir, whom I do not mean, from whence you may guess at those, whom I do. — By friends of the constitution, I mean not those, whose selfish attachments to their interest has deprived the publick of a most beneficial Law, from the want of which by your own account, *"Our staple is fallen into disgrace in foreign markets and every man's property in a degree decreasing and mouldering away."* I mean not *those few*, out of tenderness and regard to whom, the general welfare of this province has been sacrificed; to preserve *whose* salaries from dimunition, the fortunes of all their countrymen have been suffered to be impaired; I mean not *those*, who advised a measure, which cost the first Charles his crown and life, and who have dared to defend it upon principles more unjustifiable and injurious than those, under which it was at first pretentedly palliated. You see Sir I adopt the maxim of the British constitution — *The King can do no wrong*,[6] I impute all the blame to his ministers, who if found guilty and *dragged to light*, I hope will be made to feel the resentment of a free people. But it seems from your suggestions that we are to place an unlimited trust in the men, whom I have pretty plainly pointed out, because they are men of great wealth and have *"as deep a stake in the safety of the constitution as any of us."* Property even in *private* life, is not always a security against dishonesty, in *publick*, it is much less so. The ministers, who have made the boldest attacks on liberty, have been most of them men of affluence; from whence I infer, that riches so far from insuring a minister's honesty, ought rather to make us more watchful of his conduct.

[6] The maxim may be found in Blackstone's *Commentaries on the Laws of England* (London, 1821), 1:246.

You go on with this argument, and urge me thus: "*Do I conceive that such men can possibly be hired unless they be overtaken by infatuation, to engage to pull down a fair and stately edifice, with the ruins of which, as soon as it is levelled to the ground, they and their families are to be stoned to death.*" I have read of numberless instances of such infatuation; there are now *living examples* of it; the history of mankind is full of them; men in the gratification of sensual appetites, are apt to overlook their future consequences; thus for the present enjoyment of wealth and power — liberty in reversion will be easily given up; besides, a perpetuity in office may be aimed at; hopes may be entertained that the *good thing*, like a precious jewel, will be handed down from *father* to *son*. I have known men of such meanness, and of such insolence (qualities often met with in the same person), who exclusive of the above motives, would wish to be the first slave of a sultan, to lord it over all the rest; power Sir, power is apt to pervert the best of natures; with too much of it, I would not trust the milkiest man on earth; and shall we place confidence in a *minister* too long inured to rule, grown old, callous, and hackneyed in the crooked paths of policy?

2d Cit. "*I do not choose to answer this last question*" — you grow warm and press me too close. But why is all your indignation poured out against our ministers, and no part of it reserved for the lawyers — those cut-throats, extortioners — those enemies of peace and honesty, those *reipublicae portenta, ac poena fumera,*[t] to use the energetic words of Tully, because I can find none in english to convey my full meaning, but by comparing *our harpies* to those two monsters of iniquity— Piso, and Gabinius.[7]

---

[t] *Mr. Melmoth, the elegant translator of Cicero's familiar letters, makes this remark in his notes on the 8th letter of the first book, Vol. 1—"Cicero has delineated the characters at large of these consuls (Piso and Gabinius) in several of his orations, but he has in two words given the most odious picture of them that exasperated eloquence perhaps ever drew, where he calls them "duo reipublicae portenta ac poena fumera"—an expression for which moderne language can furnish no equivalent."*

---

[7] *The Letters of Marcus Tullius Cicero to Several of His Friends* (London, 1753), translated by William Melmoth. The Cicero quote is from *de prov. consul.* 1, 2, and may be translated: "those two monsters of depravity who almost ruined the state." The consuls to whom Cicero alludes are Lucius Calpurnius Piso, a plebeian nobilis whose daughter married Caesar, and Aulus Gabinius, a dependent and favorite of Pompey. They succeeded Caesar and Bibulus in this office in 58 B.C., the year Cicero went into exile.

1st Cit. From this vehemence of yours, I perceive you are one of those, who have joined in the late cry against lawyers; from what cause does all this rancour and animosity against those gentlemen proceed? is it a real tenderness for the people, which has occasioned such scurrility and abuse? or does your hatred, and that of your kidney, arise from disappointment and the unexpected alliance, between the lawyers and the people, in opposition to officers,— This alliance, I know, has been termed unnatural, because it was thought contrary to the lawyer's interests, to separate themselves from the officers; since a close and firm union between the two, would probably secure success against all patriotic attempts to relieve the people from their late heavy burthens, of which too great a part still subsists.

2d Cit. "*For heaven's sake to what purpose is all this idle talk? you well know it does not touch us, we are not galled and therefore need not wince.*" But reconcile, if you can the inconsistency of conduct, with which some of your favourites may be justly re-proached; I have one or two in my eye (*great patriots*) whose conduct, I am sure, will not bear a strict scrutiny; "*I can tell them with truth* — (Vide dialogue from the last words, to these — *glorious and patriotic particulars.*"[2]

1st Cit. Is it a crime then to be seen in the company of certain great officers of government? — surely *their* principles must be pestilential indeed, whose *very breath* breeds contagion. But you can name, "*the very appointments, they have laid their fingers upon, you are well apprised of their eager impatience to get into office*"; if you are well assured of all this, if you can name the appointments, why in God's name, do it; speak out, at once undeceive me; shew me that I have mistaken my men, that I have been imposed on; for never will I deem that man a fast and firm friend to his country, or fit to represent it; who under their circumstances applies for, or accepts an office from government; the application for, or the acceptance of a place by the persons alluded to, would in my opinion, as much disqualify them for so important a trust, as the duplicity of character which you lay to their charge.

2d Cit. Do not mistake my meaning, or wilfully misrepresent it; I do not pretend to insinuate, that a person accepting a place thereby becomes unfit for a representative, but that no dependence

can be placed in one, who declaims with virulence against *officers,*
—and yet would readily take an *office.*

1st Cit. So I understood you, have I put a different construction
on your meaning?

2d Cit. Not expressly; but you seem to think the acceptance of
a place, as exceptionable, as duplicity of conduct; I am not quite of
that opinion.

1st Cit. There we differ then; I esteem a double dealer, and an
officer equally unfit to be chosen a member of Assembly, for this
opinion I have the sanction of an Act of Parliament, which vacates
the seat of a member of the house of Commons on his obtaining a
post from Government,[8] presuming, that men under the bias of self-
interest, and under personal obligations to Government, cannot act
with a freedom and independency becoming a representative of the
people. The Act, it is true, leaves the electors at liberty to return
the same member to parliament, in which particular (be it spoken
with due deference) it is more worthy our censure, than imitation;
I have a wide field before me, but I perceive your patience begins
to be exhausted, and your temper to be ruffled. I have told some
disagreeable truths with a frankness, which may be thought by a
person *of your steadiness and importance* somewhat disrespectful;
I leave you to ponder in silence, and at leisure on what I have said
— Farewell.

[8] The Succession of the Crown Act (1707).

Antilon's Second Letter

To the PRINTERS of the MARYLAND GAZETTE

*Not having been in any manner, directly or indirectly, concerned
in any piece, that has appeared in your paper in regard to the
present political contests, I hope you will give a place to the
inclosed, in your next Gazette.*

Feb. 14, 1773.

*Malevolo nihil acerbius, imperito nihil injustius, homine im-
pudente nihil molestius.* Macrob. de Mor. Hom.[1]

The confederacy of infuriate malignancy, overweening ignorance, and habitual licentiousness, would be, indeed, formidable, if
there were no other means of defence against its attacks, than to
dissolve the union by softening rancor, correcting folly, and reforming profligacy; but, happily, little is to be dreaded from the alliance,
when the aims of all its exertions are easily exposed, and indignation, and contempt, ensuing the detection, can't fail to furnish
ample succours to repel the outrage.

---

[1] "Nothing is more sour than an envious man, more unreasonable than an
ignorant one, more annoying than a shameless one." There is no work of
this title attributed to Macrobius. These lines may be from *Commentarii in
Somnium Scripionis.*

The restriction of the Officers (on the falling of the Inspection Law) by the Governor's Proclamation, has been represented to be a measure as arbitrary and tyrannical, as the assessment of Ship-money, in the time of Charles the First, not by fairly stating the nature of each transaction, and shewing the resemblance by comparison, to convince the understanding; but in the favourite method of illiberal calumny, virulent abuse, and shameless asseveration to affect the passions.

Inveterate malice, destitute of proofs, has invented falsehood, for incorrigible folly to adopt, and indurated impudence to propagate. As the artifice employed to raise alarm, can succeed only in the proportion that it deceives, it will be my endeavour to counteract the pestilent purpose, by presenting to the reader, for his candid examination, an impartial account of the Ship-money, and the Proclamation. King Charles, having determined to govern without a Parliament, had, against the fundamental principles of a free constitution, recourse to the Prerogative for raising money on the subject, though in his answer to the Petition of Right,[2] he had recently bound himself not to levy any tax upon the people without the consent of both Houses of Parliament. In pursuance of this scheme of tyranny, "Ship-money was raised on the whole kingdom. The method fallen upon was, a rate, or proportion on each county, which was afterwards assessed upon the individuals of each. The sum raised was about £200,000 sterling. Writs were issued, directing the tax to be levied by the sheriffs, and requiring them to execute the effects of *the people for the purpose*, and *to commit to prison all who should oppose the tax, there to remain, till the King should give order for their delivery*."

The necessity, of taking measures of defence against enemies, was alleged as a justification of the arbitrary proceeding: but, "it was a fictitious, pretended necessity: for England was in no danger from enemies — on the contrary enjoyed a profound peace with all her neighbours, who were engaged in furious, and bloody wars, and by their mutual enmities further secured her tranquillity. The writs, which issued for levying the Ship-money, contradicted the supposition of necessity, and pretended only that the seas were infested

[2] The Petition of Right (1628) required consent of Parliament to the levy of all loans, gifts, or benevolences. Charles I agreed to the petition as a private act, June 7.

with pirates, a slight, and temporary inconvenience, which might well have waited a legal tax laid by Parliament — besides the writs allowed several months for equipping the ships, much beyond the 40 days requisite for summoning the Parliament, and the pretended necessity was continued for near four years."[3] — Such, in substance, was the affair of Ship money, the exaction, which Mr. Hampden opposed with the energetic firmness of genuine patriotism.

That the reader may compare the two measures, and be the better able to judge of their similarity, I shall recite the Governor's Proclamation, which was in these words:

"Being desirous to prevent any oppressions and extortions from being committed, under colour of office, by any of the Officers and Ministers of this province, and every of them, their deputies, or substitutes, in exacting unreasonable and excessive fees from the good people thereof, I have thought fit, with the advice of his Lordship's Council of State, to issue this my Proclamation, and I do hereby therefore order and direct, that from and after the publication hereof, no Officer nor Officers (the Judges of the Land office excepted, who are subject to other regulation to them given in charge) their deputies, or substitutes, by reason or colour of his or their office, or offices, have, receive, demand, or take, of any person or persons, directly or indirectly, any other, or greater fees than by an Act of Assembly of this province, entitled *An Act for amending the staple of tobacco, for preventing frauds in his Majesty's customs, and for the limitation of Officers fees*, were limited and allowed, or take or receive of any person or persons, on immediate payment (in case payment shall be made in money) any larger fee, than after the rate of twelve shillings and six-pence common current money for 100 lb. of tobacco, under the pain of my displeasure. And to the intent that all persons concerned may have due notice thereof, I do strictly charge and require the several sheriffs of this province to make this my Proclamation publick in their respective counties, in the usual manner, as they will answer the contrary at their peril."[4]

---

[3] Much of these extracts is taken from David Hume's *History of England* (London, 1767), 6:252–53, but the copy is loose and there are several omissions.

[4] The proclamation was issued November 26, 1770, five days after the proroguing of the 1770 assembly. The land office regulation was issued on November 24. They were laid before the house on Octber 17, 1771, and are printed in full in *Maryland Archives* (Baltimore: Maryland Historical So-

It must be allowed, that the table of fees, in the late Inspection Law, was the most moderate of any, ever established in the province — and that the Officers are entitled to satisfaction for the services they perform. [3]

The reader can't but perceive, that the Officers are restrained from taking *more* from the people, than the table of fees, referred to, allows, as far as the threats of the Governor's displeasure, *who has power to remove them from their offices,* can operate as a restriction, and that there is no attempt in the Proclamation to subject the people, indebted to the Officers for service performed to any *execution* of their effects, or *imprisonment* of their persons, on *any account.*

The Proclamation issued with the professed design of preventing extortion and oppression; but if it had not *ascertained* the fees that might be received, it would have been entirely ineffectual, as a preventive of extortion.

It needs not any display of argument to prove, that the Proclamation, being prohibitory, allowed the Officers to receive, with impunity, according to the rate referred to.

Extortion, according to its proper, legal signification, is committed when an Officer, by colour of his office, takes money (or other valuable thing) which is not due, or *more* than is due, or before it is due. That an Officer is entitled to compensation, for the services he performs, can't be denied, and therefore he is not guilty of extortion, *merely in taking money*, or other valuable thing for his service, unless he takes *more* than is due. It is obvious to common sense, that there *must* be some *established* measure, or there can be no *excess* — that the term *more* cannot apply, unless what is due be *ascertained*— there must be a *positive*, or there can be no *comparative*. Let the result then be considered. If *something* be undeniably due, when a service is performed, and no *certain* rule, or measure to *determine* the rate, should an Officer take *as much as he can exact*, he would not commit extortion, according to the legal acceptation of the term, *extortion*. The professed design of the Proclama-

---

ciety, 1883–), 63:109–10 and 112. The 1763 act, passed November 26, entitled "An Act for Amending the Staple of Tobacco for Preventing Frauds in his Majesty's Customs and for the Limitation of Officers Fees," is printed *ibid.*, 58:433–97.

tion was to prevent extortion, the method pursued (and it was the *only one* that could be pursued) to *effectuate* the prevention, was the *settlement* of the rates — if the Proclamation had authority to fix the rates, according to which the Officers *might* receive, and *beyond which*, they could not *lawfully* receive, it was preventive of extortion — if it had not *such* authority, it was ineffectual; but whether it had, or not, depended on its legality *determinable in the ordinary judicatories*: for, as the reader will observe, there is no enforcement provided, or attempted by the Proclamation, with respect to those, for whom services might be performed; wherefore, if the settlement of the fees was attended with a legal obligation on the Officer not to take *more* than, and the people to pay *as much as*, the rates established, the Officer's remedy to recover his due, on refusal to pay it, must be sought for, where any other creditor is entitled to relief — if on the contrary the settlement of fees was not attended with *such* obligation, the Proclamation was ineffectual except so far as the dread of the Governor's displeasure might restrain Officers from taking, beyond the rate allowed by the late Inspection Law, and this being a mere question of Law, determinable in the *same* course, that justice is administered in *other* cases, what astonishing extravagance is it to call the Proclamation, an infringement of the fundamental principles of a free constitution, and what malice and effrontery must *they* be possessed with, who have endeavoured to represent it in the odious light of an act of tyranny — a measure destitute of all enforcement, of every degree of efficacy, which the *Law does not give* in its *regular*, ordinary course of Administration! *Fortiter aspergas, ut aliquid adhaereat* (asperse plentifully that something may stick) is the favourite document of the malicious Veteran — Like Ship-money! Compare, Reader, the two transactions, and your sensibility will be severely tasked to repress the emotions of indignation.

The Proclamation binds no farther than it is legal — its legality is determinable, in the ordinary course of justice — it directs no method of compulsion to enforce a compliance from the people, nor gives any remedy to the Officer, for the recovery of his dues, to which he is not entitled by the rules of Law — if legal, it is not oppressive — if not legal, the severest epithet that justice can admit, is, that it is useless to the Officer, though of some service to the people, in the restriction to which he is subjected. But the writs, for raising Ship-money, imposed a tax, derogatory from those most essential principles of Government, on which the conservation of publick liberty depends. These writs levied about £200,000 sterling, when nothing was due — they compelled payment by means the most rigorous; by distress, or execution on the effects, and imprisonment of the people, who should oppose the levy, during the will and pleasure of a tyrant. The royal mandate imposed the tax, adjusted the proportion, and directed the collection of it — the arbitrary seizure of property, and the deprivation of personal liberty were employed to spread terror, and compel submission to a tyrant's will; I say, tyrant, though the appellation may offend *the principled delicacy of Independent Whigs, particularly characterized by their attachment to the maxim, that the King can do no wrong*, and the doctrine of divine indefeasible hereditary right — a maxim and doctrine to which the refractory *Tories*, at the *Revolution*, offered such impious violence. *Whigs*, of whose instruction Cambridge cannot boast, whatever praise may be due to the documents of St. Omers,[5] and the institution of billiard rooms and tipling houses — the former, the best seminary in the universe of the champions for civil and religious liberty, the latter, of the most finished patterns of modesty, decorum, and animated elocution. King James the second, *to be sure*, did *no wrong*, in attempting to destroy all the rights of the subject, civil and religious, and yet was cruelly driven into exile; but let not the lamentations of the confederated *Independent Whigs* be too loud in deploring this *melancholy* event, as vulgar prejudice ranks the Revolution among the most glorious

[5] St. Omers was the famous English Jesuit college in Flanders. Carroll spent the first six years there of his time abroad, 1748–1765. The college was the target of much Protestant resentment in Maryland. The Freeholders of Calvert County submitted a petition in favor of lower house anti-Catholic legislation in 1755, in which they said they were shocked to find "men highly to be suspected of Popery & who were educated at St. Omers & brought up in yt Religion, admitted into Employments of great Trust & Profit." *Maryland Archives* 52:669. There were several English statutes which, if applicable in Maryland, would have prohibited the education of children in foreign seminaries: 2 James I, c.4, par. 6; 3 James I, c.5; 3 Chas I, c.2; 11 and 12 Wm III, c.4, par. 6, cited in Lawrence H. Gipson, *The British Empire Before the American Revolution* (New York: Knopf, 1958–), 2:48–51. See also St. George L. Sioussat, *English Statutes in Maryland* (Baltimore: Johns Hopkins Press, 1903).

deeds, that have done honour to the character of Englishmen, and may be apt to consider the principles of *our Independent Whigs*, as a basis too rotten to sustain the weighty superstructure of national liberty. There was a time, when the generous and spirited behaviour of one of the Confederates nearly brought on a relentless persecution against all of the same religious profession. Unjust and merciless vengeance! Had he alone been the martyr, the pangs of his sufferance would have been more than compensated by the glory of it; but hard it would have been on those to suffer, who could have derived no consolation from a similar merit. After the experience of having nearly ruined the party, of whom the importance and powers of superior wealth, and superior talents, placed him at the head. — After the experience of greater benefits having been derived from his most implacable enmity, than could have been from the utmost exertions of his most cordial friendship (my allusion is sufficiently intelligible), what admirable firmness must *that man* have, who will persist in the same course. If actuated by the motive of the unhappy spirit, who feels some relief, in his torments, from the agonies of others, his persistence might be accounted for; but this hypothesis must fail; for miscarriage has ever attended his efforts to distress, and benefits redounded from his best concerted schemes to destroy — how forlorn his situation! tormented when inactive — disappointed when active — incapable of relief, but from anothers pangs, and incapable to inflict them.

As the full efficacy of the Proclamation, for the very purpose professed, that of preventing extortion, depends upon the authority to settle the fees, because without the standard, or measure to ascertain what is due, there can be no extortion in taking *any* sum, for a service performed; how amazingly strange is it to say, that the Proclamation was defended upon principles different from what is professed, when the arguments, applied in defence of the Proclamation, were calculated to prove the authority to settle the fees, without which the Proclamation, for the reasons assigned, would be ineffectual as a preventive of extortion. The Governor's Proclamation was "a measure that cost King Charles his crown and life, which the advisers of it have defended upon principles, more unjustifiable and injurious than those, under which it was pretendedly palliated. You see, Sir, I adopt the maxim of the British constitution, *the King can do no wrong*. I impute all the blame to his Ministers, who, if found guilty, and dragged to light, I hope will be made to feel the resentment of a free people." — I must refer the reader to the *Gazette* of the 4th instant, for this most curious specimen of the political tenets of *these modern Independent Whigs*, of the extent of their knowledge, and the force of their expression. It would be hard indeed if his Majesty was chargeable with having done wrong, because the Governor of Maryland, with the advice of his council, issued a Proclamation to prevent the extortion of Officers. There is no occasion to have recourse to any maxim of jurisprudence for his vindication, common sense will at once acquit him — there can be no difficulty in finding out his Ministers, the Governor and Council are answerable in this character. *He* cannot disavow an act to which his signature is affixed. The indignation, and contempt, such impotent vehemence and futile arrogance are wont to excite, make it difficult to speak without perplexity. — The Governor, however, in the complimental address of one of the Confederates to himself, and his coadjutors, is raised to the Throne, and graced with the attribute of indelible rectitude. Base prostitution! Is their patriotism come to this? Did they mean by this fawning servility to expiate *all* the wanton indignities they had offered him? After he had most expressly declared that "What *he* should judge to be right and just, would be the *only* dictate to determine his conduct,"[6] they represented that he was blindly led by others, and not determined by his own judgement, and then add an insult to his understanding, by such extravagant adulation, as the meanest debasement would blush to offer, delicacy must nauseate, and common sense resent with indignation, especially after having been honoured by an approbation of his conduct, he is ambitious to deserve, and the *highest* he can receive. They know not him whom they thus treat.

Cui, male si palpere, recalcitrat undique tutus[7] — so inseparable are insolence and meanness — "Had" he relied upon his own manly judgment, &c.

[6] The governor's reply to the address of the lower house, November 30, 1771. *Maryland Archives* 63:223.

[7] Horace, *Sermons* 2, 1, 20. It may be translated, "whom, like a generous steed, if you stroke awkwardly, will kick you, being always on his guard."

"EDEN had been a little God below."[8]

With what propriety did they choose the signature, INDEPEND-
ENT WHIGS? What vast knowledge must these men have, who are
acquainted with the manners of the Ancients, *who to be sure never
made use of invectives in their political contests*, as well as they
are with the principles of Whiggism? A knowledge which neither
OXFORD nor CAMBRIDGE ever taught.

The idea of tax having been annexed to the regulation of the
fees, though without any provision for their payment, other than
what the Law, on the very grounds of its legality, should afford, it
may not be amiss to examine the propriety of it. If the idea be
proper, then fees can be settled, in no case, except by the Legislature, because it requires such authority to lay a tax; but the House
of Lords, the House of Commons, the Courts of Law and Equity
in Westminster Hall, the Upper and Lower Houses of Assembly,
have each of them settled fees. If such settlement be legal, then
the idea is improper; if illegal, it is strange, indeed, that it should
have so generally obtained. When fees have not been settled by an
Act of Assembly, they have, for the most part, been settled by the
authority of Government, so that the Proclamation in 1770 was not
the invention of any daring Ministers *now in being*. The opinions of
eminent Counsel, as well before the year 1733, as since the year
1770, have been very fully given in favour of this authority, on a
full state of the case, and in the latter instance, after a consideration
of the arguments contained in the Address to the Governor, and his
Answer; but the opinion of Counsel having been intimated, the
following quotation from a pamphlet has been introduced as pertinent to the occasion: "On a question of publick concernment, the
opinions of Court Lawyers, however respectable for their candor,
ought not to weigh more than the reasons adduced in support of
them; they have been all strongly marked with the same characters;
they have been generally very sententious, and the same observation
may be applied to all of them. They have declared that to be legal,
which the Minister, for the time being, has deemed to be expedient."[9]
You have, reader, already seen in the comparison between Ship-

[8] From "Independent Whigs to the First Citizen," *Maryland Gazette*, February 11, 1773, p. 2.
[9] See First Citizen's first letter, note 4.

money, and the Governor's Proclamation, one instance of the extraordinary knack of the *Independent Whigs* at assimilation, and you will now be entertained with another.

The opinion respecting the Proclamation is on no point, which the Minister for the time being aims to establish. Opinions, in favour of the Proclamation, have been given at the different periods of 1732 and 1772, by eminent Counsel, not only unconnected with, but distinguished by their opposition to, Administration.[10] Make the comparison, how striking the resemblance! — I shall not contend that the opinion of Counsel is conclusive in any case; but presume to say, that it may have weight, as well on the affair of the Proclamation, as any other. And that they, whose sentiments coincide with the opinions of Counsel, eminent in their profession, and disinterested on the question, are not fairly represented as engines of oppression, and enemies to their country. It would be a degree of arrogance, rather too excessive, *even* for the Confederacy, *expressly to avow*, that *every* sentiment, and every measure opposite to their malignant and selfish views, ought to be treated with contempt, or received with abhorrence, and such only entitled to regard, as tend to promote them. The *prudent and politick* Ogle,[11] notwithstanding the most violent opposition that ever a governor of Maryland met with, to his measures, regardless of all the virulent abuse, with which he was attacked, acted steadily, and despised the railings, particularly, of such men, as he disappointed in their unreasonable and arrogant expectations, by doing what, he thought, justice and equity required. *He* was so well convinced of the authoritative force of the Proclamation for settling the fees of Officers, that he expressly determined, as Chancellor, by a final compulsory decree, fees should be paid upon the authority, and according to the very settlement of the Proclamation.[12] What will the Confederacy say

[10] He revealed their identities on page 118 below. See below in Antilon's third letter, note 33.

[11] Samuel Ogle (1702–1752), proprietary governor, 1732, 1733–1742, and 1747–1752.

[12] His decree was in confirmation of the fee proclamation by the proprietary April 14, 1733. The controversy over the authority to set fees was finally resolved with the Inspection Law of 1747. The council in 1735 declared the proclamation was "strictly legal and by the same Authority by which our courts of Justice are erected" and declined to join the lower house in a protest against it. *Maryland Archives* 39:183.

to this? Did *he* deserve "infamy, death, or exile," for giving an irresistible, conclusive force to the Proclamation? No, no, to be sure, not quite a punishment so severe, because the *Independent Whigs* (*Independent Whigs* risum teneatis)[13] "*highly approve the British maxim, the King can do no wrong*," and therefore (the *reasonable* postulatum being admitted that a *Governor* is *King*) Mr. Ogle did no wrong; but without doubt, according to their admirable principles, if he had been Chancellor *only*, and *not both* Chancellor and Governor, he would have deserved death, &c.

In consequence of a commission issued by the Crown, upon the Address of the British House of Commons, the Lord Chancellor of England, *by the authority of his station*, and by and with the advice and assistance of the Master of the Rolls, ordered that "the Officers of the Court of Chancery should not demand, or take any *greater* fees for their services in their respective offices, *than according to the rates he established*, and that any Officer taking *more* should be punished as for a *contempt*; and that all persons might have notice of his regulation and restriction, his Lordship was pleased further to order the same to be forthwith printed and published." An Address from the House of Commons to the King; a commission from the King in pursuance of it; an Order of the Chancellor settling the fees; this Order printed and published,[14] and, *yet the settlement of fees, a tax similar to Ship-money!* "passing strange!" The Members of the House of Commons, *to be sure, were all bribed*, or forgot the privilege they had so often and zealously asserted, or they would not have addressed the King to issue a Commission *for taxing* the subject.

Serjeant Hawkins, who was a man of experience in the profession of the Law, and whose treatise of the Pleas of Crown is in great estimation, has been *so rash*, or so great an *enemy to liberty*, as to say in print, that "the Courts of Justice, in whose integrity the Law always reposes the highest confidence, are not restrained from allowing reasonable fees for the labour and attendance of their Officers; for the *chief danger of oppression* is from Officers *being left at liberty* to *set their own rates* on their labour, and make their

---

[13] May be translated, "keep laughing."

[14] *An Order of the High Court of Chancery . . . Relating to the Fees of the Officers, Clerks and Ministers of the said Court* (London, 1744).

own demands; but there can't be so much fear of *these abuses*, while they are restrained to known and stated fees, settled by the discretion of the Courts, which will not suffer them to be exceeded, without the highest resentment."[15]

What, Mr. Serjeant, have the Court's authority to tax the people, in a manner as arbitrary as Ship-money? Shall they be allowed to do *that*, *which* brought King Charles to the block? How would the learned gentleman be confounded at this expostulation, if alive to hear it? "The general welfare of this province has been sacrificed," say the Confederates, "out of tenderness and regard to a *few*, to preserve *whose* salaries from dimunition, the fortunes of *all* their countrymen have been suffered to be impaired." What say YE to this imputation, Ye who *unanimously* dissented to the Inspection Bill? YE will hardly acknowledge the *imputed* motive of your conduct, as a compliment to your understanding, candor, or spirit. A dimunition, and that very considerable, of all fees was readily agreed to, in the election given to all persons to pay in money or tobacco, and this election was extended to the Clergy's dues; but the Bill failed.[16] I might safely refer the question to the opinion of my countrymen, whether, if an Inspection Law had passed, upon the terms offered the session before last, the general welfare of this province would have been sacrificed, and all their fortunes impaired? If not, what must they think of the principles of such profligate incendiaries, as these Confederates are? Nearly the same alteration of fees was proposed heretofore, *without giving an elec-*

[15] Serjeant William Hawkins (1673–1746), *A Treatise of the Pleas of the Crown* (London, 1762), chapter 68, sec. 3, p. 171. Antilon's emphasis.

[16] The upper house proposed in a message to the lower house, October 22, 1770, "That the Duties and Fees of the Officers and Lawyers and the Dues of the Clergy do stand as they were limitted and regulated by the said (1763) act, with this Difference, that all, who shall chuse to pay for services immediately on Performance, may be at liberty to discharge the Fees in Money." *Maryland Archives* 62:187–88. The bill was "unanimously disagreed to" by the lower house the same day, *ibid.*, p. 272. The 1763 Act was due to expire soon after the assembly convened, September 25, 1770, and on September 29 it was continued until October 22. The inability of the two houses to compromise led to its expiration on that date. The council insisted that the lower house's proposed revisal of the fee scale "would reduce them so low as not to have a sufficient and proper support for the officers," while the lower house would not budge from its reductions. The option to pay in money would have had the effect of reducing fees by one-third. The legislative deadlock is outlined *ibid.*, pp. xxix–xxx.

tion to the people to pay in money, or tobacco, but it failed. [4]
By whom was all power engrossed at that period? Whose influence,
then, put to hazard the passing of the Inspection Law, and prevented the dimunition of fees, *in every respect?* Were the fortunes
of all the people of Maryland impaired by the Inspection Act, that
then passed, though fees were not diminished by it, and the makers
of tobacco were obliged to pay in tobacco? Did this Law, which
allowed of no dimunition of fees, and compelled the planters to
pay in tobacco, pass *before*, or *since* the unfortunate æra, when
somebody was thrust into office, that *all power* might centre in *one*
family? From this insinuation, as well as other touches in the
composition of the Confederates, I am led to suspect, that they have
received instruction from the Essay on Diabolism.

> Some aukward epithets, with skill apply'd.
> Some specious hints, that something seem to hide,
> Can right, and wrong most cleverly confound,
> Banditti like, to stun us, e'r they wound.[17]

But whatever may be the demerits of the *father*, what has the *son*
done to incur the displeasure of the Confederates, that they already
prepare to malign him? As one of the Confederated *Independent
Whigs* can hardly entertain any views of personal promotion, to
what black passion shall we charge his dislike? Age must have
cooled the ardor of ambition; but malignity will not cease, "till life's
reck'ning shall forever cease."

> Wash the Æthiop white,
> Discharge the leopard's spots, turn day to night,
> Controul the course of nature, bid the deep
> Hush, at thy Pygmy voice, her waves to sleep;
> Perform things passing strange, yet own thy art
> Too weak to work a change, in such an heart.
> *That* envy, which was woven in thy frame
> At first, will to the last remain the same.
> Reason may droop, may die; but envy's rage
> Improves by time, and gathers strength from age.

[17] These lines may be by William Combe, author of *The Diaboliad* (London,
1777), but I was not able to locate them.

What could persuade thee at thy time of life,
To launch afresh into the sea of strife?[18]

What means the other? is he anxiously looking forward to the event, most devoutly wished for, when he may shake off his fetters, and dazzle the world with the splendour of his talents, and the glory of his political achievements,

And save his country, whilst he — serves himself?

Let not Sempronius suspect this — to be outwitted by one, whom, from his soul, he despises, after having

—Mouth'd at Caesar 'till he shook the senate,
Cloath'd his feign'd zeal in rage, in fire, in fury,[19]

would drive him to desperation irremediable.

Officers ought to be restrained, and ought not lawyers? If the former, without restriction, may have it in their power to oppress, may not the latter also? I mean not such a restriction, as the Act of Assembly now in force imposes, an Act which is become a dead letter from its illiberal allowance in causes of difficulty in the superior courts; nor do I mean such a restriction as a reasonable Lawyer would object to — I well know there are men of the profession, who need not the restriction of positive Law to keep them within the bounds of moderation; but since, as Blackstone observes, it may happen that profligate, and illiberal men, may sometimes insinuate themselves into the most honourable professions, to check their rapacity, and insolence is not unworthy of the legislative attention.[20]

One may easily imagine that a client, drained of his money, frequently attending with humility to have his business done, insulted with insolence when his pockets are empty, and returning home with disappointment, and chagrin, thinks it hard to be

[18] Charles Churchill, *An Epistle to William Hogarth* (London, 1763), lines 435–44. The last two lines do not appear in the original.

[19] Joseph Addison, *Cato*, act 1, scene 3, lines 39–43. Two lines are omitted and there are minor changes.

[20] "To give a check to the unseemly licentiousness of prostitute and illiberal men, (a few of whom may sometimes insinuate themselves even into the most honourable profession), it hath been holden that a counsel is not answerable for any matter by him spoken." *Commentaries on the Laws of England* (London, 1821), 3:29. Blackstone does not mention "legislative attention."

abused, because he cannot answer the demand of *Teeth Money*, and heartily wishes the Legislature would extend their care, and prevent the extortion of the Lawyer, as well as the Officer.

What do the Confederates mean "by *dragging* to light — made to feel the resentment of a free people — endeavouring to set the power of the supreme Magistrate above the Laws — punished with infamy, exile, or death — dread of such fate?"

Have they any other measure, besides the Governor's proclamation, to arraign as an attempt to set the supreme Magistrate above the Law? If they have, let them be precise in their charge, and give me another opportunity of shewing them, stripped of disguise, to be, *what they are.* Has their malice, which all the colours of language are too feeble to express, so extinguished every spark of the little sense, "niggard nature spared them,"[21] as to beget a sanguine hope, that the free people of Maryland will become a lawless mob at their instigation, and be the dupes of their infernal rage? When nature's work is so equivocal that we are at a loss to determine, whether she intended to exhibit a man for human humiliation, or a monkey for human diversion, we are inclined to pity, or to laugh, as the object happens to strike the present disposition;[22] but when we behold the animal with the torch, or firebrand, bent on mischief, we should dread its fury, if not out of the reach of it.

One more word to the Confederates, or *Independent Whigs*, if they choose the signature to *their own* panegyrick on *their own* excellencies, and then *farwel*, for the present.

---

* *A tribute exacted by some Turkish tyrants of the poor people, whom they plunder of provision, for the trouble of using their Teeth in eating it. Such plunderers vehemently declaim against regular dues, that there may be the more for themselves to spoil.*

---

[21] The phrase "niggard nature" appears in William Shakespeare, *Timon of Athens* (London, 1768), act 5, scene 4, lines 76–77, "those our droplets which from niggard nature fall."

[22] Carroll's diminutive physique was one of Dulany's leading themes in these letters and inspired the numerous references to "monkeys." Carroll's biographer, Ellen Hart Smith, wrote in *Charles Carroll of Carrollton* (Cambridge: Harvard University Press, 1942) that, though he was "small and very slight in stature, he was well made, with fine hands and regular features" (p. 64).

If the Governor, in issuing the proclamation, acted on a conviction of its propriety (and he has most expressly declared, he did) he derives a satisfaction, and honour from his firm, and open avowal, which *he* will *hardly* be induced to relinquish and shelter himself under the infamous doctrine of your most servile adulation — *"that a Governor is a King, and can do no wrong."*† So rash is your solicitude to make your court, that you do not perceive the affront you offer, *even*, to his veracity in the very nature of your address. Such patriotism now it is explained, to be sure, must command the utmost confidence of the free people of Maryland.

What would John Hampden, if alive *here*, say to such patriots?

With what indignation must the confederated *Independent Whigs* be inflamed, when informed that fees in England have been settled by the courts, that the doctrine has been there advanced, *"no Officer is bound to act unless his fee be paid"*; that a Chancellor has *"stopp'd the very hearing of a cause, because fees were not paid"*; and that a Chief Justice has declared, even from the bench, that a suitor is *"liable to an Attachment of Contempt, on his refusal to pay fees"*? *Such Tyranny* has, verily, been practised without any dread of *Infamy, Exile, or Death.* O Tempora, O Mores.[23] ANTILON

---

† *By statute, if a Governor, or deputy Governor of any plantation, or colony, be guilty of oppressing any subject within his government, or any other crime or offence contrary to the Laws of the Realm; such oppression, &c. shall be enquired of and determined in the Court of King's Bench, or before Commissioners assigned by the Crown, and such punishments inflicted as are usually inflicted for offences of the like nature committed in England*[24]—*and yet the Confederates apply the maxim, "the King can do no wrong," to a Governor—what gross ignorance, what miserable flattery!*

---

[23] "Oh time, oh customs!" Cicero, *Catiline* 1, 2.

[24] "An Act to Punish Governors of Plantations in this Kingdom, for Crimes by them committed in the Plantations," 11 & 12 William III, c. 12.

First Citizen's Second Letter

MARCH 11, 1773

—"*Though* SOME *counsellors will be found to have contributed their endeavours, yet there is* ONE, *who challenges the infamous pre-eminence, and who by his capacity,* craft, and arbitrary counsels, **is entitled to the first place among these betrayers of their country.*"

HUME'S HIST. OF ENG. VOL. V. P. 243. 4TO. EDIT.[1]

The most despotic counsels, the most arbitrary measures, have always found some advocates, to disgrace a free nation: when these men, in the room of cool, and dispassionate reason, substitute virulent invective, and illiberal abuse, we may fairly presume, that arguments are either wanting, or that ignorance and incapacity know not how to apply them.

Considering the known abilities, as a writer, of the person pointed out to be the principal adviser of the Proclamation, considering too, his legal and constitutional knowledge, we can hardly suppose, if solid reasons could be adduced in support, or extenuation of that measure, but what they would have been urged, with all the force of clear, nervous, and animated language. There will not, I imagine, be wanting lawyers, to undertake a refutation of

---

* *The words in small Roman letters are substituted instead of the words* enterprise, and courage, *made use of by the historian.*

---

[1] This edition was published in London, 1770.

Antilon's legal reasoning in favour of the Proclamation; I shall therefore examine his defence of it, rather upon constitutional principles, and endeavour to shew, that it is contrary to the spirit of *our constitution* in particular, and would, if submitted to, be productive of fatal consequences: but previous to my entering upon this enquiry, it will be necessary to expose the *"shameless effrontery,"* with which *Antilon* has asserted facts, entirely destitute of truth, and from which he has taken occasion to blacken the character of a gentleman, totally unconnected with the present dispute. Who that gentleman is, no longer remains problematical; the place of his education, and his age, have been mentioned, to fix the conjectures of the publick, and to remove all doubt. *"He, instigated by inveterate malice, has invented falshoods for incorrigible folly to adopt, and indurated impudence to propagate."* Of this *Antilon* has confidently accused him; but upon what proof? on no other than his own conjecture. The first Citizen avers (and his word will be taken sooner than *Antilon's*) that he wrote the dialogue between two citizens, published in the *Maryland Gazette* of the 4th instant, without the advice, suggestion, or assistance of the supposed *author* or *coadjutor*. But the first Citizen, and the Independent Whigs, are most certainly confederated; they are known to each other; an assertion this, *Antilon*, equally rash and groundless with your former. Why do you suppose this confederacy? From a similitude of sentiments with respect to your conduct, and Proclamation? If so, then indeed are nine-tenths of the people of this province confederated with the first Citizen. The Independent Whigs, however, as it happens, are unknown to the first Citizen; of their paper he had not the least intelligence, till he read it in the *Maryland Gazette* of the 11th instant:[2] he now takes this opportunity, of thanking those gentlemen, for the compliments, which they have been pleased to bestow on his endeavours, to draw the attention of the publick, from other objects, to the real authors, or rather *author* of all our evils.

With what propriety, with what justice can *Antilon* reproach any man with malignity, when, stimulated by that passion, he accuses others without proof of being confederated with the first

[2] Cited in Antilon's second letter, note 8: *Maryland Gazette*, February 11, 1773, p. 2.

Citizen, and from mere suspicion of so treasonable a confederacy, vomits out scurrility and abuse against imaginary foes? Not content with uttering falshoods, grounded solely on his own presumption, he has imputed the conduct of *"one of the confederates"* to a motive, which if real, can only be known to the great searcher of hearts. This *confederate* is represented *"as wishing most devoutly"* (a pious and Christian insinuation) for an event of all others the most calamitous, the death of a most loved parent; ungenerous suggestion! unfeeling man! do you really entertain such an opinion of the son?[3] Do you desire, that the assigned cause of the imputed wish should have its intended effect, create uneasiness, a coolness, or distrust? What behaviour, what incident, what passage of his life, warrant this your opinion of the son, supposing it to be real? That they have always lived in the most perfect harmony, united by nature's strongest ties, parental love, filial tenderness, and duty, envy itself must own. *That father*, whose death the son devoutly wishes for, never gave him cause to form a wish so execrable; he has been treated with the utmost affection, and indulgence by the father; in return for all that tenderness and paternal care —

> Him, let the tender office long engage,
> To rock the cradle of reposing age;
> With lenient arts extend a father's breath,
> Make languor smile, and smooth the bed of death.
> — POPE.[4]

I cannot conceive what *"the generous and spirited behaviour of one of the confederates"* (who by the bye is no confederate) on a former occasion, has to do with the present question, unless to divert the attention from the subject, or to introduce a specimen of satire, and falshood prettily contrasted in antitheses. The period, I confess, runs smooth enough; but *Antilon*, let me give you a piece of advice, though it comes from an enemy, it may be useful; whenever you mean to be severe, confine yourself to truth; illiberal calumny

---

[3] Refers to page 74 above. Carroll was supposed to wish his father's death, so that he might renounce Catholicism and launch his political career.

[4] Alexander Pope, *An Epistle from Mr. Pope, to Dr. Arbuthnot* (London, 1734), lines 408–11.

recoils with double force on the calumniator. An expression of the first Citizen has been construed into a *"preparation"* to malign the minister's son: if this intention could be fairly gathered from the words inserted in the note (*A*) (and there are no other to give the least colour to the charge) it would cause the first Citizen unfeigned concern. To wipe off the imputation, I must beg leave to refer the reader to the dialogue published by the first Citizen; he will there see, that the 2d Citizen intimates, a confidence ought to be placed in *our ministers*, because they are men of property, *"and have as deep a stake in the safety of the Constitution as any of us."* In answer to this reasoning, the first Citizen observes, that a minister's wealth is not always a security for his honesty; because, to increase that wealth, to maintain his seat, and to aggrandize his own, he may be tempted to enlarge the powers of the crown (the first Citizen speaks generally), more especially should he (the minister) have any expectation of transmitting his post to one of his own family, to his son for instance. "It has been the maxim (says a judicious historian†) of English princes whenever popular leaders encroach too much on royal authority, to confer offices on them, in expectation that they will afterwards become more careful, not to diminish *that power*, which has become *their own*." It is not even asserted, that the minister does actually entertain a hope of securing his office to his son, but that, possibly, he may entertain such a hope. It may be impolitic in the supreme magistrate, to grant offices to many of, and to continue them in the same family, but it is natural for the head of that family, to wish it; if even to wish to transmit an office to his son, should be thought culpable in the father, yet still is the son exempt from all blame.

I must answer a question or two, put by *Antilon*, before I go into an examination of his reasons, in support of the Proclamation, that the argument may be as little interrupted, and broke in upon, as possible, by topics foreign to that enquiry. *Antilon* asks, "What do the confederates mean (he should have said what does the first

(*A*) — *Hopes may be entertained that the* good thing *like a precious jewel will be handed down from father to son.*
† HUME[5]

---

[5] David Hume, *History of England* (London, 1767).

Citizen mean) by dragging to light — made to feel the resentment of a free people — endeavour to set the power of the supreme magistrate above the laws — dread of such fate." — Answer — *By dragging to light,* nothing more was meant, than that the house of delegates should again endeavour, by an humble address to the Governor, to prevail on him to disclose the ill ADVISER, or *"those ill advisers who have most daringly presumed to tread on the invaluable rights of the freemen of Maryland."*[6] — *"Made to feel the resentment of a free people"* may need a little explanation; the sense of the subsequent quotations, is sufficiently obvious; if the real *adviser,* or advisers, of the Proclamation, could be discovered, in my opinion (I do not mean to dictate, and to prescribe to the delegates of the people) they ought, in justice to their constituents, humbly to address the Governor, to remove him, or them, from his counsels, and all places of trust, and profit, if they be invested with such, not merely as a punishment on the present *transgressor,* or transgressors, but as a warning to future counsellors, not to imitate their example. I have dwelt the longer on the meaning of the words — *"made to feel the resentment of a free people,"* because I perceive pusillanimity and conscious guilt have inferred from the expression, "a sanguine hope in the *"confederates,"* that the free people of Maryland will become a lawless mob at their instigation, and be the dupes of their infernal rage."

Sleep in peace, good *Antilon,* if thy conscience will permit thee; no such hope was conceived by, a thought of the sort never entered the first Citizen's head, nor (as he verily believes) of any other person. The first Citizen rejects with horror, and contempt, the cowardly aspersion. But should a mob assemble to pull down a certain house, and hang up the owner, methinks, it would not be very formidable, when headed and conducted by a *monkey,* against a chief of such *spirit* and *resolution.* Sarcasms on personal defects, have ever been esteemed the sure token of a base and degenerate mind; to possess the strength and graces of your person, the gentleman alluded to, would not exchange the infirmities of his puny frame, were it, on that condition, to be animated by a soul like thine.

---

[6] Address of the lower house, November 21, 1771, *Maryland Archives* (Baltimore: Maryland Historical Society, 1883–), 63:200.

I have at length gone through the painful task, of silencing falshood, exposing malice, and checking insolence. The illiberal abuse so plentifully dealt out by *Antilon*, would have been passed over with silent contempt, had he not so interwoven it with positive assertion of facts, that the latter could not be contradicted, without taking some notice of the former.

I shall now examine *Antilon's* reasons in justification of the Proclamation, and after his example, I shall first compare the two transactions, the *Proclamation*, and the *assessment of ship-money*. — That the latter was a more open, and daring violation of a free constitution (B) will be readily granted; the former, I contend, to be a more disguised, and concealed attack, but equally subversive, in its consequences, of liberty. — *Antilon's* account of the levy of ship-money, though not quite so impartial as he insinuates, I admit in the main to be true — "The amount of the whole tax was very moderate, little exceeding £200,000; it was levied upon the people with justice and equality, and this money was entirely expended upon the navy, to the great honour and advantage of the king-dom."[7] — At that period the boundaries between liberty and prerogative were far from being ascertained; the constitution had long been fluctuating between those opposite, and contending interests, and had not then arrived to that degree of consistency and perfection, it has since acquired, by subsequent contests, and by the improvements made in later days, when civil liberty was much

(B) *The most open and avowed attacks on liberty are not perhaps the most dangerous. When rigorous means —* "*the arbitrary seizure of property and the deprivation of personal liberty are employed to spread terror, and compel submission to a tyrant's will*" *they rouse the national indignation, they excite a general patriotism, and communicate the generous ardor from breast to breast; fear and resentment, two powerful passions, unite a whole people, in opposition to the tyrant's stern commands; the modest, mild, and conciliating manner, in which the latent designs of a* crafty minister *come sometimes recommended to the publick, ought to render them the more suspected* "timeo Danaos, et dona ferentes":[8] *The gifts, and smiles of a minister should always inspire caution, and diffidence. There is no attempt, it is true, in the Procla-mation* "to subject the people indebted to the officers for services performed to any execution of their effects or imprisonment of their persons — on any account." — *If the judges however should determine costs to be paid, according to the rates of the Proclamation, execution of a person's effects, or imprisonment would necessarily follow his refusal to pay those rates.*

[7] Hume, *History of England*, 6:239.
[8] Vergil, *Aeneid* 2, 49.

better defined, and better understood. The assessment of ship-money received the sanction of the judges — "After the laying on of ship-money, Charles, in order to discourage all opposition, had proposed the question to the judges, *"whether in a case of necessity, for the defence of the kingdom, he might not impose this taxation; and whether he was not sole judge of the necessity."* — These guardians of law and liberty, replied with great complaisance (reflect on this, good reader) that in a case of necessity, he might impose that taxation, and that he was sole judge of the necessity."[9] The same historian speaking of that transaction concludes thus: "These observations alone may be established on both sides, *That,* the appearances were sufficiently strong in favour of the King, to apologize for his following such maxims, and *that,* publick liberty must be so precarious, under this exorbitant prerogative, as to render an opposition, not only excusable, but laudable in the people."[10] — But I mean not to excuse the assessment of ship-money, nor to exculpate Charles, his conduct will admit of no good apology.

Now let us take a view of the Governor's Proclamation, advised by the minister, and of all its concomitant circumstances. — A disagreement in sentiment, between the two branches of our legislature, about the regulation of officers fees, occasioned the loss of the inspection law in the month of November, 1770. — Some proceedings in the land-office, had created a suspicion in the members of the lower house of that assembly then sitting, "That the government had entertained a design, in case the several branches of the legislature should not agree in the regulation of officers fees, to attempt establishing them by Proclamation." To guard against a measure *"incompatible with the permanent security of property and the constitutional liberty of the subject,"* they in an address to his Excellency asserted, "That could they persuade themselves, that his Excellency could possibly entertain a different opinion, they should be bold to tell him, that the people of this province will ever oppose the usurpation of such a right."[11] To which address the Governor returned this remarkable answer in his message of the

[9] *Ibid.,* p. 251.

[10] *Ibid.,* pp. 240–41.

[11] *Maryland Archives* 62:380, from the address of the lower house, November 8, 1770. The first quote is from the lower house address of November 22, 1771, *ibid.,* 63:192.

20th day of November, 1770, "That his lordship's authority had not
yet interposed in the regulation of fees of officers, nor had he any
reason to imagine, it would interpose in such a manner to justify a
regular opposition to it." (C)[12] Notwithstanding this declaration, a
few days after the prorogation of that assembly, the Proclamation
of the 26th day of November (the subject of the present controversy) was issued, contrary to a seeming promise given by the
minister (for I consider the Governor's speeches and messages as
flowing from his minister's advice) and contrary to the opinion
entertained by the minister himself, of its legality. The accusation
will not appear too rash, when we reflect on the abilities of the
man, his experience, his knowledge of the law and constitution,
and his late flimsy and pitiful vindication of the measure. He knew
that a "similar Proclamation published in the year 1733 had agi-
tated and disjointed this province till the year 1747. The evils,
which were thereby occasioned, ought strongly to have dissuaded a
second attempt, to exercise such power." *Antilon* has admitted this
fact, and has attributed "the most violent opposition that ever a
Governor of Maryland met with" to this very measure — "He
(Ogle) was so well convinced of the authoritative force of the
Proclamation, for settling fees of officers, that he expressly determined, as Chancellor, by a final compulsory decree, fees should
be paid upon the authority, and according to the very settlement of
the Proclamation," which of his own will and mere notion he had
pre-ordained as Governor.

What is the meaning of all this in plain English? Why, that Ogle
made himself both judge and party; like the French King, he issued
out his edict, as a law, which he inforced in his own court, as judge.
I am unwillingly, and unavoidably drawn into the censure of a man,
who by his subsequent conduct, which was mild and equitable,

(C) *From the words in the text, I think it is evident, the minister had at that
very time determined on issuing the Proclamation; should he afterwards be
reproached with a breach of promise, he had his answer ready, the Proclamation was not issued in* such a manner, *as to justify* a regular opposition, *it
was only issued with a view to prevent the* extortion of officers — *for this
reason I have called the minister's promise a* seeming *promise.*

---

[12] *Ibid.*, 62:425, from the Governor's address of November 20, 1771.

fully atoned for the oppressions (shall I call them errors) of his former administration.[13]

[2] *Antilon* asks, "What did he (Ogle) deserve, infamy, death, or exile?" No, not quite so severe a punishment, *Antilon*; he only deserved to be removed from his government, and not even that punishment, if he was directed, advised, and governed by such a minister as thou art; for in that case, the disgrace, and removal of the minister would have been sufficient, and would probably have restored ease, security, and happiness to the people. But if Eden should follow Ogle's example, what then? Eden is a Governor, a Governor is a King, and a King can do no wrong, ergo, a Governor may cut the throats of all the inhabitants of Maryland, and then pick their pockets, and will not be liable to be punished for such atrocious doings; excellent reasoning! exquisite wit and humor! If you, *Antilon*, should still be hardy enough, to continue to inspire the same counsels, which have already set this province in a flame, and the Governor, when warned, and cautioned against your pernicious designs, should still listen to your advice, in opposition to the inclination and wishes of the people, over whom he has the honour to preside, I confess, I should be one of those, who would most heartily wish for his removal; Does this look like flattery, *Antilon*? I scorn the accusation. The first Citizen has always treated his Excellency with that respect, which his station commands, and with that complaisance, which is due from one gentleman to another; to flatter, or to permit flattery, is equally unbecoming that character; *Antilon* accuses the *confederates*, of *fawning servility*, *extravagant adulation*, and *the meanest debasement*; yet this very man is not entirely exempt from the imputation of flattery — "They know not the man whom they thus treat."

Cui, male si palpere, recalcitrat undique tutus[14] was an artful compliment paid by a courtly poet to the tyrant Augustus. — Ye, *Antilon*, I know the man; I know him to be generous, of a good

---

[13] Carroll was mistaken in suggesting that Ogle had issued the proclamation. Dulany referred to a decree issued by Ogle, as chancellor, confirming the fee proclamation. See Antilon's second letter, note 12.

[14] See Antilon's second letter, note 7. "Whom, like a generous steed, if you stroke awkwardly, will kick you, being always on his guard."

heart, well disposed, and willing to promote, if left to himself, the happiness and welfare of the province; but youthful, unsuspicious, and diffident of his own judgement in matters legal and political (P) failings (if they deserve the name) that have caused him to repose too great a confidence in *you*; from this opinion of the man, from a persuasion of his good intentions, I was induced to apply to *him*, the maxim of the British constitution, "*the King can do no wrong*," which you have so wittily, and humourously ridiculed. The Governor is no King; wonderful discovery! Who said he was? *You*

(P) — *It cannot be supposed that the King can have a thorough knowledge of every department in his kingdom; he appoints judges, to interpret, and to dispense law to his subjects; ministers to plan, and digest schemes of policy, and to conduct the business of the nation; generals, and admirals, to command his armies, and fleets; over all these he has a general superintendency, to remove, and punish such as from incapacity, corruption, or other misdemeanors may be unfit, and unworthy of the trust reposed in them — "the King cannot exercise a judicial office himself, for though justice and judgment flow from him, yet he dispenses them by his ministers, and has committed all his judicial power to different courts; and it is highly necessary for his people's safety he should do so, for as Montesquieu justly observes — There is no liberty if the power of judging be not separated from the legislative, and executive powers. Were it joined with the legislative, the life and liberty of the subject would be exposed to arbitrary controul, for the judge would then be legislator; were it joined to the executive power, the judge might behave with all the violence of an oppressor."*[15]

"*Here, the Governor, who exercises the executive and a share of the legislative power, holds and exercises also one of the most considerable judicial offices — for he is chancellor, a jurisdiction, which in the course of some years, may bring a considerable share of the property of this country, to his determinations.*" *The Governor is so well satisfied of wanting advice, that in determining causes of intricacy, he always chuses to have the assistance of some gentleman, who from study, and a knowledge of the law, may be presumed a good judge, and able to direct him in cases of difficulty and doubt. He has recourse to the advise of his council in all matters of publick concernment; it is therefore highly probable he took the advise of some, or of ONE in the council before he issued the Proclamation. It is well known, that in England the prime minister directs and governs all his Majesty's other ministers; in Charles the IId's time the whole care of Government, was committed to five persons, distinguished by the name of the* Cabal: *the other members of the privy council were seldom called to any deliberations, or if called, only with a view to* save appearances.[16]

---

[15] M. de Secondat, Baron de Montesquieu, *Spirit of the Laws*, translated by Thomas Nugent (London, 1773), vol. 9, chap. 6, p. 222.

[16] The Cabal (1667–1673): the five ministers were Clifford, Arlington, Buckingham, Ashley-Cooper, and Lauderdale, whose initials spelled "Cabal," the common seventeenth century designation for the king's closest councillors.

comprehend the full force, and justice of the application, and *you* best know the reason of it; in order to elude, and defeat its aim, you affect to be witty, and not to take my meaning. You want to shelter yourself under the protection of the Governor, and to draw him, and all the Council, into a justification of measures *peculiarly yours*, by endeavouring to make them responsible for *your counsels.* "There can be no difficulty in finding out his (the King's) ministers; the Governor and Council are answerable in this character; *he cannot disavow* an act, to which his signature is affixed." Have not many Kings of England revoked, and cancelled acts, to which their signatures were affixed? Have not some Kings, too, at the solicitation of their parliaments, disgraced ministers, who advised these acts, and affixed to them the royal signature? The Governor is improperly called the King's minister, he is rather his representative, or deputy; he forms a distinct branch, or part of our legislature; a bill though passed by both houses of assembly, would not be law, if dissented to by him; he has therefore the power, *loco Regis*,[17] of assenting, and dissenting to laws; in him is lodged the most amiable, the best of powers, the power of mercy; the most dreadful also, the power of death. A minister has no such transcendent privileges — To help, to instruct, to advise is his province, and let me add, that he is accountable for his advice, to the great Council of the people; upon this principle, the wisdom of our ancestors grounded the maxim, "The King can do no wrong." They supposed, and justly, that the care and administration of Government would be committed to ministers, whom, abilities, or other qualities had recommended to their sovereign's choice; lest the friendship and protection of their master should encourage them to pursue pernicious measures, and lest they should screen themselves under regal authority, the blame of bad counsels became imputable to them, and they alone were made answerable for the consequences; if liable to be punished for male administration, it was thought, they might be more circumspect, diligent, and attentive to their charge; it would be indecent and irreverential to throw the blame of every grievance on the King, and to be perpetually remonstrating against

[17] In the place of the king.

majesty itself, when the minister only was in fault. The maxim however admits of limitation.

Est modus in rebus; sunt certi denique fines, Quos ultra, citraque, nequit consistere rectum.[18]

Should a King, deaf to the repeated remonstrances of his people, forgetful of his coronation oath, and unwilling to submit to the legal limitations of his prerogative, endeavour to subvert that constitution in church and state, which he swore to maintain, resistance would then not only be excusable, but praiseworthy, and deposition, and imprisonment, or exile, might be the only means left, of securing civil liberty, and national independence. Thus James the second, by endeavouring to introduce arbitrary power, and to subvert the established church, justly deserved to be deposed and banished.

The revolution, which followed, or rather brought on James's abdication of the crown, "is justly ranked among the most glorious deeds, that have done honour to the character of Englishmen." In that light the first Citizen considers it; and he believes the Independent Whigs entertain the same opinion of that event, at least, nothing appears to the contrary, save the malevolent insinuation of *Antilon*. It is high time to return to the Proclamation; your digressions, *Antilon*, which have occasioned mine, shall not make me lose sight of the main object. "It is not to be expected that any man will bear reproaches without reply, or that he, who wanders from the question, will not be followed in his wanderings, and hunted through his labyrinths." We have seen, the Proclamation was apprehended some time before its publication, and guarded against by a positive declaration of the lower house — "*The people of this province will ever oppose the usurpation of such a right.*"[19] Nevertheless *our minister*, regardless of this intimation, advised the Proclamation. It came out soon afterwards cloathed with the specious pretence of preventing extortion in officers. I shall soon examine the solidity of this softening palliative.

In a subsequent session, it was resolved unanimously by the

[18] Horace, *Sermons* 1, 1, 106. "There is a mean in things; finally there are certain boundaries, on either side of which right is not able to exist."
[19] See note 11 above.

lower house, "to be *illegal, arbitrary, unconstitutional and oppressive.*" It was resolved also, "*That the advisers (D) of the said Proclamation are enemies to the peace, welfare and happiness of this province, and to the laws and constitution thereof.*"[20]

I shall now give a short extract from Petyt's *Jus Parliamentarium*, page 327, and leave the reader to make the application: — In a list of grievances presented by the commons to James the first, are Proclamations, of which complaining bitterly, among other things they say, "Nevertheless, it is apparent, that Proclamations have been of late years much more frequent than heretofore, and that they are extended, not only to the liberty, but also to the goods, inheritances, and livelihood of men; some of them, tending to alter some *points of the law,* and make *them new; other some made shortly after a session of parliament for matter directly rejected in the same session, and some vouching former Proclamation, to countenance and warrant the latter.*"[21]

The Proclamation is modestly called by *Antilon,* "*a restriction of the officers,*" at another time, *preventive of extortion,*" though in fact, it ought rather to be considered as a direction to the officers, what to demand, and to the people, what to pay, than a *restriction of the officers.* I appeal to the common sense and consciences of my countrymen; do ye think, that the avowed motive of the Proclama-

---

(D) *It is plain from the above resolve of the delegates, that they considered the Governor, not as my lord's minister, but as his deputy, or lieutenant, acting by the advice of others, nor pursuing his own immediate measure, and sentiments. It is no imputation on the Governor's understanding to have been guided by a counsellor, from whose experience, and knowledge, he might have expected the best advice, when he did not suspect, or did not discover the interested motive from which it proceeded; the minister has the art of covering his* real *views with* fair *pretences.*

"*And seems a saint, when most he plays the devil.*"[22]

---

20 The second resolution passed by a vote of 32–3; both passed on October 18, 1771, *Maryland Archives* 63:114.

21 William Petyt, *Jus Parliamentarium* (London, 1739), p. 327. The citation is correct.

22 William Shakespeare, *The Trajedy of King Richard the Third* (London, 1957), act 1, scene 3, line 338.

tion, was the true and real one? If no such Proclamation had issued, would ye have suffered yourselves to be oppressed, and plundered by the officers? Would ye have submitted to their exorbitant demands, when instructed by a vote of your representatives, "That in all cases where no fees are established by law, for services done by officers, the power of ascertaining the quantum of the reward for such services is constitutionally in a jury upon the action of the party?" To set this matter in a clear point of view, and to expose the hollow and deceitful shew of a pretended clemency, and tenderness for the people, it may not be improper to introduce a short dialogue between an officer and citizen.

Officer. How wretched and distressed would have been the situation of this province, if the well-timed and merciful Proclamation had not issued.

Cit. How so?

Officer. The reason is obvious, had it not issued, we should have been let loose on our countrymen to live on free quarter, for every *little* piece of service we should have exacted a *genteel* reward; in a short time your pockets would have been pretty well drained, and to mend the matter, we might have pillaged and plundered, without being liable to be sued for extortion; "for we could not be guilty of extortion merely in taking *money* or other *valuable thing* for our services, unless we were to take *more* than is due; it is obvious to common sense that there must be some established measure — or there can be no excess — That the term *more* cannot apply unless what is due be *ascertained* there must be a *positive*, or there can be no *comparitive*; let the results then be considered, if *something* be undeniably due, when a service is performed, and no *certain* rule or measure to *determine* the rate, should an officer take *as much as he can exact*, he would not commit *extortion* according to the legal acceptation of the term *extortion*."

Cit. This may be good law for aught I know, but if I could not sue you for extortion, I should still have a remedy.

Officer. What, pray?

Cit. I would only pay you what I thought reasonable.

Officer. But suppose I should not think the sum tendered sufficient, and refuse to receive it.

Cit. Why, then you might either go without any reward for your service, or you might sue me, to recover, what in your estimation would be adequate thereto, and thus leave the quantum of the recompence to be settled by a jury.

Officer. This expedient did not occur to me; your condition I own, would have not been quite so deplorable as I imagined.

The plain answer of this citizen will be understood by many, who will not comprehend the more refined reasoning of the officer upon extortion; and I fancy the citizen's resolution in a like case, would be adopted by most people — *Antilon* has admitted That "if the Proclamation had not the authority to fix the rates according to which the officers *might* receive and *beyond which* they could not *lawfully receive*, it was not preventive of extortion, but whether it had or not *such authority* depended on its legality, *determinable in the ordinary judicatories.*" I should be glad to know whether its legality be determinable by the judges, or by a jury; if determinable by a jury, the liberty and property of the people will be exposed to less danger: were we sure of always having judges, as honest and upright as the present, the question, though of the most momentous concern, might perhaps be safely left to their decision: but our judges are removable at pleasure, some of them might be interested in the cause, and if suffered to establish their *own* fees would become both judge and party — a Governor, we have seen, decreeing as chancellor fees to be paid upon the authority of his *own* Proclamation, would fall under that predicament. Let us admit, by way of argument, that the decision of this question (the legality of the Proclamation) belongs properly to the judges: suppose they should determine the Proclamation to be legal; What consequences would follow? The most fatal and pernicious, that could possibly happen to this province; the right of the lower house to settle fees, with the concurrence of the other branches of the legislature, a right, which has been claimed, and exercised for many years past, to the great benefit of the people, would be rendered useless, and nugatory. The old table of fees abounding with exorbitances and abuses, would ever remain unalterable; government would hold it up perpetually, as a sacred palladium, not to be touched, and violated by profane hands.

Reasons still of greater force might be urged against leaving with the judges the decision of this important question, whether the supreme magistrate shall have the power to tax a free people without the consent of their representatives, nay! against their consent and express declaration, I shall only adduce one argument, to avoid prolixity.

The Governor, it is said, with the advice of his lordship's council of state, issued the Proclamation: three of our provincial judges are of that council; they therefore advised a measure as proper, and consequently as legal, the legality of which, if called in question, they were afterwards to determine. *Is not* this in some degree prejudging the question? It will perhaps be denied, (for what will not some men assert, or deny?) That to settle the fees of officers by Proclamation, is not to tax the people; I humbly conceive that fees settled by the Governor's Proclamation, should it be determined to have the force of law, are to all intents and purposes, a tax upon the people, flowing from an arbitrary, and discretionary power in the supreme magistrate — for this assertion, I have the authority of my Lord Coke express in point — that great lawyer, in his exposition of the statute *de tallagio non concedendo*[23] makes this comment on the word tallagium — "Tallagium is a general word and doth include all subsidies, taxes, tenths, fifteenths, impositions, and other burthens or charge *put or set* upon any man, that within this act are all new officers erected with new fees *or old officers with new fees* for that is a tallage put upon the subject, which cannot be done without common consent by act of parliament." The inspection law being expired, which established the rates of officers fees, adopted by the Governor's Proclamation, I apprehend, the people — (supposing the Proclamation had not issued) would not be obliged to pay fees to officers according to those rates; this proposition, I take, to be self-evident; now, if the Proclamation can revive those rates, and the payment of fees agreeable thereto, can be inforced by a decree of the chancellor, or by judgment of the provincial court, it will most clearly follow, that the fees are *new*, because enforced under an authority *intirely new*, and *distinct* from the act, by which those rates were originally fixed. Perhaps my Lord Coke's position will be contradicted, and it will be asserted, that fees payable to officers, are not taxes; but on what principle, such an assertion can

[23] Sir Edward Coke, *The Second Part of the Institutes of the Laws of England* (London, 1669), chap. 1, pp. 532–33.

be founded, I am at a loss to determine; they bear all the marks and characters of a tax; they are universal, unavoidable, and recoverable, if imposed by a *legal* authority, as all other debts; universal, and unavoidable, "for applications to the publick offices are not of *choice* but of necessity, redress cannot be had for the smallest or most atrocious injuries but in the courts of justice, and as surely as that necessity does exist, and a binding force in the Proclamation be admitted, so certainly must the fees thereby established, be paid in order to obtain redress." There is not a single person in the community, who at one time, or other, may not be forced into a court of justice, to recover a debt, to protect his property from rapacity, or to wrest it out of hands, which may have seized on it with violence, or to procure a reparation of personal insults.

Why was the inspection law made temporary? With a view no doubt, that on an alteration of circumstances, the delegates of the people, at the expiration of the act, with the consent of the Governor, and upper house, might alter, and amend the table of fees, or frame a new table.

That the circumstances of the province are much changed since the enacting of that law in 1747,[24] the Proclamation itself evinces, by allowing planters to pay the fees of officers in money, in lieu of tobacco, which alternative has considerably lessened the fees, and is a proof, if any were wanting, that they have been much too great. It was insisted on by the lower house, that a greater reduction of fees was still necessary; by the upper, that the fees were already sufficiently diminished, and that they would not suffer "any further reduction of fees, than that, which must necessarily follow from the election given to all persons, to discharge the fees in tobacco, or money as may best suit them."[25] One would imagine that a compromise, and a mutual departure from some points respectively contended for, would have been the most elegible way, of ending the dispute; if a compromise was not to be effected, the matter had best been left undecided: time, and necessity would have

[24] "An Act for Amending the Staple of Tobacco, for Preventing Frauds in his Majesty's Customs, and for the Limitation of Officers Fees," *Maryland Archives* 44:595–641. The fees table is substantially the same as in the 1763 act. See Antilon's second letter, note 4.

[25] Message of the upper house, November 16, 1770, *Maryland Archives* 62: 361.

softened dissention, and have reconciled jarring opinions, and clashing interests; and then a regulation by law, of officers fees, would
have followed of course. What was done? The authority of the
supreme magistrate interposed, and took the decision of this important question, from the other branches of the legislature to itself:
in a land of freedom this arbitrary exertion of prerogative will not,
must not, be endured.

From what has been said, I think it will appear that the idea of
a tax is not improperly annexed to a regulation of fees by Proclamation "but if the idea be proper, then fees can be settled in no case
except by the legislature, because it requires such authority to lay
a tax; but the house of lords, the house of commons, the courts of
law and equity in Westminster hall, the upper and lower houses of
assembly have each of them settled fees" — they have so: the house
of lords, and the house of commons have that [3] right derived
from long usage, and from the law of parliament, which is *lex
terrae*, or part at least of the law of the land. Our upper, and lower
houses of assembly claim most of the privileges, appertaining to
the two houses of parliament, being vested with powers nearly
similar, and analgous (E) to those, inherent in the lords, and com-

(E) *I say nearly similar; a perfect similitude cannot be expected; our upper
house falls vastly short of the house of lords in dignity, and independence;
our lower house approaches much nearer in its constitution to the house of
commons, than our upper house, to the house of lords; the observation of a
sensible writer on the assembly of Jamaica may be applied to ours.* — "*The
legislature of this province wants in its two first branches (from the dependent condition of the Governor and council) a good deal of that freedom,
which is necessary to the legislature of a free country, and on this account,
our constitution is defective in point of legislature, those two branches not
preserving by any means, so near a resemblance to the parts of the* British
*legislature, which they stand for here, as the assembly does; this is a defect
in our constitution, which cannot from the nature of things be intirely
remedied, for we have not any class of men distinguished from the people by
inherent honours; the assembly, or lower house has an exact resemblance to
that part of the* British *constitution, which it stands for here, it is indeed
an epitome of the house of commons; called by the same authority, deriving
its powers from the same source, instituted for the same ends, and governed
by the same forms; it will be difficult, I think to find a reason, why it
should not have the same powers, the same superiority over the courts of
justice, and the same rank in the system of our little community, as the
house of commons in that of Great-Britain. I know of no power exercised by
house of commons for redressing grievances or bringing publick offenders
to justice, which the assembly is incapable of* — *I know of none, which it
has not exercised at times except that of* impeachment *and this has been*

mons. "*The courts of law and equity in Westminster hall have likewise settled fees*"; by what authority? *Antlion* has not been full, and express on this point: Have the judges settled the fees of officers in their respective courts solely by the King's authority, or was that authority originally given by act of parliament to his Majesty, and by him delegated to his judges? Admitting even, that the chancellor and judges of Westminster hall have settled fees, by virtue of the King's commission, without the sanction of a statute, yet the precedent by no means applies to the present case. The judges in England have not settled their *own* fees — if the Proclamation should have the force of law, the commissary general, the secretary, the judges of the land office, who are all members of the council, and who advised the Proclamation, that is, who concurred with the *minister's* advice, may with propriety be said to have established their *own* fees. The Governor as chancellor decreeing his fees to be paid "*according to the very settlement of the Proclamation*," would undoubtedly ascertain, and settle his *own* fees; Would he not then be judge in his own cause? Is not this contrary to natural equity? "Where a statute is *against common right and reason* the common law shall controul it, and adjudge it to be void; for *jura naturae sunt immutabilia.*"[27] The quotation from Hawkins given by *Antilon,* militates most strongly against him; the chief *danger of oppression,* says the serjeant, is *from officers being left at liberty to set their own rates* on their own labour, and make their *own demands.* Have not the officers who advised the *Proclamation,* and the Governor who issued it, in pursuance of their advice *set their own rates,* and

---

forborn, not from any incapacity *in that body, but from a defect in the power of the council; an impeachment by the house of commons in England, must be heard in the house of lords, it being below the dignity of the commons, to appear as prosecutors, at the bar of any inferior court." The powers therefore of the house of commons, and of our lower house being so nearly similar, their respective privileges also must be nearly the same* — see the *privileges of the island of Jamaica vindicated.*[26]

---

[26] *The Privileges of the Island of Jamaica Vindicated* (London, 1766). This is a composite quote with passages taken from pp. 48–49, 33–34, and 50–51.

[27] This maxim may be found in Lord Chief Justice Hobart's opinion in Day v. Savadge, *Hob.* 85, at 87. "The laws of nature are immutable."

made *their own* demands? Answer this question, *Antilon?* If you remain silent, you admit the imputation; if you deny it, you will be forced to disavow the advice, you gave. The Proclamation is sometimes represented by *Antilon* as a very harmless sort of thing — it has no force, no efficacy, but what it receives from its legality *"determinable in the ordinary judicatories."* He has not indeed told us expressly, who are to determine its legality; if the judges of the provincial court are to decide the question, and they should determine the Proclamation to be legal, in that case, I suppose, an appeal would lie from their judgment, to the court of appeals — Would not an appeal to such a court, in such a cause, be the most farcical and ridiculous mummery ever thought of? All that has been said against the Proclamation, applies with equal or greater force against the instrument, under the great seal for ascertaining the fees of the land office.[28] *Antilon* having noticed "That in consequence of a commission issued by the crown, upon the address of the British house of commons, the lord chancellor *by the authority of his station* and by and with the advice and assistance of the master of the rolls, ordered, that the officers of the court of chancery should not demand or take any greater fees for their services, in their respective offices, than according to the rates established" — I have thought proper to insert in the note (*F*) referred to, some

(F) Antilon *infers from this argument, that the Governor has the same power in this province. In England, the King originally paid all his own officers; nothing therefore could be more consistent with the spirit of the constitution, than that he should establish the wages,* who *paid them. It is not so in this country, nor is it at present the case in England; they are now paid out of*

---

[28] Eden indicated he intended to treat the land office question separately in his proroguing speech, November 20, 1770, saying that "his Lordship has, the clearest right to dispose of his Real Estate upon such terms, as he may think proper," *Maryland Archives* 62:425. See also his address of November 30, 1771, *ibid.*, 63:231-32. Eden thought this justified regulation of land office fees by a separate proclamation, even though those fees had always been set in the fee bills. In its November 22, 1771 address, *ibid.*, pp. 193-94, the lower house argued that the land office must be considered "publick." "It very much concerns the Land-Holders in this Province, to know by what tenure they hold their Estates; if they have no Right to recur to the Land Office Records and have Copies but at the Will of his Lordship . . . they indeed" are "only Tenants" at the proprietor's will. "These records have been considered as publick records" and "have been made up at . . . the Expence of the people."

particulars relating to a similar measure, for the information of my readers, and to shew, that a regulation of officers fees, fell under the consideration of the house of commons, and that the same encroaching spirit of office, which has occasioned such altercations, heart burnings, and confusion in this province, has prevailed also in the parent state. The settlement of fees by order of the chancellor, under his Majesty's commission, issued pursuant to an address of the house of commons, is not, I will own, a tax similar to ship-

---

the pockets of the people; sheriffs, and many other officers have therefore their fees ascertained by act of parliament, and in those cases, where the fees given originally by the crown, are now established by custom, the parliament claims, and has exercised a power of controul over them, as will appear by the following quotations: "The commons ordered in lists of all the fees taken in the publick offices belonging to the law, which amounted annually to an *incredible sum* most of it to officers for doing nothing; *but the enquiry was too perplexed, and too tedious for any effectual stop being put to the evil within the period of one session*" — *Tindal's continuation of Rapin's history.*[29] Extract of a report of a committee of the house of commons impowered to inquire into the state of the officers' belonging to the courts in Westminster hall — April, 1752.[30]
"*Among the various claims of those, who now call themselves officers of the court of chancery, none appeared more extraordinary to the committee, than the fee of the secretary, and clerk of the briefs, who upon grants to enable persons to beg, and collect alms, claim, and frequently receive a fee of forty, fifty, or sixty pounds, and the register takes besides twelve or thirteen pounds for stamping and telling the briefs, which fees, with other great charges upon the collection, devour three parts in four of what is given for the relief of persons reduced to extreme poverty by fire, or other accidents.*" The committee closing their report with "*observing how little able or* willing *many officers were to give any satisfactory account of the fees, they claim, and receive,*" came to the following resolution:
Resolved, "*That it is the opinion of this committee that the long disuse of publick enquiries into the behaviour of officers, clerks, and ministers of the courts of justice has been the occasion of the encrease of unnecessary officers and given encouragement to the taking* illegal fees."
Resolved, "*That it is the opinion of this committee that the* interest, *which a great number of* officers and clerks *have in the proceedings of the court of chancery has been a principle cause of extending bills, answers, pleadings, examinations and other forms, and* copies of them *to an unnecessary length to the great delay of justice and the oppression of the subject.*"
Resolved, "*That it is the opinion of this committee that a table of all the officers, ministers, and clerks, and of their fees in the court of chancery*

---

[29] N(icholas) Tindal, *The Continuation of Mr. Rapin's History of England* (London, 1759), 20:96–97. The commons' order was dated March 15, 1730.

[30] The date of the report is misdated in the text. It was delivered to the house April 18, 1732, *Journals of the House of Commons* (London, 1803), 21:892–93.

money. But a regulation of fees by Proclamation, contrary to the express declaration of our house of burgesses, is very similar thereto. (G)

Exclusive of the above reasons, another very weighty argument, arising from the particular form of our provincial constitution, may be brought against the usurped powers of settling fees by Proclamation, and against the decision of its legality, in our *"ordinary judicatories."* We know, that the four principal officers in this province, most benefited by the Proclamation, are all members of the upper house; I have said it, and I repeat it again, a tenderness, a regard for those gentlemen, a desire to prevent a dimunition of their fees, have hitherto prevented a regulation of our staple; in a matter of this importance, which so nearly concerns the general welfare of the province, personal considerations and private friendships, shall not prevent me from speaking out my sentiments with freedom; neither shall antipathy to the man, whom in my conscience I believe to be the chief author of our grievances, tempt me to misrepresent his actions, "or set down ought in malice" — neither a desire to please men in power, nor hatred of those, who abuse it, shall force me to deviate from truth. "But the present Proclamation is not the invention of any daring ministers now in being" who said he was the inventor? *The minister now in being* has revived it only, in opposition to the unanimous sense of the people, expressed by their representatives, after a knowledge too of the evils, and confusion, which it heretofore brought on the province. Dismayed, trembling, and aghast, though skulking behind the strong rampart of Governor and council, this *Antilon* has intrenched himself chin deep in precedents, fortified with transmarine opinions, drawn round about him, and hid from publick view, in due time to be played off, as a masked

---

should be fixed, and established by authority, which table should be registered in a book, in the said court, to be at all times inspected gratis, *and a copy of it signed and attested by the judges of the court, should be returned to each house of parliament, to remain among the records." If the commons had a right to enquire into the abuses committed by the officers of the courts of law, they had (no doubt) the power of correcting those abuses, and of establishing the fees, had they thought proper, to be paid to the officers of those courts.*

(G) Because it is a tax upon the people without the consent of their representatives in assembly, as has been, I hope, demonstrated to the satisfaction of my readers.

battery, on the inhabitants of Maryland. I wish these opinions of *"Lawyers in the opposition"* would face the day, I wish the state, on which they were given was communicated to the publick, "the opinion respecting the Proclamation is on no point which the minister for the time being aims to establish" — if in favour of the Proclamation, I deny the assertion; the Proclamation is a point which the *minister* of *Maryland* aims to establish, in order to establish his own power, and perquisites, *Antilon* asks "If they (the *confederates*) have any other measure besides the Governor's Proclamation, to arraign as an attempt to set the supreme magistrate above the law?" First evince, that the Proclamation is not such an attempt; till then, it is needless to point out others; without entering into foreign matter; I have already given you an opportunity "of shewing me stripped of disguise *What I am*," I have shewn what, *stripped of disguise*) you are —

Homo natus in perniciem hujusce reipublicæ.[31]

a man born to perplex, distress, and afflict this country.

February 27, 1773   FIRST CITIZEN

[31] Probably a corruption of one of Cicero's invectives against Catiline or Piso. Similar expressions may be found in *Cat* 1, 2; *Cat* 1, 5; *Cat* 4, 2; *Cat* 4, 22; and *Sest* 5, 3.

Antilon's Third Letter

> *Sub pectore toto*
> *Individia intimuit, stultum furor abripuitque.*[1]

BEFORE I bestow any animadversion upon other impertinences, I shall endeavour to collect, and reduce to as much method, as they will bear, those parts of the Citizen's last performance, which have any apparent relation to the proclamation, and if the intelligent reader should be mischievously inclined to entertain himself with my distress, and for this purpose have recourse to my former paper, and my adversary's answer to it, I shall readily forgive him, if he smiles at the trouble I take to arrange desultory cavils, and extract out of the effusions of ignorance, and malice objections for refutation. "It is a very unfair thing (as Swift observes) in any writer to employ his ignorance, and malice *together*, because it gives his answerer *double* work. It is like the kind of sophistry that the logicians call *two mediums*, which are never allowed in the same syllogism, a writer with a *weak head*, and a *corrupt heart* is an overmatch for any single pen, like a hireling jade, *dull*, and *vicious*, hardly able to stir, yet offering at every turn to kick."[2]

---

[1] Under every breast envy swells and frenzy steals away the fool.
[2] Possibly from Jonathan Swift, *The Examiner* essays in *Works* (London, 1755–1759).

In my former letter I laid before the reader for his examination, and comparison, the two transactions of the ship-money tax, and the proclamation, and shewed that the former imposed a direct tax on the people, and enforced the payment of it by the rigourous means of execution affecting the property, and personal liberty of the subject, and that the latter contained the sanction only of the Governor's threats of displeasure to officers dependant, and removeable without any enforcement extended to the people beyond that, which the ordinary courts might confer on the very ground of its legality. I also proved that *without some settled* rate, or standard *no* exaction of an officer could be punishable as *extortion*, and that judges and others not vested with a *legislative* authority, had settled, and ascertained the fees of officers for the very purpose of preventing the oppression of the subject, and concluded, the two transactions, were not only not equally arbitrary infractions of the constitution, but were entirely dissimilar. The Citizen professes his design to consider my reasons in defence of the proclamation, and after having "granted that the assessment of ship-money was a more open, and daring violation of the constitution, still contends that the proclamation, though more disguised, is *equally subversive in its consequence* of liberty." The reader will remember that the Citizen to support the *character* he has atrributed to the proclamation, must prove it to be an *arbitrary tax*.

He allows that the tax of ship-money was an "open and avowed attack on liberty" and seems to apply to the proclamation the epithets, "modest, mild, and conciliating." He acknowledges that the methods pursued in levying the ship-money were the "arbitary seizure of property and deprivation of personal liberty" and that there "is no attempt in the proclamation to *subject* the *people* to any execution"; but, notwithstanding his admission of *so great difference*, he endeavours to maintain his position, that the proclamation is as subversive, *in its consequence*, of liberty, as the levy of ship-money was. "The most daring attacks on liberty, he says, are not *perhaps* the most dangerous," because extreme violence excites general indignation, and opposition; but the "modest, mild, conciliating manner, in which the *latent* designs of a crafty minister come *sometimes* recommended, ought to render them the more suspected, and should always inspire caution, and diffidence," let the operation, and effect of the proclamation determine its character; but, because the manner is modest, &c. — let not suspicion at once infer, that the design of it is to violate the peoples rights; for if one measure is to be opposed, because expressed in an imperative stile, and attended with the most rigorous enforcements, and another measure is also to be opposed, because it is "modest, mild, &c." in the manner, and unattended by any enforcement, except what it derives from the law, it would be difficult, indeed, for the best intentions to escape censure. In speaking of the ship-money *exaction*, the Citizen admits my account of it to be, "*in the main* true," but intimates that "it is not *impartial*," "it is *in the main* true." In what was it then not impartial? The exility[3] of the insinuation shall not protect the principle of it, nor shall contempt so entirely extinguish indignation, as to hinder me from exposing the subdolous[4] attempt. The appelation, "Tyrant" has, I suspect, rubbed the fore. "The tax (says he) was *very moderate little exceeding*, £200,000 sterling — it was *levied* with *justice* and *equity*, &c." "moderate?" When the people were plundered of every farthing of it? "levied with justice and equity"; when extorted by the rigours of distress, and imprisonment, in the most direct violation of every principle of liberty? The moderation, justice, and equity of a robber, who should suffer the plundered passenger to retain half a crown for his dinner, might be celebrated with equal grace and propriety. Again he whines — "the boundaries between liberty, and prerogative were far from being ascertained." What, had not Magna Charta so often (at least thirty-two times) confirmed; the statute (he has referred to on another occasion) de tallagio non concedendo, the petition and act of rights (to mention no other) *most clearly* established the *principle*, that "the people could not be taxed without their consent"? The boundary could not have been more clearly marked out by the utmost precaution of jealous prudence or more outrageously transgressed by the most determined, and lawless tyranny, and yet the Citizen, *the generous friend of liberty*, though he has adopted the pretences of a *notorious apologist*,[5] has advanced them *without any view* to "excuse the assessment of ship-

[3] Shrunken or attenuated condition, smallness in number or size; thinness, slenderness, meagreness.
[4] Crafty, cunning, sly.
[5] Historian David Hume.

money, or exculpate King Charles" — he means not to apologize, though he has adopted the very principles of the tyrants apologist — again "James the IId by endeavouring to introduce arbitary power, and subvert the ESTABLISHED *church deserved* to be deposed, and banished, and the revolution *rather*" says the Citizen, "*brought about*, than *followed* King James's *abdication* of the crown."

Here reader you have another proof of the staunch whiggism of the *champion*, so *properly* celebrated by our Independent Whigs. "The revolution rather brought about, than followed King James's abdication?"

Those great men, by whom the cause of national liberty was supported, entertained very different ideas from our *Independent Whigs* and their *champion*. They received their instruction IN *a very different school*. The commons voted that, King James IId "having endeavoured to subvert the constitution of the kingdom, by breaking the original contract between king, and people, and by the advice of jesuits, and other wicked persons, having violated the fundamental laws, and withdrawn himself out of the kingdom hath *abdicated* the government, and the throne is thereby vacant, and that it hath been found by experience to be inconsistent with this protesant kingdom to be governed by a popish prince."

The abdication of James was, *the wrong done by him*, "the government is under a *trust*, and acting against, is renouncing *it*; for how can a man in reason, or sense, express a greater renunciation of a trust, than by the constant declaration of his actions contrary to that trust."[6]

"The revolution rather brought about than followed the abdication."

The principles of this champion for whiggism having been developed, the *Independents*, perhaps, may doubt the propriety of their political attachment, when they consider the effect of the Citizen's suggestions is, that the revolution was *rather* an act of *violence*, than of *justice*, unless, indeed, the regard he has expressed for the *established* church, so *consistent* with his *religious* profession, should, happily, divert their attention; for *this regard*, to be sure, is very commendabie.

[6] Quotes from N(icholas) Tindal's *The Continuation of Mr. Rapin's History of England* (London, 1759), 13:lxviii, and David Hume's *History of England* (London, 1767), 8:300.

That the proclamation restrains the officers is certain, and, having *this* effect, *if it has no other*, it is beneficial — if it has moreover, the effect of binding the people to pay, as well as the officer to receive according to the adopted rates, this effect flows from its legality, from the same principles, that the general protection, and security of mens rights are derived.

The ship-money was levied upon the people, when *no part* of it was due — the officer can receive *nothing*, when *nothing* is *due*, and yet the Citizen alleges they *equally* correspond with the idea of *tax*, and of an arbitrary, tyranical imposition — a tax cannot be laid unless by the *legislative* authority; but fees, the Citizen is constrained to admit, have been *lawfully* settled by the lords *alone*, by the commons *alone*, by the upper and lower houses separately, and by the courts of law, and equity in England — that these fees have not been settled by the *legislative* authority is *therefore* clear. What is then the plain result? *No* tax can be imposed, except by the *legislature*, but *fees* have been *lawfully* settled in the *manner premised* by persons, *not vested with legislative authority*, consequently the settlement of fees is *not a tax*. On this head the Citizen remarks, that the lords and commons derive "their right from long usage, and the law of parliament which is part of the law of the land" — be it so, but the law of parliament, which is part of the law of the land, doth not vest the lords, or the commons *alone* with authority to tax. The amount then of the Citizen's *reasoning* is, that the lords and commons *separately* settle fees, because they are *enabled* so to do so by the *law of the land*. The judges have *no* share in the *legislature*; but *their* settlement of *fees* is *lawful* too, whence is their authority derived; but from *the law of the land*? "The chief danger of oppression (says Hawkins in his treatise of crown law) is from officers being left at liberty to set their own rates, and make their own demands, therefore the law has authorized the judges to settle them."[7] How are *these settlements*, and the admission of their *legality* to be reconciled with the position that *fees*, are *taxes*? "The proclamation, says the Citizen, *is in its consequence*, as subversive of liberty, as the ship-money, if the

---

[7] Serjeant William Hawkins, *A Treatise of the Pleas of the Crown* (London, 1762), chapter 68, sec. 3, p. 171.

judges should determine costs to be paid according to the rates, because execution would necessarily follow a refusal to pay those rates."

This objection, if I am not mistaken, suggests an additional argument to prove the settlement of fees to be, not only, not an arbitrary tax, but a *legal unavoidable* act. When a suit is brought in a court of law, or equity, or carried by appeal from an inferior to a superior jurisdiction, and a final judgment, or decree is given, in which costs are awarded, these costs are *necessarily ascertained*, and the party against whom they are awarded is compelled to pay them. It will, I presume, be admitted to be just, and reasonable, that the person, obliged to apply to a court of justice, should be repaid the lawful costs attending the prosecution of his suit, and that a party, put to expence in defending himself against an illegal claim, should also be repaid by his adversary the legal costs attending his defence. What then are *these costs, which ought* to be awarded, and must necessarily be *ascertained*, by the judgment or decree? the fees of the lawyer, and of the officers constitute, sometimes, the whole, sometimes part of these costs, and the fees are not only such, as have been *actually* paid, but such too as the party is *lawfully chargeable* with. If he has paid, or stipulated to pay *more*, than the *legal* rate, he is entitled to no allowance for the excess. The *voluntary* payment or contract of the party would be a very inconvenient rule, if not controuled by some other standard — he might be induced by a *personal regard* for the lawyer, or the officer, or by *his enmity* to his antagonist to exceed the just proportion. The lawyer cannot lawfully demand, or receive his fee, which makes part of the costs, till the cause is finished; the officer, too, generally, gives credit, beyond the time of passing the judgment, or decree, for fees, which also are part of the costs; but the suitor being chargeable the fees are included in the costs awarded by the judgment or decree, which may be immediately carried into execution. That the costs not only *may*, but *must* be awarded in various cases — that the fees of the lawyer, and officers are comprehended in the costs — that the costs must be ascertained in the judgment, or decrees — that therefore there must be some established *rule* or standard to *settle* and *fix* the *rates* of the *fees* which constitute the whole, or part of the costs, cannot be denied. The fees of the lawyer are settled by an act of assembly, the fees of the officer are not. There must be then some other authority to settle these fees, because they constitute part of the costs, and the judgment or decree, awarding the costs, must *necessarily* be *precise*. Justice cannot be administered without the exercise of such authority, and what is essential to the administration of justice, I must conclude, is not only, not an arbitrary, despotick imposition *extremely like* the levy of ship-money derogatory from the most fundamental principles of a free constitution: but is most consistent with, and even necessary to the general protection of the people; wherefore the *consequence* of an execution for costs is so far from fixing the opprobrious character of an arbitrary, oppressive tax, subversive of liberty, that on the contrary, it proves the necessity of settled rates for the very purposes of justice. The Citizen *adopts* a quotation from 2d. inst. to prove that the settlement of fees is a tax; but what Coke observes may be fully admitted without any proof, that *every settlement* of fees is a tax. If this had been his assertion it would be overruled by the clearest authorities, by every one of the instances of the settlement of fees already enumerated, as well as by other, depending upon the same principle. The statute, de tallagio non concedendo, speaking in the royal name, is to this effect, "no tallage or aid shall by us or our heirs be put or levied in our kingdom *without the grant of parliament*." Coke in his exposition of this part of the statute, observes that "all *new* officers *erected* with *new fees*, or *old* offices with *new* fees are within this act; for that is a tallage put upon the subject, which cannot be done without common consent by act of parliament."[8]

The offices, to which the proclamation relates, are not within the designation, *new offices*, and therefore so far the passage from 2d inst. is irrelative. The offices are *old* and *constitutional* such as do not depend on any will or discretion of the supreme magistrate, whether they shall be continued, or cease; but must be preserved as functions, always exerciseable, and necessary to the execution of the laws. *New fees* are not to be annexed to such offices according

[8] Sir Edward Coke, *The Second Part of the Institutes of the Laws of England* (London, 1669), chap. 1, pp. 532–33.

to Coke's opinion, by which is plainly meant, that the *old*, or established fees belonging to these offices cannot be lawfully augmented, or altered without *an act of parliament*. That in the *old* offices, fees may be settled for necessary services, when there happens to be no prior provision, or establishment, and that such settlement is lawful, and in the case of costs, I have already considered, *indispensably necessary*, the instances enumerated evince.

The judges determined that an under-sheriff should receive a fee of a person brought to the bar for, and acquitted of, a felony, "because it was assigned to the officer by the *order* and *discretion* of the *court*, and that it was *with reason* and *good conscience* this fee [2] was allowed by the court to the officer, *for the trouble* and *charge* he has with prisoners, and of his attendance on the court, as a *reward* for the service." 21 H. 7. 17, 28.[9]

Fees not settled by the legislature, and which may be lawfully received, *are not taxes*, because it is not competent to *any* persons, not constituting the *legislature*, to *tax* the subject. The same authority distinct from the legislative, that *has* settled, *may* settle the fees, when the proper occasion, of exercising it, occurs. "*Where there is the same reason, there is the same law.*"[10] Wherefore I presume to think, that though the *old* or *established* fees are not to be altered, increased, or augmented, yet, when fees are *due*, and the *rates* of them are *not* established, they may be settled *without* the legislative authority, because the *principle* of the authority *remains*, and it ought to be *active*, when the *reason* of it *calls* for *exertion*. Though the Citizen had admitted that the lords *alone*, the commons *alone*, the upper and lower houses *separately*, the courts of law and equity, have lawfully settled the fees of their officers, and consequently fees so settled are not *taxes*, which cannot be laid but by the act of the *whole legislature*, yet he has cited 2d inst. to prove that *fees* are a *tax* — again from some proceedings of the house of commons, he infers a power in the commons *alone* to settle fees in the *courts*, for that he is of opinion *at one time fees*

---

[9] *Les Reports des Cases* (London, 1679). The reference is to the Yearbook for 21 Henry 7. Antilon apparently made the translations from legal French. The citations are correct.

[10] *Ubi est eadem ratio, ibi est eadem lex*, from Sir Edward Coke, *The First Part of the Institutes of the Laws of England* (London, 1629), 10a.

are a tax, at *another*, he *admits* they are *not* a tax, *again* he
asserts that they *are* a tax, and *again* that they are *not* a tax.

Quoteneam vultus mutantem Protea nodo

(with what noose may I hold this Proteus so often shifting his
forms).[11] Having given an extract of some proceedings of the
house of commons upon an enquiry into fees received by the
officers belonging to the law, and of the resolves of the committee,
that "it was their opinion the long disuse of publick enquiries into
the behaviour of these officers had been the occasion of unnecessary officers, and illegal fees — that the interest of the great number of officers was the occasion of extending the forms to unnecessary lengths, of great delay, and oppression, and that a *table* of all
the officers, and of *their fees* in chancery should be *fixed*, and
ascertained by *authority*, which table should be registered in a
book in that court, to be inspected at all times gratis, and a *copy*
of it *signed*, and *attested* by the *judges*, should be returned to
each house of parliament to remain among the records,"[12] the
Citizen makes a *sagacious*, and *pertinent* observation, which gives
an *adequate* proof of his constitutional knowledge, and logical
abilities — "if the commons (says he) had a right to *enquire*
into the abuses committed by the officers of the courts, *they* had
no *doubt*, the *power* of correcting these abuses, and of *establishing*
the fees in those courts, *had they thought proper*."

Without doubt the parliament, or the general assembly may
establish fees; but the Citizen's conclusion is, that the commons
alone can,[13] and the premises whence he draws his egregious
inference are these — the commons have authority to enquire into
the abuses committed by the law officers — so that his argument in
form is this — *whenever* the *commons* have a *right to enquire* into
any subject, *they* may *establish* whatever *they may think proper*
concerning *that subject*.

Navem agere ignarus navis timet; abrotonum ægro
Non audet, nisi, qui didicit, dare; quod medicorum est

[11] Horace, *Epistles* 1, 1, 90.
[12] Quoted above in First Citizen's second letter, pp. 96–98.
[13] See *ibid.*, p. 98.

Promittunt medici: tractant fabrilia fabri.
The ign'rant landman shakes with fear
Nor dares attempt the ship to steer;
He who ne'er learn'd the doctor's trade,
To give ev'n southernwood's afraid;
Profes'd physicians cure by rules,
And workmen handle workmens tools.[14]

The magnanimous citizen however undertakes *any thing*, though it must be confessed by his admirers, that a little more diffidence would impeach his understanding, no more than it would tarnish his modesty; but though the extract is *entirely destitute of all force in the Citizen's application of it*, yet it suggests an additional circumstance in favour of the proclamation, which his malevolence has arraigned, and his arrogance has censured: for the opinion of the commons may be justly inferred from these expressions in their resolves, "a *table of all the fees should be fixed*, and established by *authority* that a *precise settlement of the rates* would be the *proper means* of preventing extortion," according to Serjeant Hawkins' observation already recited, and from the expressions, "the table of fees should be registered in a book open to inspection gratis, and a copy of this table *signed* and *attested by the judges* returned to each house of parliament,"[15] it may also be justly inferred that the "*authority*" meant was *not reposed* in *themselves*, and *as they were to be informed by a copy, signed and attested by the judges* of the *specifick* exercise of it, that the judges, who were to give information under their signatures, and official attestation, were understood to be the persons vested with the *authority* to *fix*, and *establish the fees*. The settlement of fees a tax, and yet the commons acknowledged the authority of the judges to make the settlement.

Putat tonsor sibi poscere navim
Luciferi rudis? exclamat Melicerta, perisse Frontem de rebus —

[14] Horace, *Epistles* 2, 1, 114.
[15] See above, in First Citizen's second letter, pp. 97–98. Serjeant William Hawkins, *A Treatise of the Pleas of the Crown* (London, 1762), chapter 68, sec. 3, p. 171.

(*A*) Should a mere barber think to ask
A pilot's trust, (an arduous task)
Yet cannot, such a dunce is he,
An observation make at sea,
Well *Melicerta might exclaim
That he had lost all sense of shame.[16]

That questions ought not to be prejudged is another of the Citizen's objections. This is very true in a proper application, but extremely absurd in the Citizen's — if there were no precedents, or established rules, the measures of justice might be very unequal, and the scales uneven and unsteady. "Misera est servitus, ubi jus est vagum."[17] The utility of precedents consists in the *very effect*, which is the *ground* of the Citizen's objections, that *similar* cases are governed by them. Without *this* effect, contests would be infinite. What he calls *prejudging*, is that which is the consequence, the salutary, beneficial consequence of legal certainty, preventive of endless litigation, vexation, and distress. The judges must have therefore, some fixed, stable rule for the ascertainment of costs. Indeed, reader, I find it to be a very irksome task to encounter such extreme ignorance, blended with such exuberant vanity, pertinacious impudence, and connate malignity, and to unravel the contexture they have formed. I observed in my former letter, that the courts of law and equity had settled fees, and the Citizen asks by what authority. The passage in Hawkins, already quoted, answers the question. Admitting, however, that the judges have settled fees, the Citizen alleges the "precedent does not apply." Surely to prove that the settlement of fees is not a *tax*, which nothing less than *full legislative authority* can establish, and therefore the precedent applies to destroy the very principle on which he

(*A*) *I have taken some liberty with Perseus but not more than the Citizen has done in his motto with Pym's speech* — Neque enim lex aequior ulla est.[18]
* The marine deity.

---

[16] Persius, *Fifth Satire*, lines 102–4.

[17] "It is a wretched state of slavery which subsists where the law is vague or uncertain." Sir Edward Coke, *The Fourth Part of the Institutes of the Laws of England* (London, 1681), p. 245.

[18] "For neither is any law more fair."

has "spent his feeble efforts" to prove the proclamation an arbitrary tax, as subversive of liberty as the levy of ship-money.

Cereopithecus quam sapiens est animal, ætatem qui uno ostio nunquam committit suam, quia si unum ostium obsideatur, aliud perfugium gerit.

(*B*) So wise the monkey, that he ne'er confides
His safety to *one* passage; but provides
That, if th' adversary should *one* make sure,
Another then may his retreat secure.[19]

Lest the objection to the proclamation *that it is a tax* should be refuted, the *sagacious* Citizen has provided another *outlet* for escape. "The precedents of judges having settled fees, says he, do not apply, because they have not settled *their own* fees: but the commissary, secretary, judges of the land office, being members of the council, and advisers of the proclamation (that is) *concurring* with the advice of the *minister; may be said* to have established their own fees; and the governor (*C*) as *chancellor, decreeing* his

(*B*) *Here too, after the example of the Citizen, I have been a little free with Plautus.*

(*C*) *What the Citizen has remarked, in one of his notes, to prove it inconsistent with the security, which the constitution of England affords in the distribution of the legislative, executive, and judicial powers, for the governor to be chancellor, proceeds from his very crude ideas of the British polity —* "*were the judiciary power joined with the legislative, the life and liberty of the subject would be exposed to arbitrary controul: for the judge would then be legislator*";[20] *but this does not provide that if a branch of, and not the whole legislature exercises a judicial power, there would be this consequence. The lords who are a branch of the legislative exercise a judicial power. The king, in whom the executive power is lodged, exercises, personally, no judicial power, considering the royal dignity and preeminence the idea of his being a judge in an inferior, subordinate and controulable jurisdiction would be absurd, and if the judicial power should be reposed in him absolutely, and conclusively, and his decisions not subject to examination and controul on an appeal to a superior jurisdiction, there would be great danger of, because there would be no regular method to prevent, violence, and oppression — now the chancellor, though he exercises a judicial power, and is vested with the executive, as governor, cannot commit the violence, and oppression dreaded, because there is an appeal to a superior provincial jurisdiction, and*

[19] This quote is not from Plautus. Pliny's *Natural History* is a more likely source. "Cercopithecus" is a rare Latin word and was probably inserted by Antilon.

[20] M. de Secondat, Baron de Montesquieu, *Spirit of the Laws*, translated by Thomas Nugent (London, 1773), vol. 9, chap. 6, p. 222.

fees according to the very settlement of the proclamation, would undoubtedly ascertain and settle *his own fees*, and be *judge in his own cause.*" Here the idea of tax is dropped. Who the *wicked minister* is, we shall be puzzled to find out. The commissary, secretary, and judges of the land-office *concurring with his advice*, he is not to be sought after in *this list* of officers. "It may be said," to be sure, Mr. Citizen, *anything* may be said — the proclamation however has no relation to the chancellor;† Plain Truth has sufficiently exposed the absurdity of this imputation.[21] "The governor *decreeing* his fees as chancellor!" "He is generous, of a good heart; but youthful, unsuspicious, diffident." I shall not analyse your composition; but pray, Mr. Citizen, let me ask, what reason, what experience, what probable conjecture have you to extenuate your affrontive insinuation? Has he ever been a judge in his own cause? Has he ever betrayed any symptom of an inclination to be so? Again, at your *mischievous tricks* "tam forma & mores sunt consimiles"[22] the proclamation has no relation to the judges of the land-office, their fees are settled in a different manner, and the legality of it does not depend on any question of prerogative; but on the *power every owner has over his property*, to dispose of it upon such

---

his decrees may be reformed, or reversed, and an ultimate appeal too is provided to the king in council; and, moreover, he is removeable, accountable, and even punishable, for violence and oppression — whence then the danger to liberty from the chancellor's violence and oppression. In New York, and in the Jerseys, the governors are chancellors — in Virginia the governor, and also the members of the council, the executive, and two branches of the legislative exercise an extensive judicial power in matters of equity, law, and of crimes. Should any branch of the legislative, whether governor, upper, or lower house, assume, in any instance, all the powers legislative, executive, and judicial, without doubt, it would be an extreme violation of the constitution, and the Citizen's impartiality would severely condemn it, though a tenderness for his connexions may prevent his publick censures. A similar affection, perhaps, inclined him to pass over a question, or two, in my former letter. I do not wish him to offend any of his connexions. Let those, whom he has honoured with his regard, still enjoy it, however opposite their political walks, political attachments, and the colours of their apparent political principles may have been.

† See the Gazette, *No. 1436.*

---

[21] "Plain Truth" appeared in the *Maryland Gazette*, March 18, 1773, pp. 4–5.
[22] "To such a degree, form and customs are similar."

terms, as he thinks proper. The advice of the council was not asked on this subject.[23] This regulation too you have represented to be as arbitrary as the ship-money assessment, and with equal facility you may prove it to be a tax, or a rigadoon.[24]

The governor and council were twelve in number, of whom two only can be said (I mean with truth) to have any interest in the effect of the proclamation.[25] The governor was not to be *directed* by the *suffrage* of the council; he was to judge of the propriety of their *advice* upon the *reasons* they should offer. It cannot be asserted (I mean again with truth) that they were not unanimous, though the Citizen has the assurance to affront them with the reproachful imputation of being implicit dependants on *one man*. The proclamation was the act of the governor flowing from his persuasion of its utility. He had promised, *publickly* and *solemnly promised* that "if the prerogative should interpose in the settlement of fees, *he* would take good care to act on *mature consideration*, and what *he* should *judge* to be right and just, would be the *only* dictate to determine *his* conduct."[26] He again, has publickly, and solemnly declared that, "so clear was his *conviction* of the propriety, and utility of a regulation to prevent extortion, and infinite litigation, if it was necessary, instead of recalling, he would renew his proclamation, and in stronger terms threaten all officers with his displeasure, who should presume to ask, or receive of the people any fee beyond *his restriction*."[27] In his proroguing speech he again *declared* that "He had issued the proclamation solely for the benefit of the people, by *nine tenths* of whom, he believed it was so understood."[28] But you, Mr. Citizen, have asserted, an absolute, direct, impudent, malicious (I will give you, as it is upon paper, a *dissyllable*) falsehood, that he was

[23] The land office proclamation on November 24, 1770, is printed in *Maryland Archives* (Baltimore: Maryland Historical Society, 1883–), 63:112.

[24] A lively dance with a jump step for one couple; music for the dance.

[25] Dulany himself, as provincial secretary, and his brother, Walter Dulany, commissary general.

[26] The governor's reply to the address of the lower house, November 30, 1771. *Maryland Archives* 63:223.

[27] *Ibid.*, p. 233.

[28] The proroguing speech was also delivered November 30, 1771, *ibid.*, p. 237.

not determined by *his own* judgment, but by the dictate of a *man* whom sometimes you call a clerk, sometimes a register, and sometimes minister, and that nine tenths of the people do not believe the proclamation issued for the purpose, so publickly, so solemnly declared. The contradiction, it must be confessed, is direct and pointed, and if advanced on sufficient grounds, the veracity, sincerity, and honour of — would be — but I know it to be an infamous, impudent calumny (characteristical of the author of it) prompted by the temerity of ungovernable malignity. To atone for this insolence, the maxim, "the king can do no wrong," is introduced, and on what principle? Not such as would allow an application to a —— who should happen to be old, or middle-aged, or circumspect — He must be "youthful, unsuspicious, &c. &c." — really this seems to be an innovation, rather arbitrary — *legal maxims* have been understood to be *rather unpliant*; however as *you* can so easily *garble moral* ones, who will dispute *your* address in modifying the legal? Would he but act as he should — alas! would he but — then "he would be a little god below," and be *worshipped accordingly*; something *more* than a king. "The governor however, you say, is no king" — but yet again you tell us, "kings have *revoked* proclamations, and *therefore*, though the governor has *affixed his signature*, he may *disavow* his act." Again, "He is *improperly* called the king's *minister*, he is *rather* his *representative*, or *deputy*. He forms a distinct branch of the legislature, and he has the power of life and death," and as a representative, or deputy, cannot act *beyond*, or *out of* the *capacity* of his constituent, or principle, you have, Mr. Citizen, *clearly proved* in your *peculiar* style, that the governor is the *representative* or *deputy* of the king, *because* the king *cannot* execute a *judicial* office; and, the governor *can* — a grave refutation of such nonsense *about* the governor's being a king, and not a king, would be, indeed, ridiculous. The mean, foolish servility of the intended palliative offers an insult to HIS understanding, *whose* sincerity, veracity, and honour you have so insolently attacked. But to return to Serjeant Hawkins, and answer the question which, in the triumph of ignorance, you have proposed: "Have not the officers who advised, and the governor who issued the proclamation, set their own rates?" No, I have shewn, they have not — your *law* case is nothing to the purpose, or I would shew it, *not to be law.* You may perceive, if not quite blind, that I have not by silence admitted the imputation, neither have I denied the advice I gave "as far as I gave it": but I deny (what your impudence, and *mendacity* have asserted) that *any one* man of the council was the dictator of the proclamation, though I avow it to be my opinion, the measure was expedient, and legal. I deny what you have asserted, and without reserve charge you with having outraged truth with the most impudent, and flagitious malice, on the mean base motive of engaging the passions of those, whom you have studied to delude by a feigned regard for the publick welfare, to assist you in the gratification of a narrow, personal, sordid enmity. Take this as an answer to all your desultory, base, malevolent assertions of the controuling power of *a wicked minister*, and blush, *if* you have any sense of shame left.

> pudet haec opprobria dici,
> Et dici potuisse, & non potuisse refelli.[29]

I have been the more direct, and explicit in my disavowal, lest your unprincipled confidence should cast a blemish upon the honour of the other members of the council, whom you aim to render *contemptible*, that you may make *one* man publickly obnoxious, who, despising the impotence of it, bids defiance to all the efforts of your malice.

I alleged in my former letter that the proclamation, by restraining the officers, prevented extortion, and recited it at large that the reader might form his own judgment; but, says the Citizen "it ought rather to be considered as a *direction* to the officers what to demand, and to the people what to pay." This word *"rather"* seems to be a favourite, it does not *assert*; it only *squeaks* insinuation, what is meant by [3] "direction"? It is a vague term, it is applied by the Citizen to the officers, and to the people *equally*, and having been substituted in the place of "restriction, and *preventive of extortion*" it is proper to guard against *deception*, by *fixing* the sense of it; if it only means *pointing out*, it is harmless; but why

---

[29] "It shames me that these insults are able to be uttered and not refuted." Ovid, *Met.* 1:758–59.

then the substitution? If it means *order*, or *command*, it is fallacious: for the *people* are not *ordered* or *commanded*. I wish he had carried his appeal to the *feelings* of the people. If oppressed, they must feel the oppression — if they are not, let them not be persuaded by this political quack to think, that they are. Prudent men who possess the blessing of vigorous health, will hardly be persuaded to swallow the pill, or draught of an ignorant mountebank, who has the impudence to pronounce that they are distempered, and ought to take his drugs. It is true that the lower house called the settlement of fees by proclamation *"the usurpation of a right"* and threatened an opposition, and their resolves were afterwards extremely violent; but if the settlement of fees was lawful, and expedient, it was not to be controuled by resolves, and a submission to such intemperate vehemence would have derogated from the dignity of government, and endangered the constitutional balance of power. The other branches of the legislature were as unanimous, and clear in an opposite opinion. Other reasons, besides what the Citizen has suggested may be assigned for the temporary duration of the inspection law. As a regulation it might, from an alteration of circumstances, become in every respect inconvenient, and the utility of a law, so extensive, and important, ought to be established by infallible experience, before its perpetuity is ordained. That a similar proclamation, in 1733, was the occasion of much clamour I believe, but not that the clamour was so general, and violent, as it has *since* been, *on another topic:* resolves have been as vehement, and more expressive of apprehension, *on another occasion*, when only *three* members ventured to vote against them; the number that divided against the last resolve, respecting the proclamation.[30] The Citizen need not go far to have this matter explained, and, I imagine, he may be inclined to think resolves ought not *always* to fix mens opinions, since *sometimes*, they may be dictated by *passion*. His objection, that settling the fees is a prejudging of the question, has been answered, and besides an appeal to the supreme court of the province will hardly admit of supposition; for the sum must exceed £ 50 sterling, or 10,000

[30] The reference is to a division of the lower house March 5, 1754, in which Dulany was one of three delegates to oppose adoption of an anti-Catholic report. See note 37 below.

lb. tobacco, and it is not to be expected, that an officer would suffer any one to be indebted to him, in so large a sum. The Citizen seems desirous to be informed, how fees are to be recovered — all in good time — if in chancery, the Governor, acting upon his own judgment, in this sage gentleman's opinion, will deserve to be removed ab officio, and he will most cordially wish his removal — weighty opinion — tremendous wish! if a patriot stepping forth, *like Hampden*, in the glorious cause of liberty should be *iniquitously* compelled to pay an officer's fees, for services, *actually* performed, how alarming would be the event? The Citizen has thought proper to make me say that "Mr. Ogle met with the most violent opposition any Governor ever did, *on account* of his proclamation" but I must object to this substitution, because the fact asserted by him is absolutely false. The opposition he met with, and the railings, he despised, flowed from a very different source, and, I suspect, the Citizen only affects an ignorance of the *particular circumstances*. The proclamation was not issued by Mr. Ogle, but "he" fully atoned, "says the Citizen," by his "*subsequent* conduct, which was mild and equitable, for the oppressions (or errors) of his *former* administration" here again I must object, because the Citizen falsely insinuates, that the decree I mentioned was in his *first*, when in fact, it was in his *last* administration.[31] The opinions of eminent counsel in England, in favour of the proclamation, having been intimated, a passage in a pamphlet was cited by him to this effect, "on a question of publick concernment, the opinions of court lawyers, however respectable for their candour ought not to weigh more than the reasons adduced in support of them, &c. — for they have generally declared that to be legal, which the *minister for the time being* has deemed to be expedient"[32] and hence he seemed to infer that the opinions in favour of the proclamation should be regarded with suspicion. I answered in my former letter, that the cases were entirely different, because "proclamation was no point which the minister aimed to establish &c." and what have you replied to this, Mr. Citizen? "You deny

[31] Carroll was mistaken. See above in Antilon's second letter, note 12; and in First Citizen's second letter, note 13.

[32] Daniel Dulany, Jr., *Considerations on the Propriety of Imposing Taxes in the British Colonies* (Annapolis, 1765), pp. 12–13.

the assertion, *if* the opinions are in favour of the proclamation, because it is a point, which the *minister of Maryland* aims to establish" the minister "of Maryland" pitiful sneaking prevarication — *a'r'n't you ashamed of yourself?*

The Citizen wishes "that the opinions of the English lawyers in the opposition; would face the day" — for two reasons his request will not be complied with — the first, that he has no kind of right to make it — second, I have no power to grant it, but that I may not seem to be a mere churl, I inform him — that besides the attorney, and solicitor general of England, Serjeant Wynn and Mr. Dunning were of opinion, that the King could *lawfully* settle the fees of *constitutional* officers in the royal governments, and that this power was conferred on the proprietor of Maryland by the charter, under which we derive the power of making laws for our good government.[33] In New York, the fees of officers have been settled by the Governor, and council, in virtue of the royal commission, and the people there (not much inclined to submit to violations of their rights) submit to the settlement. By this royal commission the Governor, with the advice, and assistance of the council, was authorized to make a table of fees, and thereby a reasonable provision for officers, and in virtue of this commission, such table of fees was made, and is the fixed rule, or standard, though an act of assembly in New-York for the settlement of fees had passed a little time before, and received the royal dissent — all this Mr. Citizen, has been "endured" in New York, for want of the exertion of men of *your* principles civil, and religious.

The short extract from Petit affords a just specimen of the Citizen's candour — the Citizen did not choose to state the nature of the proclamations mentioned in Petit, but has left the reader to infer a *great deal* from his *little scraps.* To obviate this disingenuous purpose, it is necessary to observe, that the proclamations complained of "as altering some points of law, and making new" directed, who should not, and who might be *chosen* to *represent the people*, and ordered "if returns should be made contrary to this direction, they should be rejected, and warranted any person to

[33] The opinions are printed in *Maryland Archives* 32:493–501.

seize starch, and to dispose, or destroy any stuff, &c. and restrained all men, not licensed (by the crown) to make starch" — "the proclamation made for matter directly rejected the precedent session" ordered, that "houses should be built with brick" — the proclamations "touching the freehold livelihood of men" directed "the razing and pulling down houses, and prohibited them to be rebuilt, and appointed the owners land to be let by other men at what price they pleased" — former proclamations vouched "ordering country gentlemen out of London, and against buildings" — "confiscations of goods, fine, forfeitures, imprisonment, seizure, standing in the pillory threatened"[34] — now the reader may make his application, without danger of being deceived, and he may not improperly, judge too of the Citizen's *real patriotism.* (D) The Citizen it must be allowed, has a happy talent at *explanation* — I asked in my former letter, what was meant "by dragging to light" — "made to feel the resentments of a free people — punished with infamy, exile or death — dread of such a fate" — and his ingenuity has proved, nothing more was meant, than a removal from office, and a different supposition proceeded from the "conscious guilt of" a wicked minister "trembling, and dismayed" — despicable fribble, and yet you complain of ridicule — "Sarcasms, says he, on personal defects have *ever been* esteemed the sure token of a base degenerate mind" — but I insist upon this exception. "Where there is an apparent correspondence between the form, and the disposition, cum forma, et mores consimiles sunt," when the features and lineaments of the one, are directed by the motions, and affections of the other, when the countenance does the office of a dial plate, the wheels, and springs within the machine actuating its muscles.

(D) Proclamations are lawful, or not, according to their subjects. That they have been employed as instruments of tyranny is not to be denied; but they have, too, been expedient to invigorate legal sanctions. Instances may be cited of proclamations, particularly such as have affected the order, and profession of certain religionists, that have been received with great popular applause. Eos tamen lædere non exoptemus, qui nos lædere non exoptant.[35]

---

[34] William Petyt, *Jus Parliamentarium* (London, 1739), p. 327.
[35] See First Citizen's translation and discussion on p. 152 below.

The figure such, as may the soul proclaim —
We pity faults by nature's hand imprest
But with his mind, Thersites' form's a jest.[36]

When an adversary exerts all his *mischievous* powers; and the person assailed attempts to ridicule them "he gives" according to the Citizen's maxim "a sure token of a base, degenerate mind" but the extreme *mendacity*, and malice of the assailant are *just* proofs of his publick spirit — I am as little apprehensive of any attack upon my person or house, by a party of free men led on by the Citizen, as I am that the Ægyptian superstition, cultus Ægyptius cercopitheci (the worship of a monkey) will succeed the demolition of our religious establishment.

Dialogue, as he has managed it, is a manner of writing very suitable to the tenuity of the Citizen's genius, he takes care that his opponent shall always be discomfited, and himself complimented on his victory. In the short one introduced into his last piece he has very cleverly, disclosed, or concealed just so much as answers his main purpose of misrepresentation: but the officer, *in fact*, has it in his power, in various instances, to receive his fees *immediately*. If a writ be applied for, or a copy of any record, or paper in his custody — if a warrant of survey, or patent — if letters testamentary, or of administration, if an account is to be passed, an inventory to be received, a commission to be issued, if the examination and passing a certificate, if a survey is to be made, certificates of it to be made out &c. &c. the respective officers have it in their power to receive their fees immediately for their services, and, if not restrained, might oppress, so that the Citizen's expedient, "not pay," is the "baseless fabrick of a vision" the officers, who are thus paid, save the expence of collection, suffer no loss from insolvencies, and are not put to inconvenience from the irregular, or negligent conduct of sheriffs.

There is a *little mischievous* insinuation of the Citizen, which deserves some animadversion: speaking of the affair of ship-money, he says, "that the judges," the guardians of law, and liberty (*"reflect on this, good reader"*) gave a corrupt opinion — the

[36] Thersites was a misshapen fool in Shakespeare's *The Histories of Troylus and Cressida* (London, 1609).

words, "reflect on this good reader" — seem to have been thrown out to raise a suspicion of *other judges*. That judges have been corrupt, that juries *too* have been corrupt, that Kings have been tyrants, that men have professed the utmost purity of intention, and after they had gained, by the arts of simulation, the popular confidence, basely sacrificed the rights of the people, and that personal enmity has assumed the fair appearance of publick virtue cannot be denied: but are all judges, all juries to be suspected of corruption, all kings of tyranny, all patriots of venality? and is *every* man, professing a regard for the publick welfare to be suspected of a narrow, personal, rancorous enmity, because the Citizen's furious temerity has laid aside the mask, and betrayed all the turpitude, and deformity of the basest, and the blackest malignity!

Notwithstanding *your averment*, Mr. Citizen, the strong probability, on which I founded my opinion, who were concerned in the unprovoked virulent attacks, contained in the papers, still remain in full force. The many instances, in which you have shewn your utter disregard of truth in your assertions and of the most disingenuous prevarication in your answers, and explications, render *your* testimony extremely suspicious; and such is your casuistical ingenuity that *all possibility* of mean cavil and illiberal subterfuge must be absolutely precluded, before any credit will be due to *your averments*. "Advice," suggestion, "assistance," are not terms of sufficient comprehension — if, however, when attacked in the dark, I have mistaken the assailant, and directed some resentment against a person *really not privy to*, nor *approving* the outrage, it is a strong reason to dissuade from these dark attacks, which may involve men, *in no manner* concerned.

After all, who is this man, that calls himself a Citizen, makes his addresses to the inhabitants of Maryland, has charged the members of one of the legislative branches with insolence, because, in their intercourse with another branch of the legislature, they proposed stated salaries, and has *himself* proposed a *different* provision for officers; contradicted the most publick, and explicit declarations of the governor, represented *all* the council, but *one*, to be mere fools, that he may represent *him* to be a political parricide; denounced infamy, exile, and death; expressed a regard for the *established* church of England? Who is he? He has no share in the legislature, as a member of any branch; he is incapable of being a member; he is disabled from giving a vote in the choice of representatives, by the laws and constitution of the country, *on account of his principles*, which are *distrusted* by those laws. He is disabled by an express resolve from interfering in the election of members, on the *same account*. He is not a protestant.[37]

In my former letter I intimated, Mr. Citizen, that the Governor's conduct in the proceedings relative to the proclamation had been honored by the royal approbation, and yet you have *vehemently* pronounced, that the proclamation "*must not be endured.*" Softly, magnanimous citizen, softly — you have already stretched the *skin* too much, and raise not your voice to so great a pitch of *dissonance*, as, peradventure, may be *intolerable.* "Must not be endured!" These are naughty words. What then are you to do? Are you to have no employment, no amusement? Yes, be employed, be amused; but before you resolve upon a plan, consider seriously, what you are able, and what you are not able to bear,

> quid ferre recusent,
> Quid valeant HUMERI[38]

---

[37] According to Lawrence H. Gipson, *The British Empire Before the American Revolution* (New York: Knopf, 1958-), 2:48-51, "of all the British plantations in North America, Maryland had the severest anti-Catholic laws." These laws inflicted various disabilities on Catholics, including prohibition of public worship and disenfranchisement. The establishment of the Church of England by acts of assembly in 1700 and 1702 paved the way for the direct assaults on Catholic liberties, *Maryland Archives* 24:91-98, 265-73. For subsequent legislation, see *ibid.*, 26:340-41, 431-32; 30:228-29, 612-17; 33:287-89. There was an apparent lessening of anti-Catholic fervor before imperial hostilities with the French induced a new wave of attacks. These included a rider to the 1756 Supply Bill, calling for double taxation of Catholic lands. See Charles A. Barker, *Background of the Revolution in Maryland* (New Haven: Yale University Press, 1940), pp. 240-41. The new attitude of the assembly, especially the lower house, was revealed in a series of committee reports and addresses. A 1753 report claimed anti-Catholic legislation was not well enough enforced, *Maryland Archives* 50:198. The committee found that "the growth of popery within this province, is become notorious, by the public preaching of Priests, and their perverting many of his Majesty's Protestant and loyal subjects; as also corrupting the Minds of Youth by teaching School publickly." On a subsequent vote in the lower house, March 5, 1754, only three delegates, including Dulany, opposed adoption of the report. Dulany also opposed double taxation in 1756.

[38] Horace, *Ars Poetica*, line 39. "Revolve in your thoughts for a considerable time what your strength is unable and what it is able to support."

and, if you are not very perverse, you will follow my advice, (though I have shewn what, stripped of disguise you are — "stultus invidiæ furore abreptus," a foolish fellow, hurried away by the rage of malice) instead of making yourself ridiculous, perhaps, obnoxious, by endeavouring to gain the confidence of the people, who are *instructed* by the spirit of our laws, and constitution, by the disabilities you are laid under, not to place any trust in *you*, when their civil, or religious rights, may be concerned. My advice to you is to be quiet, and peaceable, and with all due application, Ædificare casas, plostello adjungere mures, Ludere par impar, equitare in arundine longa. to build baby houses, yoke mice to a go-cart, play at even or odd, (or push pin for variety) and ride upon a long cane.

ANTILON

First Citizen's Third Letter

MAY 6, 1773

Our places *are disposed of to men, that are the* ornaments *of their own dignity; to men that have the welfare of the* kingdom *wholly at heart, and who accept of* offices *only to do the necessary* drudgery *of the state, and neither to* amass estates *from their services, nor* aggrandize *any* branches *of their family: hence it happens that England can never be infamous for a* Sejanus, *who rose from the dunghill to grasp all power, and whose* working *wickedness had generally a* double plot, *upon his* prince, *and upon the* people.

TRUE BRITON, NO. 38.[1]

THE prince, who places an unlimited confidence in a bad minister, runs great hazard of having that confidence abused, his government made odious, and his people wretched: of the many instances, which might be brought to confirm the observation, none more instructive, can perhaps be selected from the annals of mankind, than the story of Sejanus. We need not however have recourse to the history of other nations, and of other ages, to prove, that the unbounded influence of a wicked minister, is sure to lead his master into many difficulties, and to involve the people in much distress; the present situation of this province is·a proof of both.

---

[1] *Memoirs of the Life of his Grace Philip Late Duke of Wharton.* By an Impartial Hand (London, 1731), p. 329. Sejanus was born of distinguished parentage. He became commander of the praetorian guard and exercised a growing influence over Tiberius. Sejanus planned to strike at the principate in 31 but the plan failed. He was arrested, brought before the senate, and executed.

It is not my intention to compare Antilon with Sejanus; yet whoever has the curiosity to read the character of the latter drawn by the masterly pen of Tacitus, and is well acquainted with the former, will discover some striking likenesses between the two. — The (*A*) "animus sui obtegens, in *alios criminator*" — The "juxta adulatio & superbia" are equally applicable to both.[2]

Does it yet remain a secret, who this wicked minister, this Antilon, is? Are ye, my countrymen, *"puzzled to find him out"*? Surely not; his practices have occasioned too much mischief, to suffer him to lurk concealed, notwithstanding all his mean, and dirty arts, to gain popularity, by which he rose to his present greatness, and the indefatigable industry of his *tools*, in echoing his praises, and celebrating the *rectitude* of his measures.

In vindication of his conduct, Antilon has not endeavoured to convince the minds of his readers by the force of reason, but *"in the favourite method of illiberal calumny, virulent abuse, and shameless asseveration to affect their passions"* — has attempted to render his antagonist ridiculous, contemptible, and odious; he has descended to the lowest jests on the person of the Citizen, has expressed the utmost contempt of his understanding, and a strong suspicion of his *political*, and *religious principles*. What connexion, Antilon, have the latter with the proclamation? Attempts to rouse popular prejudices, and to turn the laugh against an adversary, discover the weakness of a cause, or the inabilities of the advocate, who employs ridicule, instead of argument — *"The Citizen's patriotism is entirely feigned"*; his reasons must not be considered, or listened to, because his *religious principles* are not to be trusted — Yet if we are to credit Antilon, the Citizen is so little attached to those principles, "That he is *"most devoutly wishing for the event,"* which is to free him from their shackles.[3] What my speculative notions of religion may be, this is neither the place, nor time to

---

(*A*) *"A mind dark and unsearchable, prone to blacken others, alike fawning and imperious."*

If the Latin word adulatio, *implies that Sejanus was fond of flattery, and inclined to flatter, the sentiment is still more apposite to* our wicked minister, *who is known to swallow greedily the fulsome and nauseous praises of his admirers, and to bear a great deal of* daubing.

---

[2] Tacitus, *Annales* 4, 1, 16.

[3] See p. 74 above.

declare; my political principles ought only to be questioned on the present occasion; surely they are constitutional, and have met, I hope, with the approbation of my countrymen; if so, Antilon's aspersions will give me no uneasiness. He asks — Who is this Citizen? — A man, Antilon, of an independent fortune, one deeply interested in the prosperity of his country: a friend to liberty, a settled enemy to lawless prerogative. I am accused of folly, and falsehood, of garbling moral, and legal maxims, of a narrow, sordid, and personal enmity; of the first, and second accusations, I leave the publick judge, observing only, that my want of veracity has not been proved in a single instance. What moral, what legal maxims have I garbled? Point them out Antilon: you assert that my censures of your conduct flow from a narrow, sordid, and personal enmity; that I dislike your vices, is most true; that my enmity is rancorous, and sordid, I deny; you have made the charge, it is incumbent on you to prove it; should you fail in your proofs, admit you must, on your own principles, that you have exhibited the strongest tokens of a base mind: but what is evident to all, can receive no additional confirmation from your admission. Take this as an answer, the only one I shall give, to all your obloquy and abuse. — That vituperari ab improbo summa est laus. The bad man's censures are the highest commendations.

If it be irksome to be engaged against a writer of a "weak head," and *corrupt heart*, the task becomes infinitely more disgusting when we have to encounter not only the latter vice, but likewise the wilful misrepresentations of craft, and falsehoods dictated by *"shameless impudence."* It will be shewn in the course of this paper that Antilon is guilty of both charges.

The assessment of ship-money, the Citizen has said, was a more open, the proclamation a more disguised, though not less dangerous attack on liberty; it has, I hope, been proved already, that fees are taxes, and that the settlement of them by proclamation is arbitrary, and illegal: Antilon has not refuted the arguments adduced to prove both propositions; other reasons in support thereof shall be brought hereafter; at present let us consider whether the proclamation be not a *disguised, and dangerous attack on liberty*. If we attend to the time, circumstance, and *real* motive of issuing the proclamation, they will, I think, evince, beyond all doubt, the truth of the assertion. The proclamation came out a few days after the prorogation of the assembly,[4] under the colour of preventing extortion, but in reality to ascertain what fees should be taken from the people by the officers, and after a disagreement between the two houses about a regulation of fees by law. It would have been too insolent, to have informed the people in plain terms; your representatives would not come into our proposals; the governor was therefore advised to issue the proclamation for the settlement of fees, adopting the very rates of the late regulation objected to by your delegates, as unjust, and oppressive in several instances; their obstinate, and unreasonable refusal to comply with our *moderate* demands, constrained us to recur to that expedient. It would I say have been too daring, to have talked openly in this manner, and too silly, to have avowed, that, to cover the dangerous tendency of the proclamation, it was cloaked with the specious, and pretended necessity of protecting the people from the rapacity of officers. This affected tenderness for the people, considering the character of the minister, who made a parade of it, and has since assigned it as the best excuse of an unconstitutional measure, was sufficient to awake suspicion, and fears. Our constitution is founded on jealousy, and suspicion; its true spirit, and full vigour cannot be preserved without the most watchful care, and strictest vigilance of the representatives over the conduct of administration. This doctrine is not mine, it has been advanced, and demonstrated by the best constitutional writers; the present measures call for our closest attention to it; the latent designs of our crafty minister will be best detected by comparing them with the open, and avowed declarations of government in 1739, on a contest exactly similar to the present. The pursuits of government in the enlargement of its powers, and its encroachments on liberty, are steady, patient, uniform, and gradual; if checked by a well concerted opposition at one time, and laid aside, they will be again renewed by some succeeding minister, at a more favourable juncture.

Extract from the votes and proceedings of the assembly 1739:[5]

---

[4] The assembly was prorogued November 21, 1771, and the fee proclamation issued November 26.

[5] June 2, 1739, *Maryland Archives* (Baltimore: Maryland Historical Society, 1883–), 60:251.

"The conferrees of the upper house are commanded to acquaint the conferrees of the lower house, that they conceive the proprietary's authority to settle fees, *where there is no positive law* for that purpose, to be indisputable, and that they apprehend the exercise of such an authority to be agreeable to the *several instructions* from the throne to the respective governments, and therefore that the upper house cannot but think a *perpetual law* in this case, reasonable and necessary, &c."

Compare, my countrymen, the proclamation issued in 1739 with the present; compare the language of the conferees of the upper house in 1739, with Antilon's arguments, and vindication of his favourite scheme; in substance they are the same. Antilon's account of ship-money, I have admitted in the main to be true, though not intirely impartial; this sentence conveys no insinuation, but what is plain, and easily justified. A writer may give a relation of facts generally true, yet by suppressing some circumstances, may either exaggerate, or diminish the guilt of them, and by so doing, greatly alter their character and complexion. The justice of the remark will hardly be denied, and the application of it to the present case will evince its utility. Antilon has vented part of his spleen on Mr. Hume; the censured passage is taken from that author, acknowledged by a sensible writer, (*B*) and thorough whig, to be an instructing, and entertaining historian. To exculpate the *notorious apologist*, and myself, it is necessary to observe that the words "*levied* with *justice, and equality*" (not *equity* as cited by Antilon) mean, the tax was equally divided among, or assessed upon the subjects without favour and affection to particular persons, that the imposition, though applied to a good and publick use, was contrary to law, the historian has acknowledged in the most forcible, and express words.[6]

(*B*) *Daines Barrington — Observations on the statutes chiefly the more ancient.*[7]

---

[6] Ship-money "was intirely arbitrary: By the same right any other tax might be imposed: And men esteemed a powerful fleet . . . an unequal recompence for their liberties," David Hume, *History of England* (London, 1767), 6: 239–40.

[7] (Dublin, 1767). There is a reference to Hume on p. 405.

Has the Citizen anywhere insinuated, that the assessment of ship-money was legal? Has he not expressly declared, that he does not mean to excuse that assessment? That the conduct of Charles will admit of no *good* apology? Yet that there were some appearances in his favour, the passages already quoted, candid men, I think, will admit, if not as a proof to convince, at least as an inducement to incline them to that opinion; mine, I confess, it is, and I make the acknowledgment, without fear of incurring the odious imputation of abetting arbitrary measures, or of being a friend to the Stuarts.

What means the insinuation, Antilon, conveyed in this sentence, *"The appellation "tyrant" has I suspect rubbed the sore."* Your endeavours to defame, excite only pity, and contempt; your heaviest accusations, thank God, have no better foundation than your own suspicions. But to return. I again assert, that notwithstanding all the acts ascertaining the subjects rights, cited in your last admirable, and polite performance, that the boundaries between liberty and prerogative were far from being ascertained in Charles's reign, with that precision, and accuracy, which the subsequent revolutions, and the improvements our constitution in later times have introduced. (C) I must trouble my readers with a few more quotations from the obnoxious historian abovementioned, submitting the justice of his observations, and the inference drawn from them to their decision, and better judgment.

"Those lofty ideas of monarchical power *which were very commonly adopted during that age and to which the ambiguous nature of the English constitution gave so plausible an appearance*, were firmly riveted in Charles." Again, speaking of illegal imprisonment, "But the Kings of England (says he) who had not been able to prevent the enacting these laws, (in favour of personal liberty) had sufficient authority, when the tide of liberty was spent, to

(C) *"The latter years, says Blackstone, of Henry VIII, were the times of the greatest despotism, that have been known in this island, since the death of William the Norman: the prerogative, as it then stood by common law (and much more when extended by act of parliament) being too large to be endured in a land of liberty."*[8]

---

[8] Blackstone's *Commentaries on the Laws of England* (London, 1821), 4:428.

hinder their regular execution, and they deemed it superfluous to attempt the formal repeal of statutes, which they found so many expedients, and pretences to elude."

"The imposition of ship-money (the same historian remarks) is apparently one of the most dangerous invasions of national privileges, not only which Charles was ever guilty of, but which the most arbitrary princes in England, since any liberty had been ascertained to the people, had ever ventured upon." He subjoins in a note, "It must however be allowed, that Queen Elizabeth ordered the seaports to fit out ships, at their own expence, during the time of the Spanish invasion."[9] Elizabeth treated her parliaments with haughtiness, and assumed a tone of authority in addressing those assemblies, which even the tyrant Charles did not exceed: — her father governed with despotic sway. To these opinions, and unsettled notions of the kingly power, and to the prejudices of the age, candour perhaps will partly ascribe the determination of the judges in favour of ship-money, and not solely to corruption.

The Citizen has said, *"that the revolution rather brought about, than followed King James's abdication of the crown."* The assertion is warranted by the fact. James's endeavours to subvert the establishment of church and state, and to introduce arbitrary power, occasioned the general insurrection of the nation in vindication of its liberties, and the invasion of the Prince of Orange, soon afterwards crowned King of England. James, dispirited by the just, and general desertion of his subjects, and fearing, or pretending to fear violence from his son in law, withdrew from the kingdom; his withdrawing was what properly constituted his abdication of the crown: his tyrannical proceedings were the cause indeed of that abdication, and voted together with *his withdrawing*, an abdication of the government; till that event the revolution was incompleat. Will any man, except Antilon, or one equally prejudiced, infer from the last mentioned quotation, that the Citizen intended to cast any reflection on the revolution, to represent it as an *unjust* act of violence, or that he does not approve the political principles of those, by whom it was principally accomplished? — I shall now consider Antilon's main argument in support of the proclamation, first reducing it into a syllogism.

[9] Hume's *History of England*, 6:167, 253, and 253n.

"Taxes cannot be laid but by the legislative authority; but fees have been laid by the separate branches thereof; therefore fees are not taxes."

I deny the major, Mr. Antilon, in the latitude laid down by you, but admit it with this restriction, saving, in such cases as are warranted by long, immemorial, and uninterrupted usage. The very instances adduced in your paper are in exception to the general rule. The two houses of parliament have separately settled fees, as I said before, by the usage, custom, and law of parliament, which is part of the law of the land.

"*The judges in Westminster-hall have settled fees,*" you say, without defining what you mean by a settlement [2] of fees in this instance: your inference, "*therefore a similar power is vested in the governor of this province,*" I deny. The inference will not be granted, unless you prove, that the King by his sole authority, contrary to the express declaration of the commons, has settled the fees of officers belonging to the courts of law, and equity, in Westminster-hall, that is, hath laid new fees on the subject, at a time when they were no longer paid out of the royal revenue, but taken out of the pockets of the people. The fees of officers have been established for many years past in this province by the legislature, and the act establishing them was made temporary, that on a change of circumstances an alteration of the fees, if expedient, should take place; that this was the *sole* motive of making the inspection law temporary, the Citizen has not asserted, nor has Antilon denied it to be *one* of the motives. An inspection of the votes and proceedings of assembly in 1739 will evince, that the principal reason of giving a temporary existence to that act was to alter, and correct the table of fees on the expiration of it.[10]

"31 May 1739. — The conferrees of the upper house acquaint the conferrees of the lower house, that the upper house could agree to no law to establish officers' fees, but what should be *perpetual,* and were ordered not to proceed to consider of any fees, till the sense of the lower house on that point should be made known."

---

[10] The May 31, 1739, conference minutes were laid before the upper house on June 2, *Maryland Archives* 60:251. The resolutions, cited here as of June 2, were delivered to the conferees June 1 and reported to the upper house the following day.

"2 June 1739. — This house (the lower) having taken into consideration the report of their members appointed conferrees concerning the officers' fee-bill, and the proposal made by the conferrees of the upper house, of making that bill *a perpetual act*, do unanimously agree, that it would be of the *most dangerous and destructive consequence to the people of this province to make such act perpetual*."

Judge now reader what was the principal intention of the delegates in making the inspection law temporary; but if fees may be lawfully settled by proclamation, "*when there happens to be no prior provision, or establishment of them by law*," then may the fees originally settled by a temporary act, be upheld by prerogative, and made perpetual, and the province be left exposed to the same dangerous, and destructive consequences, which were apprehended from a perpetuity of the law.

Antilon asserts, "That the Citizen has been constrained to admit, that the judges in England have settled fees": This assertion I must take the liberty of contradicting; if the reader will be at the trouble of turning to the Citizen's last paper, he will there see, that the Citizen, after quoting Antilon's words, "*The courts of law and equity in Westminster-hall have likewise settled fees*," asks, by what authority? "Antilon, says he, has not been full, and express on this point" — "Admitting even, (continues the Citizen) that the chancellor, and judges have settled fees, by virtue of the King's commission, at the request of the house of commons, without the sanction of a statute, yet the precedent by no means applies to the present case." — Is this being constrained to admit that the judges in England have settled fees? Once for all, Antilon, I must inform you, that I shall never admit your assertions, barely on the strength of your *ipse dixits*, unsupported by other proof; I perceive your drift, but I know my man, and will not suffer myself to be intangled in his snares.

Vane ligur, frustraque animis elate *superbis*,
Nequiequam patrias tentasti *lubricus* artes.

Proud Antilon,
On others practice thy deceiving arts;

Thin stratagems, and tricks of little hearts
Are lost on me.[11]

"*The judges in Westminster-hall have settled fees.*" A full
enquiry into this matter, I am inclined to believe, would expose
Antilon's disingenuity, and shew how inconclusive his inference is
— "*Therefore the Governor may settle fees,*" that is, *impose fees*
on the inhabitants of this province. It has been already observed,
that the King originally paid all his officers, and that nothing can
be more consistent with the spirit of our constitution, than that he,
who pays salaries, should fix them. "Fees are certain perquisites
allowed to officers, who have to do with the administration of
justice, as a recompence for their labour, and trouble, and these
are either ascertained by acts of parliament or established by
ancient usage, which gives them *an equal sanction with an act of
parliament (D).*" Coke in his comment on Littleton, sect. 701,
observes, that it is provided by the statute of Westminster 1st, that
no sheriff, or any other minister of the King, shall take any reward
for doing his office, but that which the King alloweth. That the
subsequent statutes having permitted fees to be taken in some
instances, under colour thereof, abuses had been committed by
officers: but that they cannot take fees, but such as are given by act
of parliament. "But yet such reasonable fees as have been allowed
by the courts of justice of *ancient time* to inferior ministers, and
attendants of courts for their *labour* and *attendance,* if they be
asked and taken of the subject, is no extortion."[12] It does not
appear to me, that the judges have ever imposed *new fees* by their
sole authority. Hawkins says, "the chief danger of oppression is
from officers (E) being left at liberty to set their *own* rates, and

(D) Bacon's Abridg. 2d. Vol.[13]

*(E) Antilon has acknowledged, that two counsellors were interested in the
settlement of fees: he is, perhaps, one of them: he has acknowledged, that he
advised the proclamation as expedient and legal: he has held up the proclama-*

---

[11] Vergil, *Aeneid* 11, 715–16. Carroll substituted "Antilon" for "Ligurian."
[12] Sir Edward Coke, *The First Part of the Institutes of the Laws of England*
(London, 1629), sec. 701, p. 368b.
[13] Matthew Bacon, *Abridgement of the Law* (London, 1768), 2:463.

make their *own* demands,"[14] therefore the *law* has authorized the judges to settle them.

What law, common, or statute, has either empowered the judges to impose *new* fees? Antilon asks, how are *these settlements*, and the admission of *their legality* (take notice, reader, I have not admitted *their legality*) to be reconciled with the position, *that fees are taxes?* Before you can reasonably expect an answer to this question, it is incumbent on you, Antilon, first to fix a certain, and determinate meaning to a *settlement of fees by the judges*, and to explain in what manner, upon what occasions, and at what time, or times, the judges have *settled* fees; then shall we have some fixed, and certain notion of those settlements. After you have taken all this trouble, the information may be pleasing (man is naturally curious and fond of having mysteries unfolded) but the inference, *"Therefore, the governor may legally impose fees by his sole authority,"* will be rejected for this plain and obvious reason. Fees in this province have been generally settled by the legislature; so far back as 1638, we find a law for the limitation of officers fees;[15] in 1692, the governor's authority to settle fees was expressly denied by the lower house; it was voted unanimously by that house, *"That it is the undoubted right of the freemen of this province not to have ANY FEES imposed upon them but by the consent of the freemen in a general assembly."* — The speaker of that house attended by several members went up to the council chamber, and informed the governor, and members thereof, "That no *officers' fees* ought to be imposed upon them, but by the consent of the representatives in assembly, and that this liberty was established and ascertained by several acts of parliament, the authority of which is so great, as to receive no answer, but by repeal of the

---

tion as the standard, by which the courts of justice are to be guided in awarding costs: if all this be true, has he not endeavoured to set his own *rates? and make his* own *demands?*

[14] Serjeant William Hawkins, *A Treatise of the Pleas of the Crown* (London, 1762), chapter 68, sec. 3, p. 171.

[15] *Maryland Archives* 1:57–59, "An Act for Fees"; not necessarily good evidence for Carroll's position, as it begins, "Be it enacted By the Lord Proprietor of this Province of and with the advice and approbation of the same."

said statutes, and produced the same with several other authorities; to which the governor's answer was, that his instructions from his majesty were to *lessen*, and *moderate* the exorbitancy of them, and not to *settle* them; to which Mr. Speaker replied that they were thankful to his majesty for the same, but withal desired that *no fees* might be *lessened* or *advanced* but by the consent of the assembly, to which the governor agreed."[16] An act was passed that very session for regulating officers fees.

Here was a formal relinquishment of the claim to settle fees by prerogative; from that day to this, the claim has been constantly opposed by the representatives of the people, and in consequence of that opposition, laws have been made from time to time for the limitation of officers fees; these laws ought to be considered, as so many strong, and express denials of the proprietary's authority to settle fees, and as so many acknowledgements on the part of government of its illegality. Precedents, I know, have been brought to shew, that the power hath been exercised; so have many other unconstitutional powers; the exercise doth not prove the right, it proves nothing more, than a deviation from the principles of the constitution in those instances, in which the power hath been illegally exercised. Precedents drawn from the mere exercise of a disputed authority, so far from justifying the repeated exercise of that authority, suggest the strongest motive for resisting a similar attempt, since the former temporary, and constrained acquiesence of the people under the exertion of a contested prerogative is now urged as a proof of its legality. As precedents have been mentioned, their proper use, and misapplication, cannot be better displayed, than by a quotation from the author of the considerations. After perusing the passage with attention, the reader, I think, will be disposed to treat Antilon's argument drawn from the precedent of New York, with great contempt, perhaps, with some indignation, should he have reason to believe, that the considerations were wrote by this very Antilon. "When instances are urged as an authoritative reason for adopting a new" (or an

---

[16] Substantially verbatim from *Maryland Archives* 13:382, May 22, 1692. The "Act for limitation of Officers Fees" is printed *ibid.*, pp. 506–12. It begins, "be it enacted by the King and Queens most Excellent Majesties by and with the advice and consent of this present Generall Assembly and the authority of the same."

illegal measure, the reason is applicable to either) "they are proved to be more important from this use of them" (the countenance and support they are made to give to arbitrary proceedings) "and ought therefore to be reviewed with accuracy, and canvassed with strictness; what is proposed, ought to be incorporated with what has been done, and the result of both stated, and considered as a substantive original question, and if the measure proposed is incompatible with the constitutional rights of the subject, it is so far from being a rational argument, that consistency requires an adoption of the proposed measure, that on the contrary, it suggests the strongest motive for abolishing the precedent; when therefore an instance of *deviation* from the constitution is pressed, as a reason for the establishment of a measure striking at the root of all liberty; though the argument is inconclusive, it ought to be useful. Wherefore, if a sufficient answer were not given to the argument drawn from precedents, by shewing that none of the instances adduced are applicable, I should have very little difficulty in denying the justice of the principles, on which it was founded; *what hath been done if wrongful confers no right to repeat it*; to justify oppression and outrages by instances of their commission, is a kind of argument, which never can produce conviction, though it may *their* acquiesence, whom the terror of greater evils may restrain; and thus the despotism of the east may be supported, and the natural rights of mankind trampled under feet. The question of right therefore doth not depend upon precedents, but on the principles of the constitution, and hath been put on its proper point already discussed,"[17] whether the prerogative may lawfully settle fees in this province. Antilon has laid great stress on the authority of the English judges to settle fees, and from that authority, has inferred a similar power in the governor of this province; he has not indeed explained, as it behoved him to do, the origin, nature, and extent of that authority, nor has he shewn, in what manner it has been exercised.

No man, I believe, hath a precise, and clear idea of a settlement of fees by the judges, from what Antilon has hitherto said on that subject. What does it mean? I ask again, does the authority to

[17] Daniel Dulany, Jr., *Considerations on the Propriety of Imposing Taxes in the British Colonies* (Annapolis, 1765), pp. 40–41.

settle, imply a power to lay *new* fees? The judges it is allowed cannot alter, or increase the *old* fees; they have not therefore, I presume, a discretionary power to impose *new*; if their authority should extend to the imposition of *new fees*, why in a variety of instances, have fees been ascertained by act of parliament? Where was the necessity of enacting those statutes, if the judges were empowered *by law* to settle, that is, to impose fees by their own, or delegated authority? Here seem to be two distinct powers in the same state, capable of the same thing; if co-equal, they may clash, and interfere with each other; if the one be subordinate to the other, then no doubt, the power of the judges must be subject to the power of the parliament, which is, and must be supreme; if subject to, it is controulable by parliament. The parliament, we all know, is composed of three distinct branches, independent of, yet controuling, and controuled by each other: no law can be enacted, but by the joint consent of those three branches; now, if in a case of disagreement between them about a regulation of fees, the power of the judges may step in, and supply the want of a law, then may the interposition, and authority of parliament in that case be rendered useless, and nugatory. Suppose the leading members of one branch to be deeply interested in the regulation, that branch will probably endeavour to obtain, if it can, an *exorbitant provision* for officers: the other may think the provision contended for, too great, they disagree; the fee-bill miscarries; the power of the judges is now left at liberty to act, a necessity for its acting is insisted on, and they perhaps establish the *very fees*, which one branch of the legislature has already condemned as unreasonable and excessive. Suppose the judges should hold their seats during pleasure, suppose them strongly prejudiced in favour of government, might not a bad administration, if this power were submitted to, obtain what establishment it pleased for its officers? Should the judges discover a disinclination to favour the views of government, the removal of the stubborn, and the putting in of others more compliant, would overcome that difficulty, and not only secure to government for a time, the desired establishment of fees, but render that establishment perpetual. That a bold, and profligate minister will embrace the most barefaced, and shameful means to carry a point, the creation of twelve peers in one day, *"on the spur of the occasion,"* is a memorable proof.[18] A settlement of fees by proclamation, I still presume to assert, notwithstanding the subtile efforts of Antilon to prove the contrary, to be an arbitrary, and illegal tax, and consequently thus far similar to the ship-money assessment: my Lord Coke's authority warrants the assertion and his reasoning will support the principle; all new offices erected with new fees, or *old* offices with *new* fees, are within this act (de tallagio non concedendo) that is, they are a *talliage* or *tax* upon the people.

I never asserted, that our offices relating to the administration of justice were not *old*, and *constitutional;* but I have asserted, that we have *no old*, and *established fees;* that fees settled by proclamation, are *new* fees, and that consequently they come within the act, and Coke's exposition of it; and therefore, as *new* fees are taxes, and taxes cannot be laid but by the legislature, except in the cases heretofore mentioned; fees settled by one, or two branches thereof, are an unconstitutional, and illegal tax. What Coke observes, says Antilon, in his comment on the statute (de tallagio non concedendo) "may be fully admitted, without any proof, that *every settlement* of *fees* is a tax"; therefore, I presume, some settlement of fees is a tax, what settlement of them, Antilon, is a tax? If fees settled by act of parliament are taxes, why should they cease to be taxes, when settled by the discretionary power of the judges? if when settled by the latter authority, they come not within the strict legal definition of a tax, are they on that account less oppressive, or of a less dangerous tendency? According to Antilon, the words, *"new fees are not to be annexed to old offices,"* mean, *"that the old and established fees are not to be augmented or altered but by act of parliament"*; yet, in *"the old offices, fees may be settled."* That is, if I comprehend him right, *new* fees may be established by the judges, *"for necessary services, when there happens to be no prior provision made by law for those services."*

How is this interpretation of my Lord Coke's comment to be reconciled with his position, that fees cannot be imposed but by act of parliament, and with the doctrine laid down in 2d Bacon already recited? The *legality* of the proclamation, Antilon has said,

[18] Queen Anne created twelve Tory peers in one day in 1712.

is determinable in the ordinary judicatories; does it follow therefore, that the measure is *constitutional?* On the same principle the
assessment of ship-money would have been constitutional; for the
legality of that too was determinable in the ordinary judicatories,
and it was actually determined to be legal by all the judges, four
excepted; if in that decision the parliament, and people had
tamely acquiesced, proclamations at this day would have the force
of laws, indeed would supersede all law.

Antilon's next argument in support of the proclamation is
derived from the necessity of ascertaining precisely by the judgment, or final decree, the costs of suit, which are sometimes wholly,
sometimes partly composed of the lawyers, and officers fees. If
fees are taxes, and taxes can be laid by the legislature only, that
necessity (admitting it for the sake of argument to exist) will not
justify the settlement of fees by proclamation, who is to be judge
of the necessity? Is the government? then is its power unlimited.
Who will pretend to say, that the *necessity is urgent*, and *invincible?* Such a necessity only, can excuse the violation of this fundamental law; *"The subjects shall not be taxed but by the consent of
their representatives in parliament."* "If necessity is the sole
foundation of the dangerous power" of settling fees by prerogative,
when there is no prior establishment of them by law, "it behoves
those, who advise the exercise of that power, not only to see that
the necessity is indeed *invincible*, but that it has not been occasioned by *any fault* of their own; for, if it is not the one, the act is
in no way justifiable, and if the other, that very necessity, which is
the excuse of the act, will be the accusation of those, who occasioned it, and in place of being [3] justifiable in their conduct,
they must be chargeable, first, with the *blame of the necessity*,
and next with the danger of the violation of the law, as the
drunken man who commits murder, justly bears the guilt both of
inebriation and bloodshed (F)." To whom is the blame of the

*(F) Quoted from a pamphlet intitled a "speech against the suspending, and
dispensing prerogative" supposed to be written by my Lord Mansfield.*[19] *Mr.
Blackstone speaking of the very measure, which occasioned that speech, ob-*

[19] The attribution of this pamphlet is inaccurate. It was probably written by
George Grenville. *A Speech Against the Suspending and Dispensing Prerogative* (London, 1767), pp. 56–57.

supposed necessity, now plead as an excuse for acting against law, imputable? Is it not to those, who rather than to submit to a regulation by law of their fees, and to an apprehended dimunition of income, chose to shelter themselves under the wings of arbitrary prerogative, and to expose their country to all the difficulties, and distress, which the wanton exercise of an unconstitutional power was sure to introduce?

Who, the least acquainted with the arguments in favour of ship-money, and the *dispensing power*, does not perceive this part of Antilon's defence to be a repetition, and revival of those exploded, and justly odious topics tricked off in a new dress to hide their deformity, the better to impose on the unthinking and unwary. Antilon asserts, that the Citizen from some proceedings of the house of commons, infers a power in the commons "*alone*," to settle the fees of officers belonging to the courts of law. Want of accuracy in the expression has, I confess, given a colour to the charge; but Antilon to justify his construction of the sentence referred to, and to exclude all doubt of the Citizen's meaning, has inserted the word "*alone*."[21]

"If the commons, says the Citizen, *had a right to enquire into the abuses committed by the officers of the courts, they had, no doubt, the power of correcting those abuses, and of establishing the fees in those courts, had they thought proper*" — he should have added (to prevent all cavil) — *with the concurrence of the king and lords*. This was really the Citizen's meaning, though not expressed; his whole argument should be considered, and taken together; he endeavours all along to prove, that fees are taxes, that taxes cannot be laid but by the legislature, except in the instances already mentioned, which, as I said before, are exceptions to the general rule.

---

serves, "*A proclamation to lay an embargo in time of peace upon all vessels laden with wheat (though in the time of a publick scarcity), being contrary to law* — *the advisers of such a proclamation, and all persons acting under it found it necessary to be indemnified by a special act of parliament,* 7 Geo. 3d. C. 7."[20]

---

[20] Blackstone, *Commentaries*, 1:270–71.

[21] See pp. 96–98, 108 above.

The extracts from the report of the committee were adduced to shew, what abuses had crept into practice by officers charging illegal fees; what oppressions the encroaching spirit of office had brought upon the subject; and the controuling power of the house of commons over the officers of the courts of justice. They resolved, that all the fees should be fixed, and established by authority, that they should be registered in a book, and inspected gratis, that the rates being publickly known, officers might not extort more than the usual, ancient, legal, and established fees. It does not appear, that the commons authorized the judges to create *new* fees, or to alter, and increase the old, but insisted, that a table of all the fees should be made out under the inspection of the judges, and, to give it a greater sanction, should be signed, and attested by them, to prevent, no doubt, the secret and rapacious practices of officers. That fees are taxes, I hope, has been proved; but should it be granted, that they are not taxes, because they have been settled in England by other authority, than the legislative (which I do not admit, if by a settlement of fees under the authority of the judges, an imposition of *new* fees be meant) still I contend, that a settlement of fees in this province by proclamation is illegal, and unconstitutional, for the reasons already assigned; to which the following may be added. If a table of fees had been framed by the house of commons, confirmed by act of parliament, and all former statutes relating to fees had been repealed, and a temporary duration given to the new act, that at its expiration, corrections and amendments (if expedient) might be made in the table of fees, if in consequence of a disagreement between the branches of the legislature about those amendments, the law had expired, and the commons had resolved, that an attempt to estab-lish the late rates by proclamation would be illegal, and unconstitu-tional, would any minister of Great Britain advise his sovereign, to issue his proclamation, under colour of preventing extortion, but in reality for the very purpose of establishing the contested rates? If a minister should be found daring enough to adopt the measure, a dismission from office might not be his only punishment, although he should endeavour to justify his conduct upon legal principles, in the following manner.

The same authority distinct from the legislative, that has settled, may settle the fees, when the proper occasion of exercising it occurs: the proper occasion has now presented itself, we have no law for the establishment of fees; some standard is necessary, and therefore the authority distinct from the legislative, which used to settle fees, must interfere, and settle them again; necessity calls for its exertion, and it ought to be active; recourse, I allow, should not be had to its interposition, but in a case of the utmost urgency.

Nec deus intersit nisi dignus vindice nodus.

Nor let a god in person stand display'd,
Unless the *labouring plot* deserve his aid.[22]

Such reasoning would not screen the minister from the resentment of the commons: they would tell him, that the necessity, *"The tyrant's plea,"* was pretended, not real, if real, that it was occasioned by his selfish views, which prevented the passage of a law, for the settlement of fees; they would perhaps assert, that a power distinct from the legislative, unless authorized by the latter, had never attempted to impose fees, since they began to be paid by the people; they might possibly shew, that a settlement of fees by the judges, does not imply an authority in them to impose *new* fees, if it should, that the power is unconstitutional, and ought to be restrained; they might contend that a settlement of fees by the judges, was nothing more than a publication under their hands, and seals of such fees, as had been usually, and of ancient time received by the officers of the courts; that the publication by authority was made, to prevent the rapacious practices of officers; they would probably refer the minister to my Lord Coke, who says expressly— that, while officers "could take no fees at all for doing their office but of the King, then had they no colour to exact anything of the subject, who knew, that they ought to take nothing of them, but when some acts of parliament, changing the rule of the common law gave to the ministers of the King, fees in some particular cases to be taken of the subject, abuses crept in, and the officers and ministers did offend in most cases, but at this day,

[22] Horace, *Ars Poetica*, line 191.

they can take no more for doing their office, than they have been since this act allowed to them *by authority of parliament.*" (Westminster 1st.)[23]

But let us leave fiction, and come to reality; What will the delegates of the people at their next meeting say to *our* minister, this Antilon, this *enemy to his country*, (G) this bashaw — who calls

"Meminimus, et ignoscimus."

"*We remember, and forgive.*"

a censure of his measures,   arrogance, and freedom of speech, presumption? — They will probably tell him, *you* advised the proclamation, with *you* it was concerted in the cabinet, and by *you* brought into council; *your* artifices imposed on the board, and on the Governor, and drew them into an approbation of a *scheme, outwardly specious, and calculated* to deceive; *you have* since defended it upon principles incompatible with the freedom, ease, and prosperity of the province. If your endeavours should prove successful, if the proclamation should be enforced, we shall never have it in our power to correct the many glaring abuses, and excessive rates of the old table, adopted by the proclamation, nor to reduce the salaries of officers, which greatly overpay their services, and give an influence to government, usually converted to sinister purposes, and of course repugnant to the general good.

(G) *Voted so by the lower house.*[24] *Antilon seems to make very light of those resolves, a wicked minister is never at a loss to find out motives, to which he may ascribe the censure and condemnation of his conduct, these he will impute either to passion, to the disappointment of a faction, or to rancorous and personal enmity; however, if the proclamation is illegal, and of a dangerous tendency, the votes alluded to, so far from being justly imputable to any of those causes, ought to be deemed the result, and duty of real patriotism. Antilon has compared the votes of a former lower house against certain religionists,[25] to the late votes against the adviser of an unconstitutional measure. The unprejudiced will discern a wide difference between the two proceedings, but a review of the former would answer no good purpose, it might perhaps rekindle extinguished animosities; of that transaction, therefore, I shall say no more than —*

---

[23] Coke, *First Institute,* chapter 27, p. 210.

[24] Vote of October 18, 1771, *Maryland Archives* 63:114.

[25] See p. 116 above; also, in Antilon's third letter, notes 30 and 37.

The monies collected from the people, and paid to officers, amount annually to a large sum; officers are dependent on, and of course attached to government; power is said to follow property, the more, therefore, the property of officers is encreased, the greater the influence of government will be; fatal experience proves it already too great. The power of settling fees by proclamation is utterly inconsistent with the spirit of a free constitution; if the proclamation has a legal binding force, then will it undoubtedly take away a part of the people's property without their consent. "Whatever another may *rightfully* take from me without my consent, I have certainly no property in," (*H*) — if you render property thus insecure, you destroy the very life, the soul of liberty. — What is this power, or prerogative of settling fees by proclamation, but the meer exertion of arbitrary will? — If the supreme magistrate may lawfully settle fees by his sole authority, at one time, why may he not increase them at some other, according to his good will, and pleasure? (*I*) what boundary, what barrier shall we fix to this discretionary power? Would not the exercise of it, if submitted to, preclude the delegates of the people from interfering in any future settlement of fees, from correcting subsisting abuses, and excesses, or from lowering the salaries of officers, when they become too lucrative? — It is imagined, the salaries of the commissary, and secretary, from the increase of business, will in process of time, exceed the appointments of the governor, does not this very circumstance point out the necessity of a reduction? — But if the

(*H*) *Mollyneux case of Ireland stated.*[26]
(*I*) *Fees were actually increased by proclamation in 1739 on the application of several sheriffs.*[27]

---

[26] William Mollyneux, *The Case of Ireland being bound by Acts of Parliament in England Stated* (London, 1770), p. 129.

[27] There apparently was no such petition in 1739. Carroll may have been referring to the creation of new officers in chancery, with fees, which the house's Committee of Aggrievances and Courts of Justice considered unconstitutional. These "fees were charged by virtue of a regulation made by the Lord Baltimores Proclamation." *Maryland Archives* 40:353, May 26, 1739. The new officers performed functions hitherto performed by commissioners without charge. According to a committee report of June 1, 1739, by "the laws of our Mother Country (the Birth Right of every Subject here) . . . no new offices can be erected with new fees or new fees appointed to old offices without our Common Assent in Assembly," *ibid.*, p. 381. Dulany thought Carroll was referring to a 1735 petition. See p. 178 below.

authority to regulate officers' fees, with the concurrence of the other branches of the legislature, should be wrested from the lower house, What expectation can we ever have, of seeing this necessary reduction take place?

"That questions ought not to be prejudged, says Antilon, is another of the Citizen's objections" here again he wilfully misrepresents the Citizen's meaning.

The passage in the Citizen's last paper alluded to by Antilon is this — "The governor it is said with the advice of his lordship's council of state, issued the proclamation: three of our provincial judges are of that council, they therefore advised a measure, as proper, and consequently as legal, the legality of which, if called in question, they were afterwards to determine; is not this in some degree prejudging the question?" Antilon talks of precedents, and established rules; the Citizen says not a word about them, his meaning is too plain to be mistaken, without design. The council, it has been said, advised the proclamation, the judges therefore, who were then in council, and concurred in the advice, thought it a legal measure; the legality of it may hereafter be questioned; as judges of the provincial court, they may be concerned in the determination of the question; Is there no impropriety in this proceeding? If they should determine the proclamation to be illegal, Will they not condemn their former opinion? when they advised the proclamation, they no doubt, judged it to be, not only "*expedient*," but *legal*; possibly, the decision of this controversy may rest ultimately with the members of the council, who constitute the court of appeals; these gentlemen, it seems, unanimously concurred in advising the proclamation. "*Is not this to anticipate questions before they come to them through their regular channel, to decide first, and hear afterwards*" (K) of the twelve counsellors, says

(K) "*Whether any officer has been guilty of extortion, is a question, which neither your nor our declaration ought to prejudicate; but that your declarations held out to the publick would have, in no small degree, this effect, can hardly be doubted, and on our part particularly, such a declaration would be the more improper, the* last legal appeal *in this province being to* us; it would *be to* anticipate questions, before they come to us through their regular channel, to decide first, and hear afterwards." *Vide upper house message 20th November,* 1770.[28]

[28] *Maryland Archives* 62:366.

Antilon, "Two only were interested" — Suppose a suit to be brought before twelve judges — two of whom are plaintiffs in the cause, and these two should sit in judgment, and deliver their opinions, would not the judgment, if given in favour of the plaintiffs, be void on this principle, *that no man ought to be judge in his own cause*, such proceedings being contrary to reason and natural equity? Two counsellors only, it seems, were interested, that is *immediately* interested? But might not others be swayed by a remote interest? Are the views of thinking men confined to the present hour? Are they not most commonly extended to distant prospects? If one of the *interested counsellors*, from his superior knowledge of the law, and constitution, and from the confidence reposed in his abilities, should have acquired an uncommon ascendant over the council, may we not rationally conclude, that *his opinion* would have great weight with *those*, who cannot be supposed equally good judges of the law, and constitution? Supposing this *interested counsellor* to be an *honest man*, ought not his opinion to have the greatest weight with mere laymen on a legal and constitutional question? The proclamation has no relation to the chancellor, says Antilon. Does not the chancellor continue to receive fees in his court according to the rates of the old table? Is not the governor chancellor, and *has* not the proclamation set up the very rates of the old table? How then can it be said, that the proclamation has no relation to the chancellor? Should some refractory person refuse to pay the chancellors fees, What methods would be taken to enforce the payment of them? The chancellor, I suppose, would decree his own fees to be paid; would he not therefore be judge in his own cause? or if he should refuse to do the service, unless the fee were paid, at the instant of performing it, Would not this be a very effectual method of compelling payment?

Antilon's strictures in one of his notes on the Citizen's crude notions (L) of British polity fall intirely on another person, they

(L) *If the governor may lawfully issue his proclamation for the establishment of fees, and it should receive a legal binding force from the decree of the chancellor, who in this province is governor, or from the determination of judges appointed by him, and removable at his pleasure* — "Then may he behave with all the violence of an oppressor." *The will to ordain, and the power to enforce, will be lodged in the same person; I do not assert that the*

are the notions of Montesquieu and of the writer of a pamphlet entitled, "The privileges of the assembly of Jamaica vindicated, &c." and quoted as such.[30] Notwithstanding the appeal from the court of chancery to a superior jurisdiction, the impropriety of having the offices of governor, and chancellor united in the same person, must be *obvious to every thinking* man. "The proclamation was the act of the governor, flowing from his persuasion of its utility; he was not to be directed by the suffrage of the council, he was to judge of the propriety of their advice, upon the reasons they should offer; they were twelve in number" and no doubt each offered his reasons apart; all this may be very true, Antilon, and *you* may still remain the principal adviser, the sole *fabricator* of the proclamation; Was the proclamation thought of, at one and the same instant, by all the twelve? Who first proposed it? If you did not first propose the measure, did you not privately instigate the gentleman, who did propose it to the board, to make the motion? I know you of old; you never choose to appear openly the author of mischief, you have always fathered your "*mischievous tricks,*" on some one else — to these questions I would request your answer, and rest the truth of the accusation on your averment; but the averments of a "*cankered*" minister are not more to be relied upon, than his promises. I have charged, you say, all the members of the council with being your implicit dependents; I deny the charge; I have said, they were imposed on by your artifices; Is it the first time, that sensible men have been outwitted by a knave? You are now trying to engage them on your side, and to make them parties to *your* cause. To raise their resentment against the Citizen, you endeavour to persuade them, that they have been treated as cyphers, dependent tools, idiots, a meer rabble,

---

governor *will act tyrannically; "but the true liberty of the subject (as Black-stone justly observes) consists, not so much in the gracious behaviour, as in the limited power of the sovereign."*[29]

---

[29] Blackstone, *Commentaries*, 4:426.

[30] M. de Secondat, Baron de Montesquieu, *Spirit of the Laws*, translated by Thomas Nugent (London, 1773), vol. 9, chap. 6, p. 222; *The Privileges of the Island of Jamaica Vindicated* (London, 1766).

Nos numerus sumus, et fruges consumere nati,

We are but cyphers, born to eat, *and sleep*.[31]

To draw the governor into your quarrel, you assert, that I have contradicted him in the grossest manner; but, as usual, you have failed in your proof, "In his proroguing speech he has declared, that he issued his proclamation solely for the benefit of the people, by nine tenths of whom, he believed it was so [4] understood." That you persuaded him to think the proclamation was calculated *solely* for the benefit of the people, I easily credit, and that he really thought so, I will as readily admit: your *subdolous* attempts to involve the governor in *your* guilty counsels, and make him a partner in *your* crimes, discover the wisdom of the maxim, "*The King can do no wrong*," and the propriety, nay, the necessity of its application to the supreme magistrate of this province. I shall adopt another maxim established by the British Parliament, equally, wise, and just, "*The King's Speeches are the minister's speeches*."[32] The distinction, perhaps, will be ridiculed with false wit, and treated by ignorance, as a device of St. Omers. The proroguing speech, though perhaps not penned, yet prompted by you, suggests that nine tenths of the people understood the proclamation was issued for their benefit; how is the sense of the people to be known, but from the sentiments of their representatives in assembly? To judge by that criterion, the proclamation was not understood by nine tenths of the people as issued for their benefit. That the application of the above maxims should give you uneasiness, I am not surprised; they throw guilt of bad measures on the proper person, on you, and you only, the real author of them; the glory, and the merit of good are wholly ascribed to you, by your unprincipled creatures; the spirited reply to the petitioners for a bishop was delivered, it is said, in pursuance of your advice: be it so, claim merit wherever you can, I will allow it, wherever it is due; but cease to impose on your countrymen, think not to assume all the merit of good counsels, and of bad to cast the blame on others.

---

[31] Horace, *Epistles* 1, 2, 27.

[32] A variant of "the King can do no wrong," not included in compilations of legal maxims.

Hampden has been deservedly celebrated for his spirited opposition to an arbitrary, and illegal tax; a similar conduct would deserve some praise, and were the danger of opposition, and the power of the oppressor as great, the merit would be equal. The violent opposition, which Mr. Ogle met with, proceeded, I thought, in great measure from the cause assigned in my last paper; it certainly occasioned great discontents.

The decree for the payment of fees *"according to the very settlement of the proclamation,"* was given, as I conceived, in his first administration. A misconception of Antilon's meaning led me into this error;[33] that I would wilfully subject myself to the imputation of a falsehood so easily detected, will scarcely be credited, unless it is believed, that the hardened impudence, and *habitual mendacity* of an Antilon, become *proverbial*, had rendered me insensible of shame, and regardless of character. "The Citizen has said, the proclamation ought rather to be considered as a direction to the officers, what to demand, and to the people what to pay, than a restriction of officers" — Antilon affects to be much puzzled about the meaning of the word *direction*; it is surprising he should, when he holds up the proclamation, as the standard, by which the courts of justice are to be governed in ascertaining costs, as the only remedy against the extortion of officers, by subjecting them to the governor's displeasure, and removal from office, if they should exceed the established rates, or to a prosecution for extortion, should the legality of the proclamation be established in the ordinary judicatories. It is a common observation confirmed by general experience, that a claim in the colony-governments of an extraordinary power as incidental to, or part of the prerogative, is sure to meet with the encouragement and support of the ministry in Great-Britain. That the proclamation is a point which the minister of Maryland, (*our Antilon*) wants to establish, is by this time evident to the whole province. Every artifice has been made use of, to conceal the dangerous tendency of that measure, to reconcile the people to it, and to procure their submission. Opinions of eminent counsel in England have been mentioned, the names of the gentlemen are now communicated to the publick;[34] the state, on which

[33] See pp. 85 and 117 above.
[34] See p. 118 above.

those opinions were given, though called for, the person, who drew it, and advised the opinion to be taken, still remain a profound secret. The sacred name of majesty itself, is prostituted to countenance a measure, not justifiable upon legal and constitutional principles, to silence the voice of freedom, and of censure, and to screen a guilty minister, from the just resentment of an injured, and insulted country. The whole tenor of Antilon's conduct makes good the old observation, "That when ministers are pinched in matter proceeding against law, they throw it upon the King" (*M*). Antilon has represented the proclamation, as the immediate act of the governor, "*The governor was not to be directed, &c.*" now, to give it a still greater sanction, we are told, the governor's conduct in this very business, has met with the royal approbation. To what purpose was this information thrown out? Was it to intimidate, and to prevent all farther writing, and discourse about the proclamation? Unheard of insolence! The pride, and arrogance of this Antilon, have bereft him of his understanding; quos deus vult perdere, primo dementat.[35] Speaking of the proclamation the Citizen has said, "*In a land of freedom, this arbitrary exertion of prerogative, will not, must not be endured.*" Antilon calls these *naughty words*, and intimates a repetition of them would be dangerous. In a free country, a contrary doctrine is insufferable; the man, who dares maintain it, is an enemy to the people, perhaps, the time may not be very distant, when this haughty, self-conceited, this *tremendous* Antilon will be obliged to lower his tone, and will find perchance my Lord Coke's saying prove true, "That the minister, who wrestles with the laws of a free country, will be sure to get his neck broke in the struggle."[36] I have asserted, that the Citizen's first paper was wrote without the advice, suggestion, or assistance of any person; these words, it seems, are not

(*M*) *Grey's Debates.*[37]

---

[35] Whom God wishes to destroy, he first makes mad. A Greek maxim, attributed variously to Euripides, Sophocles, and, as preserved by Plutarch, to Aeschylus.

[36] This saying could not be located.

[37] *Debates of the House of Commons*, collected by the Honble Anchitell Grey, Esq., in ten volumes (London, 1763).

sufficiently comprehensive; What words of a more extensive import can be made use of? I have denied all knowledge of the paper wrote by the Independent Whigs, till it was published in the Maryland gazette;[38] to this moment the Independent Whigs are unknown to me. The communication to some gentleman in private, of a paper wrote against an obnoxious minister, censuring his publick conduct, though the strictures might meet with their approbation, ought not to render them so culpable, as to justify the minister in loading them with the foulest, and most virulent abuse; Does the writer even deserve such treatment? I was too well acquainted with the temper, and character of Antilon, not to be prepared against the bitterest invectives, which malice might suggest, and falsehood could propagate; such, I was persuaded, a censure of his measures, would draw on his censurer. Conscious of my integrity, confiding in the goodness of my cause, and desirous of counteracting the insidious designs of a *wicked minister*, I took up my pen, determined to despise the calumnies of a man, which I knew, a candid publick would impute to his malevolence. The event has confirmed my apprehensions, Antilon has poured out the overflowing of his *gaul*, with such fury against the Citizen, that, to use the words of Cicero applied to Anthony.

Omnibus est visus vomere *suo more* non dicere.[39]

He seems according to custom, rather to spew, than to speak.

The extracts from Petyt were to shew, that the commons had censured proclamations issued to "*establish matters rejected by parliament in a session immediately preceding*"; That, "*Former proclamations had been vouched to countenance, and to warrant the latter.*"

The Citizen had no intention to deceive the people; no wish, that more might be inferred from his "*little scraps*," than what was plainly announced. The proclamations alluded to, were contrary to law; and it is contended, and, I trust, it has been proved, that the proclamation for settling officers fees is also contrary to law. Had the Citizen designedly suppressed the titles of the proclamations

[38] On February 11, 1773, p. 2.
[39] Probably from the *Philippics*; the quote is apparently a corruption.

recorded in Petyt, would he have mentioned the authors name, and referred his readers to the very page, from which the extracts were taken? Would he not rather have imitated the conduct of Antilon, who speaking in his first paper, of a commission issued by the King to the chancellor for settling fees, neither mentions the book, from which the quotation is given, nor the time of the transaction.[40] I comprehend fully, Antilon, your threats thrown out against certain religionists, to shew the *greatness of your soul*, and your utter detestation of malice, I shall give the publick a translation of your latin sentence; the sentiment is truly noble, and reflects the highest lustre on its author, or adopter.

Eos tamen lædere non exoptemus, qui nos lædere
non exoptant.[41]

"We would not wish to hurt those who do not wish to hurt us" — in other words — I cannot wreak my resentment on the Citizen, without involving all of his religion in one common ruin with him; they have not offended me, it is true, but it is better, that ninety-nine just should suffer, than one guilty man escape; a thorough paced politician never sticks at the means of accomplishing his ends; Why should I, who have so just a claim to the character? These, Antilon, are the sentiments, and threats, couched under your latin phrase, which *you even* were ashamed to avow in plain English; how justly may I retort

pudet haec opprobria dici,
Et dici potuisse, et non potuisse refelli.[42]

The conclusion of a late excellent pamphlet (*N*) is admirably suited to the present subject; I shall, therefore, transcribe it, taking the liberty of making a few alterations, and insertions. "If we see

(*N*) *Intitled, a speech against the suspending and dispensing prerogative.*[43]

[40] *Maryland Archives* 63:114.
[41] See p. 119, note D above.
[42] Ovid, *Met.* 1:758–59; see Antilon's third letter, p. 115.
[43] [Grenville] *Speech Against Prerogative*, p. 74. The quotations are accurate.

an arbitrary and tyrannical disposition some where, the call for watchfulness is a loud"; *That there is such a disposition some where, and where, we all know* — *the proclamation, and the arrogance of its supporter, are convincing proofs.* "A tyrannical subject wants but a tyrannically disposed master, to be a minister of arbitrary power: if such a minister finds not such a master, he will be the tyrant of his prince" — *or prince's representative* — "as much as of his fellow servants, and fellow subjects — I should be sorry to see" *the governor of this province* "in chains, even if he were content to wear them — to see him unfortunately in chains, from which perhaps he could with difficulty free himself, till the person, who imposed them, runs away: which every good subject would, in that case, heartily wish might happen; the sooner, the better for all."

FIRST CITIZEN

Antilon's Fourth Letter

JUNE 3, 1773

Duceris ut nervis alienis mobile lignum.
                                                    HOR.
Thou thing of wood, and wires by others play'd.
                                                    FRANCIS.[1]

THE Citizen in a former paper expressed his expectation, that "lawyers would not be wanting to undertake a refutation of Antilon's legal reasoning, in favour of the proclamation," and signified it to be *his* design to examine the measure, on the more general principles of the constitution. His expectation I am induced to believe from various circumstances, from occurrences extrinsick to the last performance published with his signature, and from the many peculiar marks with which his work abounds, has not been disappointed. The artifice of this shifting management obliges me to enter into a minute detail, and in this to repeat some passages of my former letters, for the purpose of giving a plain view of the subject, which my adversaries have endeavoured to perplex by their cavils, and obscure by their declamations; for I am persuaded that the better the measure, which has been branded with the character of an arbitrary tax, is understood, the more will its legality, and expediency appear.

---

[1] Horace, *Sermons* 2, 7, 82. This and subsequent translations may be found in Quintus Horatius Flaccus, *A Poetical Translation of the Works of Horace*, with the original text and notes collected from the best Latin and French Commentators by Philip Frances (London, 1747).

When the late inspection law expired, as there remained no regulation of the fees of officers, so would they have had it in their power to commit excessive exactions, if there existed no competent authority to restrain their demands, or if such authority did exist, and was inactive. If such authority existed before the temporary act was made, it of course revived from the expiration of this act, and no declaration, or resolve of the lower house could prevent the exercise of it; because if the authority was competent, its competency was derived from the law, which can't be abrogated, altered, or in any manner controuled, but by an act of the whole legislature. The question related to *old*, or *constitutional* officers, who are supported not by salaries, but by casual fees, whose incomes are not fixed by stipend, but turn out to be more or less according to the services they perform. As the offices are *old* and *constitutional*, and thus supported by incidental fees, so is the right, to receive such fees, *old* and *constitutional*. There have been, as will appear hereafter, different regulations of these fees at different periods, none of which remained, when the late inspection law expired. The officers, being entitled to these rewards for their support, they could not be guilty of *extortion merely for receiving fees — when they perform services. They could not commit extortion, but by taking *larger* fees than they ought, and consequently, without some positive rule, or standard, it would not be extortion, if an officer should exact *any* fees for his services. In this situation, when there was no regulation of fees, no restriction of the demands of officers, the proclamation issued, with the professed design of preventing the excessive exactions of officers, and for this purpose ordered, that no officer should receive *greater* fees, than the rates settled by the then last regulation, under pain of the Governor's displeasure, which rates were the most moderate of any, that had before been established, and in consequence of the falling of the inspection law, less beneficial to the officers. Such in substance is the proclamation. It has, however, been objected, that it did not proceed from the *professed* design of preventing extortion; but the *real* motive was the benefit of the officers, and the time, when it issued, is urged as a proof, that this was the motive. The rectitude, or

---

* *Extortion is committed, when an officer, by colour of his office takes money, or other valuable thing, which is not due, or more than is due, or before it is due.*

impropriety of the measure is not to be determined by professions, or imputations, but by its effects. Officers, without settled rates of fees, would be under no legal restriction. The present regulation contains *no enforcement of payment from the people*, the officer being *left* to his *legal remedy*. When the inspection act was in force, his remedy was by execution. This effect of the new regulation can't be denied, viz. that the officer, being removeable, is restrained, by the threats of the person, who has authority to remove him, from receiving beyond the rates prescribed, and without this regulation, would have it in his power to demand, and receive fees, not only to the extent of the rates, but beyond it. The little suggestion, introduced by a puerile dialogue, that a party might have the service done, and refuse payment for it, if he thought the demand not reasonable, has been answered, by shewing that an officer would not have been bound to perform a service, without payment at the time of performing it. Whence then the benefit to the officer by the restriction resulting from the proclamation? and if a benefit to the officers can't be shewn, and the restriction can't be denied, how is the professed design of the proclamation, productive of the very effects explained by it, refuted by imputing to it a different motive, with which its effects do not correspond?

As to the time, when the proclamation issued, the new regulation was then if ever proper, because the former then ceased, and the two houses having disagreed on the subject there remained no regulation at all, so that as to this imputation,

> Cum ventum ad verum est, sensus moresque repugnant,
> Atque ipsa utilitas, justi prope mater et aequi.*[2]

But the grand objection to the new regulation of fees is, that it *imposes a tax upon the people*, and consequently is competent only to the legislature. Whether this idea be proper or not, I shall consider. If when fees are due, a regulation, allowing the officer to

---

* "*When we appeal to truth's impartial test, /Sense, custom, social good, from whence arise/All forms of right, and wrong, the fact denies.*" FRANCIS.

[2] Horace, *Sermons* 1, 3, 97.

receive them at a certain rate, be a tax, there can be no legal regulation of fees, *in any instance*, except by the legislature; but if it can be proved, that there may be legal regulations of fees *without* a legislative act, then the idea of tax is improper. I have already observed, that the lords, and commons, and the upper, and lower houses of assembly, *separately*, have allowed fees to be taken by their *necessary* officers, and since taxes *can't* be imposed but with the *concurrence* of *all* the branches of the legislature, I have concluded, that *these* fees are *not* taxes; but the proposition that taxes can't be laid, but by the legislative authority, is denied by my adversaries, who, in order to evade the direct consequences of the instances put, add this restriction, "saving such cases, as are *warranted* by long immemorial, and uninterrupted usage." This exception, they have not attempted to prove, and therefore have not advanced any reasoning for particular discussion; but their principle may be ascertained, and it will be incumbent upon them either to give up their exception, or to maintain this position, that there is *an authority to tax, warranted* by long, immemorial, and uninterrupted usage, *distinct* from the legislative; for the exception being applied to qualify the general, or major proposition that "taxes can't be laid, but by the legislative authority" necessarily implies, that there *may* be *taxes lawfully* established by *some other*, than the legislative authority, and the exception being expressed to result from "such cases, as are *warranted* by long, immemorial, and uninterrupted usage," it remains to be proved, that there are such *warranted* cases of *tax*, or the exception stands on a mere supposition to evade the force of my conclusion, without any proof to support it. Now I call upon my adversaries to prove, on the principles of our constitution, that there are cases of *tax, warranted* by usage, *known* to have received *no* legislative sanction, but to have been established by the lords or commons, the upper or lower house of assembly, separately, or by the judges. If they fail in their proof, my argument, that "no tax can be imposed except by the legislature; but fees have been lawfully settled by persons not vested with a legislative authority, consequently the settlement of fees is not the imposition of a tax," remains in full force. If the original settlement of any fees was a tax, it continues a tax, if it was not a tax, it can't become so from the acts of officers, and parties receiving, and paying the fees. The *origin* of it being *ascertained*, and not left to *presumption*, if the settlement of fees was originally a tax, and therefore unlawful in the commencement, the usage, or, in other words, the repeated acts of paying, and receiving, can't make it lawful: for it is an established maxim of law, if, on enquiry into the legality of custom, or usage, it appears to have been derived from an illegal source, that it ought to be abolished — if originally invalid, length of time will not give it efficacy.

It is, indeed, strange that they, who object to the argument from precedents, should rely altogether upon them in support of a doctrine so extraordinary, as that the legality of even taxes, not laid by the legislature, may be maintained by the precedents of their having been paid, and received! For what constitutes usage; but the frequent repetition of the same acts, or examples for a long time? Wherefore, I presume, the settlement of the fees of *old constitutional* offices, *to which the right of fees was annexed when the offices were created* is not a tax, and that the lawful allowance of fees to their necessary officers by the lords &c. who are not vested with a legislative authority, is a proof of my position. Saying that these allowances are founded on the law of parliament, which is part of the general law, amounts to no more than saying, they are lawful; but the proof is wanting, that either branch of the legislature, *alone*, can impose taxes on the subject by the law of parliament.

The judges are not governed by the law of parliament; they have no authority to tax the subject; but their allowance of fees to their necessary officers is lawful. It appears by the 21st Hen. 7th, that an officer was entitled to receive a fee of a person acquitted of a felony *on this principle*, that it was assigned him by the *order*, and *discretion of the court;* and with reason, and good conscience, for his trouble, charge, and attendance on the court with prisoners.[3] This is a pointed authority, and I believe, has never been impeached. In the case of Shurley and Packer, Hill 13 Jac. Coke observed, that by the statute of Westm. 1st. no sheriff could take money for serving process, and that the receipt of money for such

[3] See above in Antilon's third letter, note 9.

service would be extortion; but *that the judges may allow him fees*, and with such allowance he may receive them, and he cited the 21st Hen. 7th.[4]

Hawk. 1 book, cap. 68, speaking of the statute of Westm. 1st, observes that "it can't be intended to be the meaning of it to restrain the *courts of justice*, in whose integrity the law always reposes the highest confidence, *from allowing reasonable fees* for the labour, and attendance of their officers; for the *chief danger* of oppression is from officers being at liberty to set their own rates, and make their own demands; but there can't be so much fear of these abuses while they are *restrained* to known, and *stated fees, settled by the discretion of the courts*, which will not suffer them to be exceeded without the highest resentment."[5] Do my adversaries deny this authority, have they any distinction to evade the force of it, or do they admit it? If it is admitted, it directly applies to, and supports, my position, that the settlement of fees, and restraining officers to known, and stated rates, by the allowance, and order of the judges, is not taxing the subject. To prove that fees can be settled only by act of parliament, or antient usage, they have quoted a passage from Bac. abrid. 2 Vol. 463, but in the next page of the same book, this passage, which they have omitted, occurs, "such fees as have been *allowed* by the *courts of justice* to their *officers* as a *recompence* for *their labour and attendance* are established fees,"[6] a position which corresponds with Hawkins's doctrine. Coke's exposition of the statute de tallagio non concedendo is again cited. "All *new* offices erected with *new* fees, or *old* offices with *new*, fees, are a tallage (or tax) put upon the subject, and *therefore can't be done without common consent by act of parliament.*"[7] Whenever therefore, a fee is a tax, it can't be established *without an act of parliament*. This was the result of my major, or general proposition, which they have endeavoured to restrain by the exception, such cases as are warranted "by long,

---

[4] Cited in Sir Edward Coke, *The Second Part of the Institutes of the Laws of England* (London, 1669), sec. 701, p. 368b.

[5] Serjeant William Hawkins, *A Treatise of the Pleas of the Crown* (London, 1762), chapter 68, sec. 3, p. 171.

[6] Matthew Bacon, *Abridgement of the Law* (London, 1768), 2:464.

[7] Coke, *Second Institute*, chap. 1, pp. 532–33.

immemorial, uninterrupted usage," an exception directly repugnant
to Coke's opinion. When fees are taxes, only the legislature can lawfully grant them; but that fees are not taxes, in the instances I have
put of allowances made by the lords &c. and the judges, the legality
of these allowances is a plain proof. What construction then shall
the passage cited from Coke receive, that it may be reconciled
with the other authorities? "new offices erected with new fees," my
adversaries admit are out of the question, that fees may be settled
or ascertained at a time subsequent to the institution of offices, the
cases, I have cited, prove, and if the construction of the passage
from Coke be carried so far as to include these settlements, or
rates, he is contradicted by those cases, and appears to be inconsistent with himself, not only from the case of Shurley and Packer,
but the doctrine he has laid down in his 1st inst. which I shall
presently consider. This being the state of the matter, there is a
necessity for putting such a construction upon his words, as may
reconcile his opinion with the other authorities, or it will be overruled by them. Fees may be due, without a precise settlement of
the rate, and the right to receive them may be coeval with the
institution, or first creation of the offices, as in the case of our old,
or constitutional offices; when such fees are settled, they are not
properly *new* fees, and therefore a regulation, restraining the officer from taking beyond a stated sum for each service, when he was
before entitled to a fee for such service, is not granting, or annexing
a *new* fee to an *old* office; but when the officer is not entitled to
receive a reward from the party in the execution of an old
office, or is entitled to a certain sum from him, the granting of a
fee, when nothing was before due, or augmenting the sum the
officer was before entitled to, creates a *new* fee, according to
Coke's exposition. When a man, in consideration of receiving an
adequate recompence for the service, performs work, and labour
for another at his request, without a special contract fixing the
sum to be paid, he, for whom the service is done, becomes
indebted. If the parties to the contract afterwards ascertain the
sum due for the service, this settlement does not create a *new* debt,
but fixes, or regulates the quantum or rate payable on the original
contract. In this sense I understand Lord Coke, and admit that,
when fees are settled, they ought not to be augmented — when

services ought to be performed without a fee, a fee ought not to be granted; but oppose any construction contrary to the authorities I have cited to establish this point, *that when officers are entitled to fees, not precisely settled as to the quantum or rate*, they may be fixed, or ascertained by the authority of the judges incident to their functions, or offices, and that it is not a just objection to their exercise of this authority that "the settlement of fees is the imposition of taxes on the subject."

Co. Litt. 368 is also quoted, to this effect: "it is provided by the statute of Westm. 1st, That no [2] sheriff or other minister of the King, shall take any reward for doing his office, *but only that which the King allowed him*, on pain that he shall render double to the party, and be punished at the King's pleasure," and this was the antient common law, and was punishable by fine, and imprisonment; but the statute added the aforesaid penalty. "Some latter statutes having permitted them to take in some cases, by colour thereof, the King's officers, as sheriffs, coroners, escheators, feodaries, jailers, and the like, do offend in most cases, and seeing this act yet standeth in force, *they can't take any thing*; but where, and so far as latter statutes have allowed to them. Yet such reasonable fees as have been allowed by the courts of justice of antient time to inferior ministers, and attendants of courts for their labour, and attendance, if they be asked, and taken are no extortion."[8]

In his exposition of the statute de tallagio non concedendo, Coke lays down the position, that where the grant of fees would amount to a tax, "it can't be done without act of parliament." In the passage just cited from the 1st inst. it appears that "such reasonable fees, as have been allowed by the courts of justice of antient time, &c." may be taken, and therefore these fees fall not under the predicament of tax, which can be laid only by act of parliament.

I must first observe, that this statute of Westm. relates only to officers supported by salaries, and not by fees from suitors. "*They are to take only that, which the King allowed them.*" The constitutional officers in Maryland, derive no support from salaries, or any other allowance, than the fees they receive from those, for whom

---

[8] *Ibid.*, sec. 701, p. 368b.

they perform services; the right to demand, and receive such fees is coeval with the institution of their offices, and therefore they are not within the purview of this statute, which describes, and relates to, officers prohibited from taking *"any* reward for doing of their office; *but only that which the King alloweth"*; but yet notwithstanding the absolute terms of this statute, Lord Coke observes, that "such reasonable fees, as have been allowed by the courts &c." may be taken. The statute is so far from permitting the taking even of these fees, that the words of it are in the negative, "not any reward shall be taken" beyond the crown's allowance, and yet, by construction, fees allowed of antient time by the judges may be taken with impunity. I have already remarked, and shewn, that this statute does not extend to constitutional officers in Maryland, whose right to receive fees is coeval with the institution of their offices, and who have no other support, than what they derive from these fees. The objectors having, however, observed, that it does not appear, "the judges have ever imposed *new* fees by their sole authority," I will pursue the subject a little farther, though I have already given an answer to their case, and inferences from it. The passage cited from Coke shews that fees allowed by the courts may be lawfully received even by officers described in the statute of Westm. 1st — upon the allowance of these fees, surely they were *new*, the allowance was by the judges, and therefore without doubt, when made, *new* fees were allowed by the judges by their sole authority. If the fees, thus allowed, were originally, when they were *new*, taxes, they have not ceased to be taxes, in consequence of the frequent repetition of the acts of payment, and receipt, and of their having obtained the denomination, "antient fees." Serjeant Hawkins having taken notice that, "at the common law affirmed by Westm. 1st, it was extortion for any minister of the King, whose office did in any way concern the administration, or execution of justice, or the common good of the subject to take any reward for doing his service, except what he received from the King," makes this remark, "surely this was a most excellent institution, highly tending to promote the honour of the King, and the ease of the people, and hath always been thought to conduce so much to the publick good, that *all prescriptions whatsoever*, which have been *contrary* to it, have been holden to be void, and upon this ground it hath been resolved, that the prescription by virtue whereof the clerk of the market claimed certain fees for the view, and examination of all weights and measures, was merely void."[9] The allowance therefore of the judges was lawful, when made, and when the fees were *new* or it could not become so by length of time, since *no* prescription contrary to the common law, affirmed by the statute of Westm. 1st is good. Hence it appears that the judges have an authority incident to their office to settle the rates of fees. That the settling, or fixing the rates of fees has been deemed to be a proper preventive of excessive exaction will, moreover appear from the following proceedings. Among the rules, and orders of the court of chancery published in the year 1739,[10] the following order occurs — "it is his Majesty's pleasure, that the judges of all his Majesty's courts at Westminster do impanel juries of the officers, and clerks of the same court, to enquire what fees have been usually taken by the several officers for the space of thirty years last past, upon certificate whereof his Majesty will take such course for settling fees, as to his wisdom shall seem meet, and the lord keeper is to signify this his Majesty's pleasure to the judges of the other courts, that they may perform the same this term!" Among the rules, and order of C. B. published in 1708 is one, to the following effect, "a jury of able, and credible officers, clerks, and attornies once in three years shall be impanelled, and sworn to inquire of new, exacted fees, and of those, who have taken them under whatever pretence, and to prepare, and present a table of the due, and just fees, and the same may be fixed, and continued in every office."

In the year 1743, an order was made in chancery by Lord Hardwicke,[11] reciting that "the King *upon the address of the commons* had issued his commission for making a diligent, and particular survey, and view of all the officers of the said court, and inquiring what fees, rewards, and wages everyone of these officers might, and ought lawfully to have in respect to their offices, and

[9] Hawkins, *Pleas of the Crown*, chapter 68, sec. 2, p. 170.

[10] *Rules and Orders of the Court of Chancery, for regulating the practice of the said Court . . . 4th ed., with great additions* (London, 1739).

[11] *An Order of the High Court of Chancery . . . Relating to the Fees of the Officers, Clerks and Ministers of the said Court* (London, 1744).

what had of late time been unjustly encroached, and imposed upon
the subject, that the commissioners should propose in writing means
and remedies for reforming abuses, and certify their proceedings
to his Majesty in chancery, reciting also the execution of this commission, and the certificate of it, and that his lordship, being
desirous that the suitors should enjoy the benefits proposed in the
certificate, had thought proper the same should be established by
the authority of the court, and observed, till some further or other
provision should be lawfully made touching the premises, therefore his lordship by the *authority* of this honorable *court*, and with
the *advice* and *assistance* of the master of the rolls, doth hereby
order, and direct, that the masters, or their clerks do not demand,
or take any greater fees, or rewards for business in their respective
offices, than the fees or rewards following, viz." Then are added
tables of the fees of the respective officers. Among the fees settled
by this order, with the advice of the master of the rolls, are the fees
claimed by the *latter*, and the officers, not observing this order, are
threatened with the same punishment, as for a contempt of court.
A provision is made for the payment of the fees of chancery by
this rule, "if any cause be set down for hearing, in which the fees
have not been paid, this may be alleged by the officers to stop the
hearing of the cause," and the hearings of causes have been accordingly stopped by the court, on the clerk's insisting to have his fees
paid, or secured. 2d P. W. 461. 2 Vez. 112. Roll, chief justice,
declared that "if a client, when his business is dispatched, refuse
to pay the officer in court the fees due to him for doing the business, and attachment upon motion will be granted against him for
commitment, till he pay the fees due: for the not paying fees is a
contempt of the court, and the court is bound to protect their
officers in their rights." P. R. 598.[12]

How has the greater part of fees been settled, or ascertained,
but by the allowance of the courts on the principle explained by
Hawkins, in pursuance of the authority incident to the offices of
chancellors, and judges? Every instance of a fee so settled, contradicts the notion, that the settlement of the rates of fees is a tax,
because it is not competent to any other than the legislative

---

[12] These three citations to chancery reports are correct.

authority to tax. This power of the judges is founded on utility, justi prope mater & aequi,[13] for, without the restriction of fixed rates, officers might commit excessive exactions to the grievous oppression of the people. If it should be asked, how does it appear, that the far greater part of fees hath been settled by the allowance of the courts, and not by statutes? I answer, because the officers entitled to fixed rates can derive this right only from the determination of the courts, or the provision of statutes, and it does not appear by the statutes, to which we may have recourse, and collect the instances, wherein fees are settled by them, that the legislative provisions extend to any considerable proportion of the fees of officers.

The proceedings of the commons in 1752,[14] as I observed in my former letter, shew the opinion of the committee to have been, that tables of fees fixed and established by the authority of the judges would be the proper means to prevent excessive exactions, and the committee could not but know, that the greater part of the fees was claimed by the officers, independent of statutes, and this claim would be more firmly established by the proposed tables. If these fees were taxes, and therefore unlawful, it is not to be imagined that a measure would have been recommended by the commons, tending in any degree to countenance an infringement of the privilege, they are so peculiarly tenacious of, that of their being the first spring of all taxes. This remark applies to the order of Lord Hardwicke in 1743, in consequence of the address of the commons, and the commission from the king. When fees are due to officers, and the rates not fixed, the judges, in very many instances, are obliged by statute law to settle or assess the fees. For at the common law, costs were not given to plaintiffs, though the justices in eire, in assessing damages, usually assessed a sum sufficient to satisfy the costs expended; but the statute of Gloucester[15] is the first principal act, which gives costs, and though only the costs of the writ are taken notice of in this statute, yet the provision hath been extended by construction to the other charges of suit. Where

---

[13] The mother of both right and equity. Horace, *Sermons* 1, 3, 98.

[14] Quoted above pp. 97–98, discussed by Antilon on p. 108.

[15] "A Statute of Quo Warranto, made at Gloucester," 6 Edw. I.

costs are due, the judges are *obliged* to award them. The sum, or amount of them *must* be ascertained — in this amount are the fees of the officers, which must therefore be ascertained, if not otherwise fixed, by the allowance of the judges. When fees are due, and the rates not fixed, the judges are not only authorized, but obliged by statute to settle the rates, because they are obliged to award costs, a duty they can't perform without ascertaining the fees. I have already observed, that justice can't be administered without the exercise of this authority, the statute law can't be carried into execution without it, and have still the presumption to conclude, that what is essential to the administration of justice, to the execution of the law, to the general protection of the people, is not like the ship-money, an arbitrary, despotic imposition derogatory from the fundamental principles of a free constitution, though an orator on a table, magne blaterans clamore[16] (sputtering with great vociferation) should bellow out his horrible indignation.

I shall now proceed to examine, such of the objections to the present regulation of fees, as are not already directly obviated, without paying much attention to the flowers, and ornaments of declamation, with which they are most admirably bedecked.

Objection. The act of assembly, which regulated the fees of officers was temporary, principally on this consideration, that there might be frequent opportunities of correcting and altering the table of fees; but if fees may be settled by any other, than the legislative authority, upon the expiration of the temporary act, then the regulation of the fees by the temporary act may become perpetual, against the intention of the delegates, who concurred in enacting the temporary law.

Answer. Though such was the motive, as the objection assigns, for making the act temporary, yet when the act expired, the authority, which existed before the enaction of the temporary law, of course revived, so that the question is, whether there was an anterior authority to settle the rates of the fees due to the officers? which I have already considered. The rates settled by the temporary act might justly be adopted in the new regulation, and very properly, because the most moderate of any, that had ever been

[16] Horace, *Sermons* 2, 7, 35.

established; but the whole regulation could not be continued because it gave the remedy of execution to the officers. At any time before, or after the expiration of the temporary act, the table of fees, without doubt, might have been corrected, or altered, by the whole legislature, *not by the delegates alone*, but the operation of the temporary act did not, in any degree, extend beyond its limited duration. Whilst in being, it controuled all other authority; when it ceased, all its controul of any pre-existent authority ceased.

Objection. If the judges have authority to settle the rates of fees, when fees are due, but their rates not fixed, there was no occasion for the parliament to ascertain fees, in a variety of instances. If the judges can settle fees, as well as the parliament, there would "*seem*" to be two distinct powers capable of the same thing, and, "*if co-equal*," they may clash. If the legislative branches should disagree, and in consequence of such disagreement, there should not be a regulation of fees by an act, the interposition of parliament may be rendered nugatory, should the want of a legislative regulation be supplied by the authority of the judges.

Answer. Parliament may have peculiar motives for settling fees in various instances — when laws are enacted, requiring the services of officers, the merit of such services are very properly considered, and the reward ascertained. Peculiar penalties, which judges can't inflict on the general principles of law, may be deemed expedient on many occasions. Judges may establish rules of practice in their courts; but the practice of courts has been regulated by parliament in various instances, and without doubt, may be in all. The notion of parliament, and the judges having a co-ordinate power, which might clash in the exercise of it, is too whimsical to require a serious answer. Parliament consists of three branches, and they must all concur to establish laws, and how the judges, by supplying the want of a legislative regulation when there is none, can render the interposition of parliament nugatory, is beyond my conception. The interposition of parliament, declaring the legislative will, is a law, without such a declaration constituting law, there can be no interposition of parliament. The power of the judges will prevail against the declaration, or resolve of one branch of the legislature, because this power is controulable only by a law, and such declaration, or resolve is not a law, nor has it any degree of constitutional efficacy either in prohibiting the exercise of any prior legal authority, or in conferring a right to exercise an authority, not before legal.

Objection. Should the leading members of one branch of the legislature be deeply interested in the regulation of fees, that branch would probably endeavour to obtain an exorbitant provision, which another branch would dissent to. The two branches disagree, and no law is made. A necessity for the judges to act is insisted upon, and they may, "*perhaps,*" establish the very fees, perpetually, which one branch condemend as excessive — judges who hold their seats during pleasure.

Answer. I might in my turn, suppose leading members of turbulent dispositions requiring what they expect will be opposed, with the view of having a subject for clamour; who would be of very little importance in times of tranquillity, and order, whose ambition it is — "to ride on the whirlwind, and direct the storm."[17]

The fact, I believe, was, that both branches agreed so far, that if a regulation had been established by an act to the extent of that agreement, the fees settled by the late inspection law would have been reduced on the average, one-third — I mean by the alternative extended to the planters to pay in money, or tobacco, and that a regulation of fees, according to the old tables, adopting this alternative, would have given general satisfaction. One branch held this to be a sufficient dimunition of fees, the other contended for a greater. The power of the judges, not having been restrained by the superior authority of the legislature, remained in full force. It will not, I trust, be directly affirmed, that the proposition of the one branch, dissented to by the other, has the force of a law, though some consequences, drawn from the resolves of one branch opposite to the sentiments of the other, seem to imply an opinion, that they have some degree of obligatory sanction, which they can't have, if they are not laws: for there is no medium between an obligatory declaration, or resolve of one branch, constituting any rule of conduct, when the subject is such, that the concurrence of all the branches of the legislature is necessary to establish a compleat act, and a full compulsory law. The judges, not having been

[17] Alexander Pope, *The Dunciad* (London, 1728), 3:264, with slight changes.

restrained by the proceedings of the two houses, might, for the reasons explained, adopt the regulation approved of by the one, and condemned by the other. The action, and re-action being equal, no force remained. Their regulation having been established, it may be perpetual; but this depends upon the legislature: for it may be abolished by a law. It is true, that the judges hold their seats during pleasure, but whilst they thus hold them, they have the legal powers annexed to their stations, and their situation is such, that they rather confer a favour upon, than receive any from, government. It is even difficult to prevent their resignation, so little is their dread of removal. We must consider legal consequences, on the principles of the constitution as it is; that it may be very much improved, I have no doubt, by altering the condition of our judges, by making them independent, and allotting them a liberal income, instead of a scanty allowance hardly suffi[3]cient to defray their daily expences. Such an alteration, I am persuaded, would be productive of a very great dimunition of the fees both of officers, and lawyers, by promoting the dispatch of juridicial business, and, of course, by discouraging litigousness.

Objection. Though the legality of the late regulation of fees be determinable in the ordinary judicatories, and course of proceeding, yet that does not prove any difference between this regulation, and the levy of ship-money: for the legality of ship-money was determined in the same course.

Answer. This, at best, is a weak cavil founded on disingenuous misrepresentation. When the regulation of fees was pronounced to be an imposition of tax, as arbitrary, and tyrannical, as the ship-money, I stated each measure, to prove their dissimilarity. I shewed that the proclamation issued with the professed design of preventing excessive exactions — that it restrained the officers — *that there was no enforcement provided or attempted against the people* — that the officer was to seek his remedy, where every other creditor is entitled to relief — that the effect of the regulation, as to the people's payment, "depended upon its legality determinable in the ordinary judicatories," *there being no degree of enforcement, except what should be derived from the law in its regular, ordinary course.* — That King Charles having determined to govern without a parliament had, against the fundamental principles of a free constitution, recourse to the prerogative for raising money on the subject, and in pursuance of this scheme of tyranny, the ship-money was raised on the whole kingdom, that writs, directing the collection of the tax, required the sheriffs to execute the effects of the people, and to commit to prison all who should oppose it, there to remain till the King should give order for their delivery; but these expressions, occurring in the state, "its legality is determinable in the ordinary judicatories," are selected by the objectors, as if the proof of the transactions of the ship-money tax, and of the regulation of fees, having different principles, and effects, rested merely on this circumstance; and moreover, the egregious misrepresentation of my argument turns out to be of no use in the application, through their extreme ignorance of the subject: for the question, respecting the legality of the ship-money tax was not determined in an ordinary judicatory, and course of proceeding.

Objection. There has been no such necessity on account of the costs, as will justify the regulation of fees: for if fees are taxes, and taxes can be laid by the legislature only, the necessity of settling the rates ought to have been urgent, and invincible, which was not the case; but if the necessity was invincible, they, who advised the regulation, ought to have seen, that it was not occasioned by their fault; for if so, the necessity is their accusation, and not their excuse. The blame of the supposed necessity is imputable to those, who apprehended a dimunition of income by a legal regulation of fees, and have exposed their country to all the difficulties, and distress, "which the wanton exercise of arbitrary power was sure to introduce."[18] This objection is principally drawn from some publications, on the affair of the embargo in the 6th or 7th year of the present King.

Answer. The occasion, and nature of the necessity to ascertain the fees, the officers were entitled to, for the purpose of enabling the judges to award costs, administer justice, and execute the laws, have been fully explained, and the question, whether these fees are taxes, has been already discussed in this paper — the fixing of the rates of fees *always due*, I contend, is not a tax, and if not, the objection made on the hypothesis that it is, of course fails. The

---

[18] See p. 140 above. Note Antilon's substitution of "arbitrary" for "unconstitutional."

reasoning applied, in the publications on the affair of the embargo, to *that sudden, and peculiar necessity*, which, if not immediately provided against, would endanger the publick safety, it would be easy to prove, if not entirely impertinent, is quite foreign to our question. The necessity, I mentioned, is that ordinary obligation on those, who act in a judicial capacity, to discharge their duty. The necessity of awarding costs flows from the obligation the judges are under to give them by the statute law. The necessity of settling the rates flows from the obligation they are under by the same law to award certain costs. Whose fault it was, that a legislative regulation did not take place, in consequence of the disagreement between the two houses, is a question not determinable in any jurisdiction, or by any legal authority, neither branch being amenable to any superior court. Uncommonly indistinct must the ideas of the objectors be, who confound the authority of a branch of the legislature to propose, or reject, with the functions of ministers?

On the question, which of the two branches was blameable, very opposite suppositions may be made, imputations cast, and with equal decency, and propriety. On the one side it has been supposed, that avarice prevented the regulation of fees, because it would have been productive of a dimunition of income — on the other side it may be alleged, that a very considerable dimunition was agreed to, at least of one-third, in the alternative to pay in money, or tobacco, and that the imputation of avarice might be cast by men, disposed to find fault, and who have the arrogance to expect, that their dictate ought to be a rule to govern the conduct of others, if a dimunition of two thirds had been agreed to, and their proposition of a still greater reduction rejected — that if the regulation of the clergy, and officers had been established on the terms proposed by the upper house, general satisfaction would have been given, and therefore this branch deserves no reproach, who offered their consent to a measure, which, if adopted by the other, would have been thus satisfactory — that this regulation was rejected through the influence of men, whose aim it was to create confusion, and popular discontents, which they have many opportunities of fomenting by their declamations and harrangues, in which they affirm, with very little scruple, what may subserve the purposes of pleasing their vanity, magnifying their importance, celebrating their own pure, and immaculate virtues, and gratifying their spleen against their political antagonists. A declaimer of this kind —

Confidens, tumidus, adeo sermonis amari,
Sisennas, Barros ut equis precurreret albis.*[19]

hic, si plostra ducenta,
Concurrantque fore tria funera, magna sonabit
Cornua quod vincatque tubas.†[20]

must speak with great energy, and pursuasive force. Thus suppositions may be made, and imputations cast on either side; but they concern not the question whether the regulation of fees always annexed to *old*, or constitutional officers, *not granting fees not before due*, but fixing their rates, be a tax, or not.

Objection. The council advised the regulation of fees. Such of the provincial judges as were of the council, concurred in the advice. The legality of the regulation may be questioned before them, as judges; but this question was, *"in some degree,"* prejudged by the advice they gave in council. The court of appeals is constituted of the council, and the question may ultimately receive a decision in this court. The council in Nov. session 1770 declined giving an opinion upon the question put by the lower house, "whether any officer had been guilty of extortion by the usual charges," upon this principle, that "it might come before them for decision in the court of appeals."[21]

Answer. Upon the principle of this objection, the judges ought

---

* *Confident, and boisterous, of such bitterness of speech that he would outstrip the Sisennæ, and Barri (most infamous for their virulence) if ever so well prepared to exert their talent.*

† *"When two hundred waggons croud the street,*
  And three long funerals in procession meet,
  Beyond the fifes, and horns, his voice he raises,
  And sure such strength of lungs a wonderous praise is."
                                                    FRANCIS.

---

[19] Horace, *Sermons* 1, 7, 7.
[20] *Ibid.*, 1, 6, 42.
[21] See above, in First Citizen's third letter, p. 145, note K; *Maryland Archives* (Baltimore: Maryland Historical Society, 1883–), 62:366.

to establish no rule, 'till the legality of it is brought in question before them by the contest of parties, because the rule would, in some degree prejudge the question of its legality, which a party may choose to advance, therefore no rules or ordinances ought to be made by the courts, 'till a case between A. and B. is brought before them, and lawyers heard pro, and con, on the legality of them. This objection is, to be sure, very ingenious, though an observance of the method suggested is liable to the dull exception, that it would promote litigation, and a considerable consequential expence. The judges, without paying a *just* regard to the principle, have settled the rates of fees; they have occasionally informed themselves, *by impanelling a jury of officers.* The rates of fees have been settled in consequence of a royal commission issued on the address of the commons — the commons in 1752 thought the establishment of fees, the proper means of preventing excessive exactions. Various orders, and regulations of practice have been established by the courts, frequent have been the conferences of the judges for the purpose of settling general rules, and an uniformity of conduct. Judges have been called upon, in council, to advise their sovereign on questions of law. Judges, in inferior jurisdictions, have acted as judges, in the house of lords in the same cause. In all the cases put, the objection would apply with equal force; but I suspect, he would be deemed to be rather an odd sort of a person, who should make it, in any of them — it would be a very difficult thing, such are the *narrow* prejudices of judges, to establish the *liberal* sentiment — expedit reipublicæ ut (*non*) sit finis litium, (it would be of publick advantage to have no end to suits,)[22] and bring into contempt the adage, misera est servitus, ubi jus est vagum, (wretched is the slavery where the law is unsettled.)[23] The question put by the lower house, and which the upper declined answering, related to the construction of an act of assembly, and transactions under it, whether certain charges were criminal or not, and consequently whether *penalties had been incurred, or not.* The principle, on which the upper house acted,

[22] Antilon added the "no." The maxim is found in Sir Edward Coke, *The First Part of the Institutes of the Laws of England* (London, 1629), p. 303b.
[23] Sir Edward Coke, *The Fourth Part of the Institutes of the Laws of England* (London, 1681), p. 245.

will best appear from their own words.‡ The regulation of fees was *in prospect*, the question was put to obtain an answer, *with retrospect*. The one to prescribe a rule for the *future* conduct of officers, the other to draw a censure, of what *they had done*.

Objection. Two of those, who advised the governor, were interested, and if a suit be brought before twelve judges, and two of them plaintiffs, should those two sit in judgment on their own case, and deliver their opinions in favour of their own claims, the judgment would be void. Besides in the present cases the other advisers might be swayed by the prospect of a remote interest. The governor, as chancellor, might decree his own fees, under his own regulation, or refuse to affix the seals, without immediate payment.

Answer. This is putting one case, in the place of another of a very different nature. The advisers of the proclamation, restraining the officers, did *not act in the capacity of judges*; it flowed from the governor's authority over officers removeable by him, and as I have already said, his conduct was not to be directed by the votes of the majority of the advisers, they having no authoritative influence. I have already shewn that Lord Hardwicke had the advice, and assistance of the master of the rolls in settling the table of fees, in which the fees, due to the latter, were included[24] — that officers, and clerks of the courts have assisted the judges in their establishment of tables of fees. Their opinions were not binding, but their information was called for. The authority to regulate

‡ *"The questions, as you have proposed them, are of a very extraordinary nature, and of a tendency inconsistent with the spirit of our constitution. The resolves, or declarations of one, or both houses, however assertive in opinion, and vehement in expression, are not laws, nor ought they to be promulgated to influence the determination of the legal appointed courts. Juries, and judges ought there to give their decisions without prejudice, or bias. Whether any officer has been guilty of extortion, is a question, which neither your, nor our declaration ought to prejudicate; but that our declarations held out to the publick would have, in no small degree, this effect, can hardly be doubted, and on our part, particularly such a declaration would be the more improper, the last legal appeal in this province being to us: it would be to anticipate questions before they come to us through their regular channels, to decide first, and hear afterwards."*[25]

24 See above, p. 71.
25 Upper house message, November 20, 1770, *Maryland Archives* 62:366.

was reposed in the chancellor, and judges, and the establishments flowed from *their* authority. As to the supposition that the other advisers might be swayed by their prospects, it is of such a kind, that it may be applied on all occasions — it may be applied to the *most violent demagogues*, and *experience* would give it a colour. The absurdity in supposing, that the governor is included in a proclamation threatening those officers with *his* displeasure, who should not obey *his* orders, has been sufficiently exposed. If he should have occasion to sue for fees due to him as chancellor, he could not, in the court, where he is the sole judge. He receives his fees now, and would be equally entitled to receive them if the proclamation had not issued. This part of the objection is not more extraordinary, on account of the extreme ignorance it betrays, than on this, that the fee for the seals was the same in all the proposed regulations.

Objection. Any person, the *least* acquainted with the arguments in favour of ship-money, and the dispensing power, will perceive that Antilon's defence of the regulation of fees is a repetition, and revival of them "tricked off in a new dress to hide their deformity, the better to impose on the unthinking and unwary."

Answer. A person, the *least* acquainted with those arguments, may *imagine* they have been revived; but no one, *well*, or *even a little* acquainted with 'em, can. The assertion of the objectors is at random. They might as well have called the defence, a papal anathema, or bull in caena Domini[26] — such imputations, unsupported by proof, would almost disgrace the character of a spouting declaimer, too contemptible to be regarded.

Objection. That the argument from precedents, doth not prove the right; it proves nothing more than a deviation from the principles of the constitution, in those instances, wherein the power hath been *illegally* exercised — that the inference from the precedent in New-York ought to be treated with great contempt, perhaps, even with some indignation, and a pamphlet is quoted to shew, that the argument from precedent is inconsistent with the doctrine advanced by the author of it. The quotation is too long to repeat

---

[26] A series of excommunications of specified offenders against faith and morals which was issued regularly in the form of a Papal bull. It was a major target of Protestant Reformation resentment.

here, and therefore I refer the reader to the Citizen's last letter.[27]

Answer. This pointless shaft hath been before thrown, without reaching the object, and "*if I comprehend it right,*" there would be no difficulty in ascertaining the quiver, whence it was supplied.

"The use of precedents must be perceived, when the inconveniences of contention, which flow from a disregard of them are considered and especially when they are severely felt: when we reflect, that the intercourse of the members of political bodies, the measures of justice in contests of private property, the prerogatives of government, and the rights of the people are regulated by them." See the message from the upper house, December session 1765.[28]

But I most readily admit that, "if what has been done, be *wrong*, it confers no right" to repeat the wrong, that "*oppression*, and *outrage* can't be justified by instances of their commission," and that "*if* a measure be *incompatible with the constitutional rights of the subject*, it is so far from being a *rational* argument, that consistency requires an *adoption* of the proposed measure, that, on the contrary, it suggests the strongest motive for *abolishing* the precedent, and therefore when an instance of *deviation* from the constitution is pressed, as a reason for an establishment *striking at the root of all liberty*, it is inconclusive."[29]

The precedents, I have cited, directly apply. I have not attempted to draw any consequences from them, in support of a "measure incompatible with the constitutional rights of the subject, or an establishment striking at the root of all liberty." The common law results from general customs, precedents are the evidences of these customs, judicial determinations and decisions the most certain proofs of them, and the arguments therefore from precedents, the practice of the courts, the decisions of judges respectable for their knowledge, and probity, and from the convenience of uniformity, are of great weight. I have proved that justice can't be administered, nor the laws duly executed without a settlement of the rates of fees, that an authority to settle them is

[27] Daniel Dulany, Jr., *Considerations on the Propriety of Imposing Taxes in the British Colonies* (Annapolis, 1765), pp. 40–41, quoted above pp. 135–36.

[28] Upper house message of December 19, 1765, *Maryland Archives* 59:104.

[29] See note 27 above.

necessary to the protection of the people, who, if officers were not restrained, would be exposed to the hazard of very great oppression. The *conclusion*, I confess, is *not very favourable to the liberal* sentiments, and *generous* views of *those, who are adverse* to the *narrow* restrictions of *systematical certainty*, and *if allowed to choose their ground* would, like Archimedes, undertake to turn the world, which way they please.[30]

"*You* knew *me* of *old*." *You* have the advantage, if *your memory* hath not been impaired, for *I* did not know *you*, and *yet* Cimex, you have my wish,

ut dique, deæque,
Vestrum ob consilium, donent tonsore*[31]

take back your shaft, and preserve it. There may be a future occasion, for its use.

Objection. If fees may be settled at one time, they may be increased at another, as happened in the year 1739, when the fees of sheriffs were increased by proclamation.

[4] Answer. The end, or design of settling fees being once accomplished, I apprehend, on the principles I have fully explained, that the rates of them can't be altered, and therefore, if the fees of sheriffs were increased in 1739, the measure was wrong; but I don't know, or believe that the fees of sheriffs were increased in 1739, having searched for the proclamation without being able to find it. In 1735 there was a petition from several sheriffs to the Governor in council for an allowance of several fees, alleged to have been *omitted* in the table, settled by the proprietary in 1733, and always established, and allowed either by acts of assembly, or by the governors in council, and the fees so omitted

---

* "*may the powers divine,*
  For this same friendly assistance of thine,
  Give thee a barber in their special grace."

---

[30] Archimedes (ca. 287–212 B.C.), mathematician and inventor, was supposed to have said, "give me a place to stand on and I will move the earth."
[31] Horace, *Sermons* 2, 3, 17. Cimex is an insect of the genus cimicidae, including the common bedbug.

were particularized in an annexed schedule.[32] The order on this petition was, that such of the fees omitted in the table, as had been settled by any act of assembly, or former order, should be allowed to the sheriffs for their services, and *no more*. If this be the order meant by the objectors, it does not justify the idea they would convey, that the sheriffs' fees *settled* by the proclamation in 1733 were *afterwards increased*: for the order extended *only* to the fees *omitted* in the table, settled by the proprietary.

Objection. If there was originally an authority, in this province, distinct from the legislative, to settle fees, that authority has been relinquished, because, as far back as 1638, a law passed for the limitation of the fees of officers, and, in 1692, the Governor's power to settle fees was expressly denied by the lower house; who insisted, that "no officers fees ought to be imposed upon them, but by the consent of the representatives in assembly, and that this liberty was established, and ascertained by several acts of parliament, and produced the same with several other authorities. To which the Governor's answer was, that his instructions were to lessen, and moderate exorbitant fees, and not settle them. To which the speaker replied, that they were thankful to his Majesty for the same, but withal desired that no fees might be lessened, or advanced, but by the consent of the assembly, to which the Governor agreed, and an act passed the same session for regulating officers' fees." And "fees in this province have been generally settled by the legislature."[33]

Answer. When the Governor, in 1692, undertook to regulate fees, there *was an act of assembly for the purpose*, and *therefore* he had no authority. When the last proclamation issued, there was *no* act of assembly. There was no act of parliament in 1692 to prevent the settlement of fees by an authority distinct from the legislative, when an act of the legislature does not exist, by which fees are

---

[32] First Citizen referred to a 1739 petition in a note on p. 144 above. A petition was read before council, June 19, 1735, stating that "several fees are omitted which have been always established and allowed either by the several Acts of Assembly made heretofore for limitation of Officers fees, or by the Governors in Council," *Maryland Archives* 27:77–79. Proprietor Charles Calvert's proclamation setting fees was issued April 14, 1733, and is printed *ibid.*, pp. 31–44.

[33] See above, p. 134.

settled; but there were various statutes, and authorities to prove, that the supreme magistrate *can't control the operation of an act of the legislature.* That this branch of the argument may be the better understood, I shall proceed to shew, how fees have generally been settled in this province, observing in the first place, that the charter, under which we derive the power of making laws, contains a grant to Lord Baltimore of "all rights, jurisdictions, prerogatives, royalties, and royal franchises, in as ample a manner, as any bishop of Durham, within the county palatine of Durham, then, or at any time before, had." And also of power, "to appoint judges, justices, magistrates, officers and ministers," and to "do *all, and every other thing* belonging unto the compleat establishment" of justice, courts, tribunals, and forms of judicature, and manner of proceeding."

"Between 1633, and 1637, the officers appointed by Lord Baltimore, or his Governors were authorized by their commissions to demand, and receive such fees, as were usually paid in England, or Virginia for similar services."

In 1637, a bill for fees was framed, but not passed, in 1638 an act passed, in which there is this clause "all fees shall be paid according to a bill upon the record of this assembly, viz." that of 1637. In March 1641, it was continued to the next assembly, in 1642, *the day after the session of assembly*, a table of fees was settled, and published by the governor, and council,[34] the act having expired, in 1669, on the petition of J. Gittings, for settling the fees of the clerk of the assembly, the Governor, and council

---

[34] The charter of June 20, 1632, is printed in the original Latin in *Maryland Archives* 3:3–12. For an English translation, see John L. Bozman, *The History of Maryland* (Baltimore, 1837), 2:9–21. The references are to sections IV and VII, pp. 11 and 13, respectively. The commission to Gov. Leonard Calvert and the Council, April 15, 1637, makes no direct reference to fees, but execution of judgments was to be determined "according to the Orders Laws and Statutes of that our said Province . . . and in default of Such Laws . . . then according to the Laws and Statutes of England," *Maryland Archives* 3:53. The 1637 fees act passed the house March 17 but did not receive the proprietor's assent, *ibid.*, 1:21. The 1638 act is printed *ibid.*, pp. 57–58. It was to expire at the end of the next assembly. A fee bill was discussed at the October 1640 session, but did not pass, *ibid.*, p. 93. The fee table of 1642 was published by the governor and council August 1, *ibid.*, pp. 162–64. The long quotes on these pages are lifted from the governor's message of November 30, 1771, *ibid.*, 63:228–30, with numerous revisions and omissions.

ordered that he should receive treble the fees of a county clerk.[35]
"In the year 1676, an act passed for limitation of officers' fees; but
before this act was framed the lower house were acquainted in a
message from the upper house that the chancellor's fees were,
settled by the then late proprietary, and his present lordship would
not consent for an act for settling the same, it being his prerogative;[36] but that the list might be recorded in the journals of the
house — whereupon the lower house voted, that they did not desire
to intrench on his lordship's prerogative; but all they aimed at was,
that the inhabitants might *certainly* know what fees they had to
pay, and since nothing could be more reasonable, and that the
same should be settled, and published, *they requested his lordship
to ascertain the fees of all* his officers, and that fair lists thereof
might be drawn out with his lordship's assent, and copies sent to
the county courts to be published, and recorded, and *that an act
might be drawn up for fining every officer exceeding the same.*"
Pursuant to this the perpetual act of 1676 passed with this proviso,
"if any fees belonging to the several officers, and by the proprietary, or governor, *so allowed, and adjudged*, and not in this act
mentioned, then it shall be lawful to have such fees as the proprietary and council shall allow, and no more; under the penalty, &c."
and there is a similar proviso in the other acts to the year 1725. In
1692, in a bill from the lower house for recording conveyances,[37]
the clerk's fees for the service were rated, to which the upper
objected, that "the settling of fees is a matter vested by their
Majesties in the governor with the advice of the council." The
indefinite act of 1676 fell under the general repealing act of
1692.[38]

"Governor Copley was empowered by his commission, and
instructions from the crown to settle with the council, the fees of
officers. In the commission from their Majesties to Mr. Blackiston,

[35] A petition from John Gittings, assembly clerk, was presented to the house
May 1, 1666, *Maryland Archives* 2:122. His fees were settled on May 6, *ibid.*,
p. 192. Governor Eden asked in his November 30, 1771 message, *ibid.*, 63:224,
under what authority those fees had been set. "You, alone, are not the assembly."

[36] *Maryland Archives* 2:489, 498–500, 532–37.

[37] *Ibid.*, 13:473–75.

[38] *Ibid.*, pp. 379, 506–14.

in 1692, to be commissary general, he was impowered to receive all such dues, and fees belonging to his office, as should be settled by their Majesties, or their captain general, and council." "Governors Nicholson, Blackiston, Seymour, and Hart, the successive governors, after Copley, appointed by the crown, till Lord Baltimore was restored,[39] were also respectively empowered to settle the fees of officers." I have already observed, that the fees of officers in New York are settled under a royal commission — In 1733, the temporary act that regulated fees having expired, Lord Baltimore, in council, settled tables of fees, and the rates, thus settled, were adopted by all the courts, and in all their judgments, and decrees prevailed as the rule, in awarding costs from 1733 to 1747, when the first inspection act passed.[40] I have already taken notice of a decree of Mr. Ogle, ordering fees to be paid according to his lordship's settlement — in 1739 the upper house insisted, that "the proprietary's authority to settle fees, *when there is no positive law for that purpose*, is indisputable, and apprehended the exercise of such authority to be agreeable to the several instructions from the throne to the respective governments."[41] In 1755, the proprietary,[42] asserted his authority to regulate fees, and objected to the inspection act, because the fees of officers were regulated by it,[43] and the lower house being informed of it, in their address to the governor expressed their concern that, "a regulation of fees agreed upon *after the most mature deliberation*, that had subsisted *for five years*, been *revived*, and *continued*, should be objected to by his lordship, and declared it to be their opinion, that the parts of the act, respecting officers fees, and foreign coins

[39] Sir Lionel Copley, governor 1692–1693; Nehemiah Blackiston, named to the council in 1692; Sir Francis Nicholson, governor 1693–1698; John Seymour, governor 1704–1709; John Hart, governor 1713–1720; and Charles Calvert, governor 1720–1727.

[40] See note 32 above.

[41] *Maryland Archives* 40:252.

[42] Frederick Calvert, sixth Lord Baltimore, never ruled Maryland in person. His governor from 1753 to 1769 was Horatio Sharpe.

[43] Gov. Sharpe told the upper house, March 8, 1755, that the proprietor had objected to the limiting of officers' fees enacted in a tobacco inspection act in the October 1753 session. He would have dissented to it but for his "sense of the great Utility of that part of the Act which relates to the Staple of Tobacco," and now requested a repealing act, *Maryland Archives* 52:9–10.

were of *great advantage*, and *highly conducive to the ease, and quiet of the people.*" Such were the sentiments of the lower house in 1755.[44]

It appears, I presume, from these proceedings, there is but a very slight foundation for the objection, that there has been a relinquishment of any original authority to settle fees — temporary acts, after their expiration, cease to have any controul, and even these acts are the less material, on this account, that the regulations of fees by them had an effect, which no authority but the legislative could give: for as it might be inconvenient to many people to pay the officers immediately for their services, and to the officers, when they give credit to those who employ them, not to have festinum remedium (a speedy remedy) for the recovery of their dues, the several acts, regulating the fees of officers, have required a credit to be given, and allowed the fees to be collected by execution. I did presume to say in my last letter, that "the same authority, distinct from the legislative, which hath settled fees, may settle them, when the proper occasion of exercising it occurs," having the countenance of the maxim, "ubi est eadem ratio, ibi est eadem lex" (where there is the same law, there is the same reason)[45] and if maxims are disputed, there can be no end to controversy: for they can't be proved per notiora. (By any thing more known, or certain.) If it be said that the maxim has not been denied, I must observe that the attempt then was to evade it: for my position is not, that *new* fees may be imposed by the judges, but that, *when fees are due*, under a *right, coeval* with the *original institution of the offices*, and the *sum, or rate is not otherwise fixed*, it *may* be settled by the judges; that their authority in this is necessarily incident to their offices, and that they can't discharge their duty without an actual exercise of it.

The objectors have drawn all the inferences they could, to favour their purpose, from every precedent they have been able to collect, and yet, when apprehensive the argument would be retorted, they would have the proofs from precedents disregarded. Their definition of liberty, if corresponding with their conduct, I

[44] Delegates' address, March 11, 1755, *ibid.*, p. 73.
[45] Coke, *First Institute*, 10a.

suspect, would be "a license to say, and do, as they please, with a power to controul the words, and actions of others."

Objection. If the fees of some of the officers should not be occasionally reduced, they would in time exceed the governor's income.

Answer. Such an event is not probable. As the governor's income must also increase, with the increase of fees, the trouble, and expence must increase. Stated salaries would prevent this effect. Such salaries were proposed by the upper house, and rejected by the lower.[46]

Lord Coke, and serjeant Hawkins have bestowed great commendations on this mode of provision, because officers, having *stated salaries*, would be under no temptation to increase, or multiply fees; but our *wiser* men determined differently. The attorney, and solicitor general of England, serjeant Wynn, and Mr. Dunning have *presumed* to be of opinion, that there may be a regulation of fees, in Maryland, without an act of assembly; but our *wiser* men have *declared* the contrary, and who will be so *"daring"* as to question *their infallibility*.[47] "Homines indicium peritissimi investigatores, veri juris, et germanae justitiae solidam effigiem tenentes, non scientiarum umbras, et imagines sequentes."*[48]

Having examined the legal reasoning, with which the profound knowledge, eminent candour, and immense patriotism of his learned, and very worthy associates have supplied him (associates

---

* *The most skilful* index-hunters, *possessed by the solid model of true law, and genuine justice, not followers of the shadows, and illusions of* science.

---

[46] The upper house proposed in a message to the lower house, November 10, 1770, that, in lieu of fees, the secretary, commissary general, and judges of the land office receive annual salaries of £ 600 sterling, *Maryland Archives* 62:353. On the same day, the lower house "Unanimously Resolved" against salaries, *ibid.*, p. 391. In a message to the upper house November 12, the delegates explained that "£ 600 sterling is too much for the Trouble and Risk" of those offices, adding that any salaries "might involve us in fresh Difficulties," since salaried officers would have no incentive to be "ready" and "diligent" in their jobs, *ibid.*, p. 315.

[47] Coke, *Second Institute*, sec. 701, p. 368b; Hawkins, *Pleas of the Crown*, chapter 68, sec. 3, p. 171; *Maryland Archives* 32:493–501.

[48] This is apparently not a classical quotation because of the peculiar wording and construction. It may date from the eighteenth century.

whose honest indignation is naturally roused by *every breach* of the *laws*, which have been *ordained, in the clearest* terms, to prevent *exaction of excessive fees*, because *they* have exhibited the most *conspicuous* examples of *their own pure moderations, and strict observance of them*) I shall now more immediately address the first Citizen.

"His grave observation, that the prince, who places an *unlimited* confidence in a *bad* minister, *runs great hazard* of having that confidence abused &c." has the *merit of being true.*

Ille magno conatu magnas nugas dixerit.[49]

(The man in troth, with much ado,
Has found that one, and one make two.)

But I must, in the most direct terms, contradict all his assertions of the influence of a minister in Maryland; assertions most infamously false, dictated by the most corrupt heart, and persisted in with the most profligate, impudence. It is very merciful, indeed, that "he has not compared Antilon, with Sejanus" — that he has not insinuated there is an Apicius, dives, et prodigus, and included stuprum &c.[50] and that he has only referred to some qualities in the character of Sejanus, which I have the comfort to know are most opposite to the character of Antilon. How plainly do such foul emanations indicate their putrid source? Should I, Mr. Citizen, represent you to be a man "tetra inflatus libidine, et consuetus alienas permolere uxores," (of the most abandoned lust accustomed to debauch other men's wives) and refer the gentle reader to Trivetas's character of Clodius,[51] would you not be apt to exclaim, "I debauch other men's wives! At what calumny will falsehood, and malice stop? I debauch other men's wives! Nothing in the world can be more remote from my character."

[49] I was unable to locate this citation.

[50] Tacitus, *Annales* 4, 1, 10. The quoted words mean "rich, prodigal, and debauchery." Apicius was a famous gourmet.

[51] Horace, *Satires* 1, 2, 35. Trivetas may be a corruption of Trivetus, Latinized form of Nicholas Triveth, author of several works, including *Annales Sex Regum Angliae* (Oxford, 1719). Clodius, born ca. 92 B.C., was a notorious debaucher of women.

Unde petitum
Hoc in me jacis? Est auctor quis denique eorum
Vixi cum quibus?[52]

(Is there, with whom I live, who know my heart?
Who taught you how to aim your venom'd dart.)
Mea sufficit una.

"I am no rover." Indeed, Mr. First Citizen, I don't believe you are,
any more than I believe you to be a man of honour, or veracity.
Your assertion that the proclamation proceeded from the
advice, and overruling influence of one man, I have most expressly
contradicted. The governor's declarations have contradicted it. The
members of the council know it to be absolutely false — many of
them have already avowed the part they took in the measure, and
expressed their resentment of the indignity of your imputation.
What I have advanced on this topic is a direct appeal to those,
who are acquainted with the transaction, and the *only* persons
acquainted with it, and still you persist in your asseverations, as
if you expected, that the most pertinacious impudence would cover
the deformities of the basest malignity, and the most profligate
mendacity.

Multa malus simulas, furiata mente laboras,
Improbus, & stultus nullo moderamine vinctus
Virtutis[53]

(The knave and fool together join'd,
No rules restrain, no tie can bind,
Perpetual slave to fraudful art,
Whilst rage, and malice swell your heart.)

My appeal, he alleges, is with the view of "engaging the governor,
and council in my *quarrel.*" A man is charged with being the sole
author of a measure published as the act of several persons, and
these *only* are acquainted with the origin, progress, and conclusion
of it. The accuser was not only no party in the measure; but was
entirely excluded from all knowledge of the manner, in which it

[52] Horace, *Sermons* 1, 4, 80.
[53] This quotation is probably from Vergil.

was conducted. The accused appeals to those who were concerned in, and perfectly acquainted with, the whole transaction, and this appeal is attributed to the motive of engaging them in his quarrel. Again — the members of the council, the accuser suggests, "though sensible men, may have been *outwitted*," but they must still continue under the delusion, if they were "*outwitted*," or they would not, as men of honour, avow their opinion of the legality, and expediency of the measure, and that they were equally concerned in it with the accused. If they have discovered, that they were "*outwitted*," their conduct would be very different; they would naturally express their indignation against the man, who had deceived them — to what an astonishing pitch of impudence has this Citizen arrived! The absurd application of the maxim, "the king can do no wrong," to the governor ("*because he is youthful and unsuspicious*") accountable for his conduct, and punishable by statute for acts of oppression, has been already shewn; but the Citizen, in his last gallimausry,[54] has introduced another maxim, as he calls it, that "the king's speech is the minister's," and applied this to the governor ("*because youthful and unsuspicious*"). There is no end to such babbling —

> break one cobweb through,
> He spins the slight, self-pleasing thread anew;
> Destroy his lie, or sophistry, in vain,
> The creature's at his dirty work again.[55]

What answer should I give, if hereafter he should think proper to assert, that the governor ought to be chosen by the council out of their own body, because the pope is chosen by the cardinals. He has given some smart proofs of a versatile genius. Though a papist by profession, he can be an advocate for the established church of England, when he speaks of the revolution. Such is his address, that he may hold one candle to St. Michael, and another to the dragon.[56]

---

[54] A hodgepodge, a meat ragout.

[55] Alexander Pope, *An Epistle from Mr. Pope, to Dr. Arbuthnot* (London, 1734), lines 89–92.

[56] St. Michael was the archangel, leader of angels against the dragon and his host in *Revelation* 12.

"You knew me of old." Indeed. Pray, when did our acquaintance begin, how has it been improved into knowledge? Perhaps your knowledge has been gathered in your flights, when you was gifted with the powers of Ariel. Hard is it upon a poor mortal to encounter such supernatural intelligences. "I have always fathered my mischievous tricks upon others" — roundly asserted; but what proof have you? An unhappy wretch you are, haunted by envy, and malice.

Invidia Siculi non invenere tyranni
Majus tormentum[57]

(Sicilia's tyrants could not ever find
A greater torment, than an envious mind.)

"I want to engage you in a quarrel with the governor, and council." I have, indeed, been led by your false, and impudent accusations to take notice of the publick insult you had offered them; but the *know*[5]*ledge of their own conduct*, and *the feelings of their own honour*, not my suggestions, or instigation, will influence their behaviour towards you. I have no spleen against Mr. Hume (as you have foolishly supposed) by whom I have often been entertained, and whose ingenuity, and literary talents I admire; but that his history is a studied apology for the Stuarts, and particularly Charles the first, all men, conversant with English history, and constitution, and not blind by prejudice must acknowledge. Without having recourse to the "letters written upon his history,"[58] I could point out very many instances to fix this character, if suitable to the design, and limits of this reply. The bill of rights, which Charles the first endeavoured to evade by mean prevarication, shews that the constitution was most clearly settled in the very point infringed by the ship money levy. That the abdication "*rather* followed, than preceded the revolution," is the assertion of ignorance, or prejudice — the very defence of jacobitism. The principle of it was stated in my former letter, from the reason-

[57] Horace, *Epistles* 1, 2, 58.
[58] D. MacQueen, *Letters on Mr. Hume's History of Great Britain Under the House of Stuart* (Edinburgh, 1756).

ing of Hampden, Sommers, Holt, Maynard, and Treby.[59] The Citizen may profess his attachment to the principles of the revolution, his regard for the established church of England, and his persuasion that it is inconsistent with the security of British liberty, a prince on the throne should be a papist, and expect his assurances (though he is a papist by profession) will be credited, because, as he informs us, "his speculative opinions, in matters of religion, have no relation to, or influence over, his political tenets"; but we are taught otherwise and put upon our guard by our laws, and constitution, which have laid him under disabilities, because he is a papist, and his religious principles are suspected to have so great influence, as to make it unsafe to permit his interference, in any degree, when the interests of the established religion, or the civil government, may be concerned.[60] When in the ardour of his zeal, the Citizen ascribed to the resolves of one branch of the legislature an operation, which is the attribute only of a perfect legislative act, to check his temerity, I referred to former resolves of the same branch, on a subject, towards which, I imagined, he was not indifferent, and left him to reflect, what would have been the consequence of these resolves, *on his principle.*

The Citizen's remark, on this intimation, is in general, evasive words, his usual manner. "The unprejudiced will discern a wide difference between the two proceedings" — popery and officers fees were not compared. The force of the resolves was the consideration, not the subjects of them; and whatever constitutional force resolves may have on the subject of officers fees, the same they can't but have, on the subject of popery; but says the Citizen "meminimus & ignoscimus" — *we* remember, and *we* forgive." This is rather too much in the imperial style. *We!* It is as little my wish, as the Citizen's, to rekindle extinguished animosities; tho' I think his conduct, very inconsistent with the situation of a man, who owes even the toleration, he enjoys, to the favour of government. His threats, of what the next assembly may do, as if his influence would sway, his assistance be sought, or his advice admitted, in the proceedings of the delegates, notwithstanding he

[59] See above, p. 103.
[60] See above in Antilon's third letter, note 37, for a summary of anti-Catholic legislation. On the vote mentioned below see Antilon's third letter, note 30.

is not even allowed by our constitution to vote for, or, in any manner, to interfere in the choice of, a delegate, are extremely impertinent. If, indeed, there should be a meeting of very different persons, at a very different place, Stentor, animated by the "ear-piercing fife, and spirit-stirring drum," and "mounted high on stage or table," might perform wonderous feats, *demonstrate by loud assertion*, and *condemn by furious obloquy*, his exertions invigorated by the applauses of surrounding admirers.

> Magno veluti cum flamma sonore
> Virgea suggeritur costis undantis aheni,
> Exultantque æstu latices; furit intus aquæ vis
> Fumidus, atque alte spumis exuberat amnis:
> Nec jam se capit unda, volat vaporater ad auras.[61]

> As when to the boiling cauldron's side
> A crackling flame of brushwood is apply'd,
> The bubbling liquors there, like springs, are seen
> To swell, and foam to higher tides within,
> Above the brims they force their fiery way,
> Black vapours climb aloft, and cloud the day.

I shall adhere to the document of Minucius, "let us not wish to injure those, who do not wish to injure us,"[62] and I sincerely believe, that there are but few papists, natives of Maryland, who are not justly entitled to indulgence, on this principle. The Citizen's exposition of the quotation exceeds his usual absurdity, and is too contemptible for animadversion.

I shewed at large the Citizen's scandalous misrepresentation of Petyt, and what is his answer? He could not mean to mislead, because he referred to the jus parliamentarium,[63] so that the reader was to turn to the work (which is in the hands of very few) to escape deception. Again — in answer to the rebuke I gave him for the extreme ignornace, his reflections on the proceedings of the house of commons in 1752[64] betrayed, he denies that he

[61] Vergil, *Aeneid* 7:462–66.
[62] For earlier references to this maxim, see above, p. 119, note D, and p. 152.
[63] See above in First Citizen's second letter, note 22: William Petyt, *Jus Parliamentarium* (London, 1739).
[64] Quoted above, pp. 97–98.

meant what his words imported. The commons enquired into the abuses committed by officers, and the Citizen's reflection on this proceeding was in these words, "if *the commons* had a right to enquire into the abuses committed by the officers, *they* had (no doubt) *the power* of correcting those abuses, and of establishing the fees, had *they thought proper*." His extreme ignorance having been exposed, he seeks to cover it by this pitiful prevarication, that he did not say the *commons, alone,* but that *the commons* had the power, and meant that *they* had *not* the power, but with the concurrence of the other branches — for shame! I said in my last letter, that the Citizen had been constrained to admit, fees had been settled by the judges; but this he denies, and quotes a passage from his letter, to which I did not allude, to justify his denial. I had observed, "if the idea of tax be proper, then fees can be settled in *no* instance, except by the legislature; but the lords, the commons, the courts of law, and equity in Westminster hall, the upper, and lower houses in Maryland have each of them settled fees." Having himself quoted this part of my letter, his words are, "*they have so.*" Was not this then a direct admission? How pitiful the evasion, when he was pressed with the consequence of his direct admission?

He having quoted Montesquieu, I observed, how crude the Citizen's ideas of the British polity were, and shewed how little countenance was given to his suggestions by that celebrated writer; but let him have his way, and he will always have an answer in some tiny evasion, or puny cavil — "Antilon's strictures on the Citizen's crude notions fall entirely (says he) on Montesquieu, and the writer of a pamphlet."[65]

> Velut ægri somnia, vanae
> Tingentur species[66]

> (He, like a sick man's dreams,
> Varies all shapes, and mixes all extremes.)

But here I take my leave of him, till he shall have made a new collection of law from the bounty of his learned associates in poli-

[65] See note C, pp. 111–12 above.
[66] Horace, *Ars Poetica*, line 7.

ticks, as little school-boys do of *sense* by *begging it* of their seniors, when their masters set them themes. "Id maxime quemque decet, quod est cujusque suum maxime," (that most becomes a man, which is most properly his own) was the saying of a wise man;[67] but a fool may choose,

> in florid impotence to speak,
> And, as the prompter breathes, like a poor puppet squeak.[68]

ANTILON

P.S. The First Citizen has admitted my account of the ship-money to be, "*in the main, true*, and yet (he says) it is *not entirely impartial*: *for* there *may* be a relation of *facts, generally true*, and *yet* by *suppressing* some circumstances, the writer may either *exaggerate*, or *diminish*, and *so, greatly alter their character*, and *complexion*." *Thus*, reader, according to this Citizen's *conscience*, an account of a transaction may be, "*in the main*," or *substantially*, true, though "the *character*, and *complexion* of it be *altered* by *exaggeration*, or *dimunition*" — unwarily, has he betrayed the principle, on which he has *affirmed*, or *denied*, with the *most infamous mendacity*.

[67] Cicero, *De Officiis* I, 31.
[68] Pope, *Epistle to Dr. Arbuthnot*, lines 317–19.

First Citizen's Fourth Letter

JULY 1, 1773

"*Though* our kings can do no wrong, *and though they cannot be called to account by any form* our constitution *prescribes, their* ministers *may. They are answerable for the* administration of the government, each *for his* particular part, *and the* prime *or* sole minister, *when there happens to be one for the* whole: *he is the more so, and the more justly, if he hath affected to render himself so, by usurping on his* fellows, *by* wriggling, intriguing, whispering, *and* bargaining *himself into this dangerous post, to which he was not called by the* general suffrage, *nor perhaps, by the deliberate choice of his* master *himself.*"

Dedication to the dissertation upon parties.[1]

The noble author of the dissertation upon parties begins his fourth letter with the following sentiment taken from Cicero's treatise on the nature of the gods — "Balbus, when he is about to prove the existence of a supreme being, makes this observation (opinionum commenta delet dies, naturæ autem judicia confirmat): Groundless opinions are destroyed, but rational judgments, or the judgments of nature, are confirmed by time."[2] The observation may be applied to a variety of instances, in which the sophistry and ingenuity of man have been employed to confound common

---

[1] Lord Bolingbroke, *A Dissertation upon Parties* (London, 1754), p. ix.
[2] *Ibid.*, pp. 44–45.

sense, and to puzzle the understanding, in order to establish opinions suited to the views of interest, or of power.

An examination of Antilon's arguments, and answers to mine, will show how forcible the judicious remarks of Balbus applies to the legal subtleties and metaphysical reasoning of my adversary. I shall take his arguments and his answers nearly in the order they occur in his last paper.

The revival of the governor's authority to regulate the fees of officers, on the expiration of the inspection law, is admitted, provided that authority had a legal existence; but the legality of the authority is denied; for, whether it be legal or not, is the very matter in debate — "The offices being old and constitutional, and supported by incidental fees, the right to receive *such* fees is old and constitutional," and therefore my adversary would infer, that the fees settled by proclamation are old and constitutional.

This inference does not follow from the premises notwithstanding the crafty insertion of the word *such*. The offices being old, the right to receive fees may be old; but the question recurs, what fees? of whom? where resides the authority of fixing the rates? for, fixed they must be, by some authority. That they may be fixed by the legislature, is admitted on all sides; should the different branches of the legislature disagree about the settlement, what authority must then interpose, and settle the rates hitherto unascertained? Antilon contends that in such case, the supreme magistrate, or the judges acting under an authority delegated from him, may settle them. If this doctrine be constitutional, what security have we against the imposition of excessive fees? Does it not give a discretionary power to the governor of making what provision he may think proper for his officers, and of rendering them independent of the people? When a service is performed, the performer is clearly intitled to some recompence, but whether he is to receive the recompence from the person served, or from another, may be a matter of doubt; the quantum of the recompence may not be ascertained, either by contract, by usage, or by law; and then in case of a dispute, must be settled by the verdict of a jury.

If the authority to regulate the fees of officers by proclamation be illegal, the proclamation can prevent the extortion of officers only by operating on their fears of the governor's displeasure, and of a removal from office; "But if the proclamation had not issued prohibiting the officers from taking *other*, or greater fees than allowed by the late inspection act, then would the officers have had it in their power to have demanded *any fees.*"

Their rapacity perhaps might have prompted them to demand most excessive fees; but under what obligation were the people to comply with their exorbitant demands?

Suppose a person should carry a deed to be recorded in the provincial office; the clerk refuses to record it, unless the party will pay him fifty guineas; must he submit to this unreasonable exaction, or run the risk of losing his property by suffering his title to remain incompleat? To avoid that danger, the money is paid; will he not be intitled to recover of the officer by the verdict of a jury, what they might think above the real value of the service? or suffering his title to remain incompleat, might he not sue the officer for damages, first tendering a reasonable fee adequate to the trouble and expence of recording the deed? Answer, Antilon, without equivocation, yes — or no. If the officer might be indicted for extortion, what benefit could the people expect from such a prosecution, when the power of granting a noli prosequi[3] is confessedly vested in the government? The present regulation, we are told — "contains no enforcement of payment from the people, the officer being left to his legal remedy." There is not, it is true, any immediate enforcement of payment, unless indeed the officer should refuse to do the service, if not paid his fee, at the very instant of performing the service, which as I formerly remarked, would be in most instances an effectual method of enforcing payment.

Suppose the officer should not insist on an immediate payment, and that his account of fees should be contested: he brings an action to recover his fees, according to the very settlement of the proclamation; to whose decision is this question to be left? To the judges? or to a jury? If to the former, and they should be of opinion, that the governor has a right to regulate fees by proclamation, when there is no prior establishment by law, and the defendant should refuse to submit to the sentence of the court, he will be

[3] Should read, nolle prosequi: An entry on the record denoting that the prosecutor or plaintiff will proceed no further in his action or suit.

committed to jail, or the sum will be levied by execution of his effects; distress, though delayed for some time, will surely overtake him in the end. Some of the judges discover a disinclination to remain in office; they solicit a removal; granted, and approved of; others are requested to succeed them; should we not have cause to suspect the rectitude of applications made to men, who have publickly declared their opinion of the legality of the measure, attempted to be enforced by the sanction of the courts of justice?

Other methods may be employed to enforce the proclamation. The frowns of government will awe the timid into a compliance: the necessitous cannot withstand the force of temptation, or the threats of power; the disobedient, and refractory must relinquish all hopes of promotion, or of promoting their friends; who have favours to ask at court, must merit court-favour by setting examples of duty, and submission.

It has been alleged that fees are taxes; to prove the assertion, the authority of Coke, and reasons grounded on the general principles of the constitution have been produced: mark, how Antilon has endeavoured to get over the authority, and confute the reasons. One of the great objections to the proclamation is, that it imposes a tax on the people, and consequently is competent to the legislature only. Antilon contends, that fees are improperly stiled taxes, because they have been settled by the separate branches of the legislature, which only can impose a tax. I have already exposed the sophistry of this argument, I hope, to the satisfaction of the unprejudiced; some farther elucidation however, may be necessary to men not thoroughly conversant with the subject. The lords and commons, and the upper and lower houses of assembly have each separately settled the fees of their respective officers by the particular usage of parliament, which must be deemed an exception to the general law, and ought, as all exceptions, to be sparingly exercised, and in such cases, and in such manner only, as the usage will strictly warrant. It was foreign to my purpose to inquire into this usage, custom, or law of parliament, to investigate its origin, or examine its constitutionality. On an inquiry, it would perhaps be found co-eval with parliaments. But do you, Antilon, admit the right of the lower house to rate the fees of its officers? If you do not admit the right, to argue from the mere exercise of it, is certainly unfair in *you*. You will insist, that I have admitted the right of the judges to settle the fees of officers attendant on their courts; be pleased to turn to the passage in my answer to your first paper, part of which you have cited, and then be candid enough to acknowledge, if you have not wilfully misrepresented, that you have mistaken my meaning.

The major proposition, that taxes cannot be laid, but by the legislature, I have admitted with this exception, "*saving in such* cases, &c."

It was not incumbent on me to prove the exception, it is sufficiently proved by the journals of parliament; the *right*, or the *power*, if you like that word better, has been frequently exercised, whether constitutionally, or not, is another question. The two houses of parliament are the sole judges of their own privileges, with which I shall take care not to intermeddle. Inconsistencies in all governments are to be met with; in ours the most perfect, which was ever established, some may be found.

A partial deviation from a clear and fundamental *maxim* of the constitution cannot invalidate that *maxim*.

To explain my meaning. It is a settled principle of the British constitution, that taxes must be laid by the whole legislature, yet in one instance, perhaps in more, the principle hath been violated. The separate branches of the legislature have settled the fees of their own officers. Antilon has inferred from that exception to the general rule, or maxim, which exception should be considered as the peculiar privilege of parliament, "that fees are not taxes." He has admitted, (if I comprehend his meaning) that fees are sometimes taxes, that is, when imposed by the legislature; but when regulated by the judges they come not within the legal definition of a tax.

Thus the fees regulated by the late inspection law were taxes: the same fees now attempted to be established by proclamation cease to be taxes because regulated by an authority distinct from the legislative; but are their nature and effects altered by these two different modes of settlement? should an act of parliament pass for the payment of the identical fees, said to be paid to officers, under the sole authority of the judges; according to Antilon's doctrine, the fees thus established by act would become instantly taxes; but are they less oppressive, because settled by the discretion of the judges? I presume to think them more oppressive, because of a more dangerous tendency, particularly if on a disagreement between the branches of the legislature, that authority may interpose, and establish the very fees, and along with them a variety of abuses, which the representatives of the people wish to have reformed. "The judges are not governed by the law of parliament, they have no authority to tax the subject, but their allowance of fees to their necessary officers is lawful" — of *ancient fees* — admitted. I have observed — "*It does not appear that the judges have ever imposed new fees by their sole authority.*" In answer to this Antilon remarks: — "that the fees when originally allowed were *new*, and the allowance being made by the judges therefore they originally, allowed *new* fees, and if fees were originally taxes when *new*, they have not ceased to be taxes in consequence of the frequent repetition of the acts of payment and receipt, and of their having obtained the denomination *antient fees*" — It will be proper to remind Antilon of another observation, which I made in my former papers on this very subject, and of which he has taken no notice. The King originally paid *all his officers* out of his own revenue; the subject was not taxed to support the civil establishment; in extraordinary emergencies, as foreign, or civil wars, tenths, fifteenths, and other impositions were granted by the commons in parliament to defray extraordinary expences.

It was consistent with the principles of the constitution, and agreeable to justice, that the King who paid *all his officers* out of his own purse, should have the right of ascertaining their salaries, or of delegating that right to his judges.

The antient fees so often spoken of, were those perhaps, which the King formerly paid, and were settled by the judges. I say perhaps, for in a matter so obscure, it would be rash to pronounce decisively. If I am right in this conjecture, *antient fees* were not originally taxes, because not paid originally by the people. *Ancient usage* according to Bacon gives fees an *equal sanction* with an act of parliament,[4] upon this principle I apprehend, that *such fees* are presumed to have been originally established by the proper authority, although their commencement and the authority, which imposed them at this day be unknown — "At common law, none of

[4] Matthew Bacon, *Abridgement of the Law* (London, 1768), 2:463.

the King's officers, whose offices did *any way* concern the administration of justice, could take any reward for doing their office, but what they received of the king"[5] — These words are sufficiently comprehensive to take in all the inferior ministers and officers of the courts of justice. The fee of 20s. commonly called the bar fee — was "*an antient fee,* says Coke *taken time out of mind* by the sheriff — of every prisoner acquitted of felony";[6] and therefore according to the above principle laid down by Bacon, acquired an equal sanction with fees established by law — "an office erected for the publick good, though no fee is annexed to it, is a good office, and the party for the labour and pains, which he takes in executing it, may maintain a *quantum meruit,* if not as a fee, yet as competent recompence for his trouble."[7] This clearly relates to an office newly erected; but what follows seems to include the unsettled fees of all offices new and old. "Where a person was libelled in the ecclesiastical court for fees, upon motion, a prohibition was granted — *for no court has a power to establish fees*; the judge of the court may think them *reasonable,* but this is not *binding.*" But if on a *quantum meruit* — a jury think them *reasonable,* then they become *established fees* — probably the fees, which now go under the denomination, *antient fees,* and not expressly given by act of parliament, were originally established by the verdict of a jury, and their having been long allowed by the courts of justice, may be deemed presumptive evidence of such establishment. The method of reforming abuses in the courts of justice by the presentment of experienced practicers upon oath, appointed by the judges, to enquire what fees had been exacted other than "*the antient and usual fees,*" seems to favour this conjecture.

"In the year 1743 an order was made in chancery by Lord Hardwicke[8] reciting, that the King upon the address of the com-

[5] Serjeant William Hawkins, *A Treatise of the Pleas of the Crown* (London, 1762), chapter 68, sec. 3, p. 170.

[6] Sir Edward Coke, *The First Part of the Institutes of the Laws of England* (London, 1629), p. 368.

[7] Bacon, *Abridgement,* 2:464. Quantum meruit: as much as he deserved.

[8] *An Order of the High Court of Chancery . . . Relating to the Fees of the Officers, Clerks and Ministers of the said Court* (London, 1744).

mons, had issued his commission for making a diligent and particular survey, and view of all officers of the said court, and inquiring what fees, and wages every of those officers might, and ought *lawfully* to have in respect of their offices, and what had of *late time* been unjustly incroached, and imposed upon the subject &c." — "Then are added" — continues Antilon "tables of fees of the respective officers, and among the fees settled by this order are the fees of the master of the rolls," who advised and assisted the chancellor in making the settlement. How is this transaction to be reconciled with the doctrine of Hawkins, "that the courts of justice are not restrained from al[2]lowing reasonable fees to their officers, as the chief danger of oppression is from officers being left at liberty to set their *own* rates and make their *own demands?*"[9] In this instance certainly, if by the settlement aforesaid an imposition of *new fees*, and not an authentication of *old and established fees* be understood, the master of the rolls was advised with, and assisted in settling his own rates. Is this proceeding consonant to the principles of justice? What says Hawkins? "There can't be so much fear of abuses when officers are restrained to *known* and *stated fees*, settled by the discretion of the courts, because the chief danger of oppression" — &c. Should the judges be any ways interested in the settlement (*A*) of their officers fees, would not the reason assigned by Hawkins for the interposition of their authority, in the manner explained by Antilon, operate most forcibly against the exercise of it? Would it for instance be agreeable to equity and natural justice, to permit the secretary of this province to settle the fees of the county clerks, on the gross amount of whose lists he receives a clear tenth; carry the case a little further: suppose the practice had long prevailed of offering the secretary a genteel present on every grant of a commission for a county clerkship, Would it not be his interest to enhance the value of county clerkships? The gratuity would probably bear some proportion to the value of the place bargained for. Do the judges in Westminster-hall receive gratuities

---

(*A*) *If such settlement implies a discretionary power in the judges to fix the precise rates to be paid to their officers, when they are not fixed by ancient usage, the verdict of a jury, or by act of parliament.*

---

[9] Hawkins, *Pleas of the Crown*, chapter 68, sec. 3, p. 171.

on granting offices in their appointment? — If they do, Hawkins' reason is felo de se[10] — it is the strongest that can be urged against the power, which it is meant to support.

If the judges have an interest in the offices in their disposal, a discretionary power to allow fees to their officers, is in some measure a power of settling their *own rates* and making their *own demands*. Coke's authority proves most clearly, that *new fees* annexed to *old* offices are taxes: whether the fees settled by proclamation are *new fees* remains to be considered; "fees, says Antilon, may be due without a precise settlement of the rates, and the right to receive them, may be co-eval with the first creation of the offices, as in the case of our old and constitutional offices; when such fees are *settled* they are not properly *new* fees, and therefore a regulation restraining the officer from taking beyond a stated sum for each service, when he was before intitled to a fee for such service, is not granting or annexing a *new fee* to an old office."

The question therefore is now reduced to these two points — 1st. Has not government attempted to settle the rates of officers fees by proclamation? 2dly. Are not fees so settled — new fees? If they are, upon Antilon's own principles, government hath no right to settle them. The restraint laid on officers, by the proclamation from taking *other*, or *greater* fees, than allowed by the late regulation, can be considered in no other light, than an implied affirmative allowance to take *such fees*, as were allowed by that regulation, and of course must be deemed an *intended* settlement of the rates (*B*). The fees payable to our old, and constitutional officers, have been differently rated, by different acts of assembly; those various rates, were never meant to be extended beyond the duration of the temporary acts, by which they were ascertained, for, one principal reason of making those acts temporary, we have seen, was to reduce the rates occasionally, and to lessen the burthen of them. On the expiration therefore of the late inspection law, the regulation of officers fees expired with it, that is, there remained no obligation on the people to pay the rates settled by that, or any

(*B*) *I say* intended, *because the settlement by proclamation being illegal, is in fact no settlement.*

---

[10] Self-defeating.

former regulation, and consequently the fees, as to the *quantum*, or precise sum, were then unsettled. Government entertained the same opinion, and issued a proclamation to ascertain the rates, or as is sometimes pretended, to prevent extortion, because the rates being *unsettled*, the officers might have demanded *any fees*; the fees therefore not being *settled*, when the inspection law fell, the settlement of them by proclamation was a *new* settlement, and of course the fees so settled were *new*; but *new* fees according to Coke cannot be annexed to *old offices* unless by act of parliament; his authority therefore, even as explained by Antilon, proves that a settlement by proclamation of fees due to *old* offices is illegal. A mere right in officers to receive fees, cannot be oppressive; the actual receipt only of excessive or unreasonable fees is oppressive, now, who are the properest judges whether fees be excessive or moderate? Officers certainly are not, the same objections, which may be made to their decision, apply to the governor, and most of them to the judges — juries may be partial, or packed. All these considerations plead strongly for a legislative regulation, which is liable to none of the objections hinted at. The doctrine laid down by Antilon in opposition to Coke's, teams with mischief and absurdities — "Old officers have a right co-eval with their institution to receive fees," the inference therefore *"when their fees are not ascertained by the legislature, the judges may ascertain them"* is by no means logical, it contradicts the most notorious and settled point of the constitution, it lodges a discretionary power in the judges appointed by the crown, and formerly removeable at pleasure, to impose excessive fees, and consequently to oppress the subject, without a possibility of redress, should the king, or lords refuse to concur with the commons in passing a law to moderate the rates, and to correct abuses — *"The governor adopted the late rates as the most moderate of any"* — If he might have adopted *any other* rates, his *exceeding lenity* deserves our *warmest* thanks; but then we are more indebted to his indulgence, than to the limitation of prerogative; we cannot therefore be said to enjoy true liberty, "for that, (as Blackstone justly observes) consists not so much in the gracious behaviour as in the limited power of the sovereign."[11] According to Antilon — "The late regulation of fees

---

[11] Blackstone's *Commentaries on the Laws of England* (London, 1821), 4:426.

expiring with the temporary act, the governor's authority to settle
the rates revived," and he insinuates, "that it was optional in him
to adopt the rates of the late, or of any prior regulation, or even to
prescribe rates intirely new." If the old and constitutional officers
have a right to receive fees, have they not, it may be asked, a
remedy to come to that right, and if so, What remedy? The remedy, which the constitution has given to every subject under the
protection of the laws. If a contest should arise between the officer
and the person for whom the service is done about the quantum
of the recompence, the former must have recourse to the only true,
and constitutional remedy in that case provided, the trial by jury.
Among other great objections to the proclamation, at least to
Antilon's defence of it, are his endeavours to set aside that mode
of trial, the best security against the encroachments of power, and
consequently the firmest support of liberty. The person, who calls
himself Antilon, has filed a bill in chancery for the recovery of fees
principally due for services done at common law: by appealing to
the court of chancery, of which the governor is the sole judge, and
in whom, he contends, the will to ordain the rates, and the power
to enforce them are lodged, he has endeavoured to establish a
tyranny in a land of freedom (C). In answer to the declaration
of chief justice Roll[12] — I shall give the declaration of a subsequent chief justice, of greater, at least, of equal authority. The
case I allude to is reported by Lord Raymond 1 vol. p. 703 — It
was asserted by council that the court of King's bench, or judge
of assize respectively, would exert their authority and commit
persons refusing to pay fees due to the *old officers* of the courts,
and that this was the constant practice. "But Holt, chief justice
said, he knew of no such practice; he could not commit a man for
not paying the said fees. If there is a right, there is a remedy; an
indebitatus assumpsit will lie, if the fee is certain, if uncertain, a

(C) *See the governor's answer to the address of the house of delegates in
1771.*[13]

---

[12] See p. 164 above.

[13] November 30, 1771, *Maryland Archives* (Baltimore, Maryland Historical
Society, 1883–), 63:219–33.

quantum meruit" — and in both instances, a jury is to be judge.[14] From hence it may be collected, that when the fees claimed by the *old* and *constitutional officers* were *unascertained* recourse was had to a jury, that their verdict might ascertain them. When fees are due to old officers, and not settled by the legislature, a jury only, upon the principles of our constitution, can settle them.

The uniform practice of the courts cannot establish a doctrine inconsistent with those principles. "If on enquiry into the legality of a custom, or usage, it appears to have been derived from an illegal source, it ought to be abolished; if originally invalid, length of time will not give it efficacy" — It has been already noticed, that the authority exercised by the judges of settling fees, that is, of ascertaining the *antient* and *legal fees*, in pursuance of a commission issued by the king, on the address of the house of commons, is very different from the authority now set up, of settling fees by proclamation, issued contrary to the declared sentiments of the lower-house of assembly; if judges in this province may settle fees, because the judges in England have settled them, in the manner above-mentioned, where was the necessity of ascertaining fees by proclamation? Was it to influence and guide the decision of our judges? If they have a right to exercise their own judgment in settling fees, in fact, in imposing them, Why was a standard held up by the supreme magistrate for their direction? In setting up that standard, is it not notorious, that he was advised, and principally guided by the very man, who is most benefited by that illegal settlement? Notwithstanding the misrepresented power of the English judges to regulate fees, and the different orders of the courts in Westminster-hall, for restraining the exaction of illegal fees, the encroaching spirit of office had rendered all the precautions of the judges ineffectual; insomuch, that the commons in the year 1730 were obliged to take the matter under their own consideration. I mentioned in a former paper that transaction. In consequence of the enquiry — a report was made by the committee in 1732 to the house of commons,

---

[14] The citation is correct. Indebitatus assumpsit: being indebted, he promised or undertook. "This form of action is brought to recover in damages the amount of the debt or demand and upon the trial the jury will, according to evidence, give verdict for whole or part of that sum." Blackstone's *Commentaries*, 3:155.

from which I gave some extracts in my first answer to Antilon.[15] It appears from the report, "That orders had been sometimes made for the officers to hang up publickly lists of their fees, most of which lists are since withdrawn, or have been suffered to decay and become useless; that the officers themselves seemed often doubtful what fees to claim, and *most of them* relied upon no better evidence than some information from their predecessors, or the deputies of their predecessors, that such fees had been demanded, and received" — it is hereby evident, that the regulation of officers' fees had been long neglected, that in consequence of such neglect, excessive abuses had crept into practice, and had grown from length of time into a kind of established rights: that a thorough discovery and reformation of those abuses required more time and attention, than the commons could spare from more important objects. As well might they have attempted to cleanse the Augean stables, a work, which the strength only of a Hercules could accomplish;[16] disgusted with the tediousness and intricacy of the inquiry, they probably chose to refer the correction of abuses to the judges, men of integrity, and best acquainted with the practices of their own officers, and of course, best qualified to reform them. It is asserted by Antilon that the legislative provisions do not extend to any considerable proportion of the fees of officers and therefore, that by far the greatest part of officers fees hath been settled by allowance of the courts, and not by statutes — this fact may be admitted, and the inference he would draw from it be denied; that judges have allowed fees to their officers in the first instance, without the intervention of a jury to ascertain them. If the judges have acted thus, they have certainly assumed a power contrary to the petition of right, contrary to the first and most essential principle of the constitution, "that the subject shall not be compelled to contribute to any tax, tallage, aid, or *other like charge*, not set by common consent in parliament"[17] — All levies of money from the subject,

[15] See pp. 96–98 above. The commons committee report was first quoted on pp. 97–98. The correct date is 1732.
[16] Seeking purification for various murders, Hercules submitted to twelve labors imposed on him by King Eurystheus of Tiryns. The fifth labor was the cleansing of the Augean stables, made filthy by a herd of 3,000 cattle.
[17] The text of the Petition of Right (1628) may be found in *The Stuart Constitution 1603–1688 Documents and Commentary*, edited and introduced by J. P. Kenyon (Cambridge: Cambridge University Press, 1966), pp. 82–85. The quotation is from sec. 8.

by way of loan, or benevolence, are also cautiously guarded against by the petition of right. The very *putting* or *setting* a tax on the people, though not levied, has been declared illegal; even a *voluntary* imposition on merchandize *granted* by the merchants, without the approbation of parliament, gave umbrage to the commons, was censured and condemned. "This imposition though it were not set on by assent of parliament, yet it was not set on by the *king's absolute* power, but was granted to him by the *merchants themselves*, who were to be charged with it. So the *grievance* was the *violation* of the *right* of the people in *setting it on* without *their assent* in parliament, not the *damage*, that grew by it, for that did *only touch* the *merchants*, who could *not justly complain thereof*, because it was *their own act and grant*" — Petyt jus parliam. page 368, 369.[18] — A tax may be defined a rate, settled by some publick charge, upon lands, persons, or goods. By the English constitution the power of settling *the rate* is vested in the parliament alone, and in this province in the general assembly.

Representation has long been held to be essential to that power, and is considered as its origin; upon this principle the house of commons, who represent the whole body of the people, claim the exclusive right of framing money bills, and will not suffer the lords to amend them. The regulation of officers fees in Maryland has been generally made by the assemblies. The authority of the governor to settle the fees of officers, has twice only, as we know of, interposed,[19] but not then, without meeting with opposition from the delegates, and creating a general discontent among the people, a sure proof, that it has always been deemed dangerous, and unconstitutional. The fees of officers, whether imposed by act of assembly, or settled by proclamation, must be considered as a publick charge, rated upon the lands, persons, or goods of every inhabitant holding lands, or possessed of property within this province. That they have been looked upon as such by the officers themselves, is evident, from their lodging lists of their respective fees with the deputies from this province, to the congress at New York, who might thereby be enabled to make known to his majesty, and to the parliament, the great expence of supporting our civil establishment. The author of the considerations once

[18] The citations are correct.
[19] By proclamation in 1733 and 1770.

entertained the same idea, but such is the versatility of his temper, such his contempt of consistency, that he changes his opinions, and his principles, with as little ceremony as he would change his coat. Speaking of the sundry charges on tobacco — "The planter (says he) pays a tax, at least, equal to what is paid by any farmer of Great-Britain possessed by the same degree of property, and moreover the planter must contribute to the support of the *expensive internal government of the colony*, in which he resides."[20] Now, the support of civil officers, unquestionably constitutes a part of the expence — he then refers to the appendix, where we meet with the following note:

"The attentive reader will observe, that the nett proceeds of a hogshead of tobacco at an average are 4 £ and the taxes 3 £ together 7 £. — Quære — how much per cent does the tax amount to which takes from the two wretched tobacco colonies 3 £ out of every 7 £. — and how deplorable must their circumstances appear when their vast debt to the mother country and the *annual burthen of their civil establishments* are added to the estimate."[21]

Impressed with the same idea were the conferrees of the upper house in the year 1771. In their messages of the 20th of November they assert — "Publick offices were doubtless erected for the benefit of the community, and for the same purpose are emoluments given to support them."[22] All taxes whatever are supposed to be imposed, and levied for the benefit of the community. If then fees are taxes, *or such like charges*, it may be asked, how came parliaments to place such confidence in the judges, as to suffer them to exercise a power, of which those assemblies have always been remarkably tenacious, and which is competent to them only? I might answer this question by asking another; how came many unconstitutional powers to be exercised by the crown, and suffered by parliament? for instance, the dispensing power[23]

[20] Daniel Dulany, Jr., *Considerations on the Propriety of Imposing Taxes in the British Colonies* (Annapolis, 1765), pp. 26–27.

[21] *Ibid.*, p. 54.

[22] November 20, 1771, *Maryland Archives* 63:53–57.

[23] The dispensing power was the prerogative crown right to make individual exceptions to the general operation of the laws. It was a major source of Parliamentary discontent and was determined illegal by the Bill of Rights in 1689.

— the answer is obvious; it required the wisdom of ages, and the accumulated efforts of patriotism, to bring the constitution to its present point of perfection; a thorough reformation could not be effected at once; upon the whole the fabrick is stately, and magnificent, yet a perfect symmetry, and correspondence of parts is wanting; in some places, the pile appears to be deficient in strength, in others the rude and unpolished taste of our Gothic ancestors is discoverable —

hodieque manent vestigia ruris.[24]

It does not appear in what instances, upon what occasions, and in what manner, the judges have allowed fees to their officers — that is, have permitted them to take fees, not before settled by law, usage, or the verdict of a jury. The power if conclusive on the subject, and if exercised in the manner explained by Antilon, is unjustifiable, and may be placed among those contradictions, which formerly subsisted in the more imperfect state of our constitution, and of which, some few remain even unto this day. How it came to be overlooked by parliament, may perhaps be accounted for somewhat after this manner. The liberties which the English enjoyed under their Saxon kings, were wrested from them by the Norman conqueror; that invader intirely changed the ancient constitution by introducing a new system of government, new laws, a new language and new manners. The contests, which sometime after ensued between the Plantagenets, and the barons,[25] were struggles between monarchy, and aristocracy, not between liberty, and prerogative; the [3] common people remained in a state of the most abject slavery, a prey to both parties, more oppressed by a number of petty tyrants, than they probably would have been by the uncontrouled power of one. Towards the close of the long reign of Henry the 3d,[26] we meet with the first faint traces of a house of commons; that house, which in process of time, became

---

[24] And today traces of the country remain; a variation on Varro, *Ling* 5, 42.
[25] The Barons' Wars of 1215–1217 and 1264–1267, in which attempts were made to overthrow Kings John and Henry III respectively. The barons were led by Simon de Montfort in the second war and enjoyed considerable success before his death in 1265.
[26] Henry III (1207–1272) became king in 1216.

the most powerful branch of our national assemblies, which gradually rescued the people from aristocratical, as well from regal tyranny, to which we owe our present excellent constitution, derived its first existence from an usurper (D). Edward the first[27] has meritted the appellation of the English Justinian by the great improvements of the law, and wise institutions made in his reign. He renewed, and confirmed the great charter, and passed the famous statute, de tallagio non concedendo, against the imposition of, and levying taxes without consent of parliament. Within the meaning of which act, says Coke, are *new* fees annexed to *old* offices. Have any new fees been annexed to old offices since that period by the sole authority of the judges? or have they increased the old and established fees? if either, they have certainly acted against law. If Coke was of opinion, that the judges had a discretionary power to settle the fees of old offices, it is most surprizing he did not intimate as much in his comment on this statute, so often quoted. He not only ought to have declared his opinion on that occasion, but also to have shewn the difference between a settlement of fees due to old and constitutional offices, and the annexing new fees to old offices. I believe it would have puzzled him, as much as it has Antilon, to shew the difference; in reality, there is none, they are but different names for the same thing. Although the necessities of Edward, and the exigency of the times, forced him to submit to those limitations of prerogative, he frequently broke through them; from whence we may conclude, that publick liberty was imperfectly understood in that rude and unlettered age, and little regarded by a prince impatient of restraint, and fond of arbitrary power, though inclined to dispense equal

(D) *Simon Montfort earl of Leicester. Vide 1st. volume parliamentary history.*[28]

---

[27] Edward I (1239–1307), the son of Henry III, became king in 1272. The Statutes of Westminster I (1275) and Gloucester (1278) were written during his reign.

[28] *Cobbett's Parliamentary History of England, From the Norman Conquest, in 1066, to the Year 1803* (London, 1806), 1:30–31. De Montfort (1208–1265) established a short-lived government during the Barons' Wars and is accorded an important role in the early growth of Parliament.

justice among his subjects. The fatal catastrophe of his son,[29] and the causes which occasioned it, are well known. In those times of discord and distraction, the greatest enormities were committed by the very men, who under a pretence of reforming abuses, sought to promote their own power.

Equally unfortunate, and equally unfit for improving the constitution, was the reign of Richard the 2d.[30] Hume teaches us what idea we ought to form of the English government under Edward the 3d[31] — "Yet, on the whole it appears that the government at best was only a barbarous monarchy, not regulated by any fixed maxims, nor bounded by any certain undisputed rights, which were in practice regularly observed. The king conducted himself by one set of principles, the barons by another, the commons by a third, the clergy by a fourth; all these systems of government were contrary and incompatible; each of them prevailed according as incidents were favourable to it."[32]

This short historical deduction may seem foreign to my subject, but it really is not.

The frequent and bare faced violations of laws favourable to the people, the pardoning offences of the deepest dye, committed by men of the first distinction, or the inability to punish the offenders, the corruption and venality of the judges, all tend to discover that practices as subversive to liberty, as a discretionary power in the judges to impose fees, went unnoticed, or remained unredressed.

From the deposition of Richard the 2d. to the battle of Bosworth,[33] the English were continually involved in wars, foreign, or domestick. Silent inter arma leges.[34]

[29] Edward II (1284–1327) ascended to the throne in 1307. He was forced to abdicate by his wife's lover Mortimer, a baron leader, in 1326. He was murdered in 1327 by means of a red hot spit thrust in his entrails.

[30] Richard II (1367–1400) became king in 1377.

[31] Edward III (1312–1377) became king in 1327.

[32] David Hume, *History of England* (London, 1767), 2:515.

[33] The Battle of Bosworth, August 22, 1485, marked the end of the Wars of the Roses. Henry Tudor, crowned Henry VII, was victorious over the Yorkists and Lancastrians under Richard III.

[34] The power of law is suspended during war. Sir Edward Coke, *The Fourth Part of the Institutes of the Laws of England* (London, 1681), p. 70.

We may presume, during that period, the courts of justice were but little frequented, and the business transacted in them inconsiderable; from whence we may infer, that the rules of practice, and orders established by the judges in their courts being slightly known to the nation at large, escaped the notice of parliament, in a time of general poverty, and confusion. Frequent insurrections disturbed the peace of Henry the 7th.[35] The first parliament of his reign was chiefly composed of his creatures, devoted to the house of Lancaster, and obsequious to their sovereign's will. The 2d parliament was so little inclined to inquire into abuses of the courts of law, or into any other grievances, that the commons took no notice of an arbitrary taxation, which the king a little before their meeting, had imposed on his subjects. His whole reign was one continued scene of rapine and oppression on his part, and of servile submission on that of the parliament. "In vain (says Hume) did the people look for protection from the parliament; that assembly was so overawed, that at this very time, during the greatest rage of Henry's oppression, the commons chose Dudley their speaker, the very man, who was the chief instrument of his oppressions."[36] Henry the 8th[37] governed with absolute sway; parliaments in that prince's time, were more disposed to establish tyranny than to check the exercise of unconstitutional powers (*E*). During the reigns of Edward the 6th, Mary and Elizabeth,[38] these assemblies were busily engaged in modelling the national religion to the court standard: their obsequiousness in conforming to the religion of the prince upon the throne, at a time, when the nation was most under religious influence, leaves us no room to expect a less compliant temper in matters of more indifference.

In truth; under the Tudors, parliaments generally acted more like the instruments of power, than the guardians of liberty.

(E) An Act was passed in his reign to give proclamations the force of laws.

---

[35] Henry VII (1457–1509), who became king in 1485, had to quash two invasions and a domestic uprising.

[36] Hume's *History of England*, 3:409–10.

[37] Henry VIII (1491–1547), son of Henry VII, became king in 1509.

[38] Edward VI (1537–1553) became king in 1547; Mary I (1516–1558) succeeded Edward in 1553; Elizabeth I (1533–1603) became queen at Mary's death.

The wise administration of Elizabeth made her people happy; commerce began to flourish, a spirit of industry, and enterprize seized the nation; it grew wealthy, and law, the usual concomitant of wealth, increased.

"In the 40th year of her reign, a presentment upon oath of 15 persons for the better reformation of sundry exactions and abuses supposed to be committed by the officers, clerks, and ministers in the high court of chancery was shewed to the committee," (appointed by the house of commons in 1739, to inquire into the abuses of the courts of law and equity)[39] "by which presentment it plainly appeared, who were the officers of the court at that time and what were their legal fees." It appears from the same report, that the officers of the court of chancery had exceedingly increased, since the 40th of Elizabeth to that time, by patents and grants, and in consequence, I suppose of the increased business of the court. It likewise appears from the report aforesaid, that commissions had frequently issued in former times to inquire into the behaviour of the officers in the courts of justice, with power to correct abuses. The enrolment of two such commissions in the reign of James the 1st, and four in the reign of Charles the 1st, were produced to the committee, but they certify, that no such commission had issued since the reformation.

During the reign of Charles the 2d,[40] parliaments were sedulously employed in composing the disorders consequent on the civil wars, healing the bleeding wounds of the nation, and providing remedies against the fresh dangers, with which the bigotry and arbitrary temper of the king's brother threatened the constitution. Since the revolution parliaments have relaxed much of their antient severity, and discipline. Gratitude to their great deliverer, and a thorough confidence in the patriotic princes of the illustrious house of Brunswick have banished from the majority of those assemblies, all fears and jealousies of an unconstitutional influence in the crown. Parsimonious grants of publick money have grown into disuse; a liberality bordering upon profuseness has taken place of a

---

[39] Another extract from the committee report of April 18, 1732. The date in the text is incorrect. *Journals of the House of Commons* (London, 1803), 21: 892–93.

[40] Charles II (1630–1685) ascended to the throne with the collapse of the Commonwealth in May 1660.

rigid and austere œconomy; complacence and compliment have succeeded to distrust, and to parliamentary inquiries, into the conduct, and to impeachments of *ruling ministers*. While parliaments continue to repose this unbounded confidence in his Majesty's servants, we must not expect to see them very solicitous to lessen the profits of officers appointed by the crown. Political writers in England, have complained bitterly of the vast increase of officers, placemen, and pensioners, and to that increase have principally ascribed an irresistable influence in the crown over those national councils. Will any impartial man pretend to say that these complaints are altogether groundless? exaggerated they may be. Let us, my countrymen, profit by the errors and vices of the mother country; let us shun the rock, on which there is reason to fear, her constitution will be split.

The liberty of Englishmen, says an admired writer, can never be destroyed but by a corrupt parliament, and a parliament will never be corrupt, if government be not supplied with the means of corrupting; among these various means, we may justly rank a number of lucrative places in the disposal of the crown.[41]

(F) A member of the house of commons speaking on this very subject, before the house, expressed himself in the following manner. "But the crown having by some means or other got into its possession the arbitrary disposal of almost all offices and places, ministers soon found that the more valuable those offices and places were, the more *their* power would be extended; therefore, they resolved to make them lucrative as well as honourable, and from that time they have been by degrees increasing not only the number of offices and places but also the profits and perquisites of each. Not only large salaries have been annexed to every place of office under government, but many of the officers have been allowed to *oppress the subject by the sale of places under them, and by*

(F) *Edward Southwell, Esq; vide debates of the house of commons for the year 1744, anno 18 George 2d.*[42]

---

[41] Bolingbroke, *Dissertation upon Parties*, p. 116. This is not a quote.

[42] Edward Southwell, Esq., in House of Commons, December 8, 1744. *The History, Debates and Proceedings of Both Houses of Parliament*, printed for J. Debrett (London, 1792), 1:423. Carroll's emphasis.

exacting extravagant and unreasonable fees, which have been *so long suffered*, that they are now looked upon as the *legal perquisites* of the office, nay, in many offices they seem to have got a *customary right* to defraud the publick, and we know how careful some of our late ministers have been to *prevent* or *defeat any parliamentary inquiry into the conduct and management of any office.*"* I am inclined to think that some of our former assemblies foresaw the great power, which the offices established in this province for the furtherance of justice, and administration of government, would sooner or later throw into the hands of the persons invested with those offices; a little foresight might have discovered, that their incomes would increase amazingly with the rapid increase of population, trade, and law. Aware of the danger they wisely determined to provide a timely remedy, and fell upon the true, and only expedient, by passing temporary laws for the limitation of officers fees, not by delegating that most important trust to judges removeable at pleasure, liable to be swayed, perhaps, disposed to overlook the evil practices of their officers, and even to countenance "the *new invented and colourable charges of combined interest and ingenuity*." I have mentioned the great abuses, which had infected the courts of justice in England, the methods there pursued to correct them, and to prevent the exaction of *new* and illegal fees, and the long interruption of those methods, or inquiries.

The grievance had become so intolerable that the commons were at last forced to take cognizance of it themselves; from the necessity of their interposition, either a neglect in the judges to reform abuses, or a want of power is deducible; and hence this other inference may be drawn, that a law, limiting the fees of officers, is the best method of preventing their encroachments and illegal practices. Notwithstanding the late law many abuses had been committed by officers in the manner of charging their fees under that law. These abuses, if the proclamation should be enforced, will continue and go on increasing till they become insupportable to a free people, or the people be enslaved by a degenerate and abject submission to that arbitrary exertion of prerogative.

The necessities of the English kings, which constrained them to have frequent recourse to parliamentary aid, first gave rise to, then gradually secured, the liberty of the subject.[43]

In this colony, government is almost independent of the people. It has nothing to ask but a provision for its officers: if it can settle their fees without the interposition of the legislature, administration will disdain to owe even that obligation to the people. The delegates will soon lose their importance, government will every day gain some accession of strength; we have no intermediate state to check its progress: the upper house, the shadow of an aristocracy, being composed of officers dependent on the proprietary and removeable at pleasure, will, it is to be feared, be subservient to his pleasure and command.

I shall now proceed to examine Antilon's answers to my former arguments against the power of regulating fees by proclamation.

The whole force of his first answer, depends on the revival of the authority, which he contends existed before the enaction of the temporary law; if that authority is illegal, it did not exist, and consequently could not revive. The reasons already assigned prove the illegality.

2d Answer. "Parliament may have peculiar motives, &c. &c." Parliament, it is true, may have many motives for settling fees in various instances. To preclude a discretionary power in the judges, incompatible with the spirit of our constitution, and to obviate the inconveniences resulting from uncertainty, and to endless litigation, should induce parliament to settle the fees in every instance. The notion of the judges and the parliament having a coordinate power, which might clash, was never entertained; from the absurdity of two co-equal powers subsisting in the same state, a subordination of the judges to parliament was inferred; but if mercenary officers, or an artful intriguing minister, by obstructing a legislative regulation of fees, may leave the power of the judges uncontrouled by parliament, and at liberty to act, then do I insist, that the authority of parliament to regulate fees may be rendered altogether useless and nugatory.

3d Answer. "I might in my turn suppose, &c. &c." Thus may the most insolent, profligate, and contemptible minister, that ever dis-

---

[43] Taken from Hume's *History of England*, 6:142.

graced a nation, or his prince, suppose every opposition to his measures flows from similar motives. I argue not upon supposition, but from facts. The late regulation of fees was unequal, therefore unjust. A planter paid 20s for the same service, which cost the farmer only 10s.

To place all the subjects on equal footing was doing equal justice to all; it was bringing back the law to its true spirit and original intent. Abuses had crept into practice, owing either to design, or to a misconception of the act, or to a doubtfulness of expression; among others, fees were often charged for services not done; the delegates attempted to reform these abuses, and to lessen the rates where excessive; in this laudable attempt they were disappointed by the obstinacy and selfishness of men, who made themselves judges of their *own merits*, and *own rewards*. I agree with Antilon, "That our constitution may be much improved by altering the condition of our judges, by making them independent, and allotting them a liberal income" — But I fancy the delegates would disagree with him about the means. They perhaps would propose to lessen the exorbitant income of an inferior officer, who does little to deserve it, who grows more insolent as he grows more wealthy, and by a reduction of fees annexed to his, and to other offices not attended with much trouble, they would probably endeavour to make such savings, as might enable them to allow the judges a genteel salary without loading the people with any considerable additional charge.

Another very great improvement might be made in our constitution, by excluding all future secretaries, commissaries general, and judges of the land office from the upper house; till that event takes place we may despair of seeing any useful laws pass, without some disagreeable tack to them, should they clash with their particular interests. Those officers have long been connected with the law for the regulation of our staple, a law of the most salutary and extensive consequence to the community, and which has hitherto been purchased by a particular attention to their interests, and a deference to their demands, as impolitic as unaccountable in the representatives of a free people.

4th Answer. A great part of this answer has been already obviated. It has been noticed, that the excessive exactions so much talked of, and so much dreaded by our *merciful minister*, are mere bugbears. Freemen are not to be terrified with visionary fears, over solicitude to protect us from imaginary dangers, and a strong inclination discovered at the same time to pick our pockets, look a little like mockery. Fees being taxes; to impose them on the subject by proclamation, was as illegal as to levy ship-money by proclamation. The design of the two measures was nearly the same.

Charles wanted to raise money without a parliament, and our upstart minister wanted to provide for himself and his brother officers without an act of assembly, as the delegates would not provide for him, and them, in a manner suitable to their wishes. Was not the legality of the ship-money assessment determinable in the ordinary judicatories? Did it not receive the most solemn sanction? The sanction of eight judges out of twelve? You still retain, Mr. Antilon, all the low evasive cunning of a pettifogger.

Quo semel est imbuta recens, servabit odorem Testa diu.[44]

5th answer. When fees are not ascertained by law, the verdict of a jury must ascertain them, when thus ascertained — the judges in awarding costs are obliged, by statute to include them in the costs; the necessity [4] therefore of fixing the rates of fees, either by proclamation, or by the allowance of the judges, is a *pretended* and *false* necessity; consequently not *urgent* and *invincible*. If such a necessity really exists when there is no legislative regulation of fees, it was foreseen in 1770, and ought to have been guarded against by passing an act of assembly for settling the rates. The *pretended* necessity therefore aggravates *their* crime, who from a mercenary motive prevented a regulation by law. The famine, which occasioned the embargo, was not a *sudden and peculiar necessity*; it was apprehended long before it was felt; parliament might have been assembled, it's advice taken, and a law passed to enable his majesty to lay the embargo. The ministers were blamed for not calling the parliament in proper time, and the *necessity* of acting against law flowing from *that neglect*, was urged as *their*

[44] Horace, *Epistles* 1, 2, 69. A cask will long preserve the flavor with which it was once impregnated.

accusation, not their excuse. Although the question *"whose fault was it that a legislative regulation did not take place"* — be not determinable in any jurisdiction or by any legal authority, yet, has a discerning publick already decided it, and has fixed the blame on the proper person. Although he cannot be punished by the sentence of an ordinary judicature, yet might he be removed from office, on application made to the governor by the delegates of the people. Encomiums on the disinterestedness of officers, and censures of some obnoxious members, in fact, of the whole lower house, come with peculiar propriety and decorum from a man, who is an officer, and was particularly levelled at in the spirited and patriotic resolves of that house. It might have given satisfaction to *many* to have had the regulation of the clergy and officers established on the terms once proposed by the upper-house; but this satisfaction would not have resulted from a conviction, that the terms offered were just and advantageous to the publick, but from a despair of obtaining better; if this despair should become general, the cause of the publick must yield to the interest of a few officers. Disgraceful, and afflicting reflection! Not a single instance can be selected from our history of a law favourable to liberty obtained from government, but by the unanimous, steady, and spirited conduct of the people. The great charter, the several confirmations of it, the petition of right, the bill of rights, were all the happy effects of *force* and *necessity*.

I am not surprized that Antilon's resentment should be directed against a man, who has publickly spoke some very home truths. The wit and verses borrowed from Horace cannot destroy the evidence of facts. I am restrained by the limits of this paper from descanting on the merits of tub oratory; it has its use, and abuse, like most other institutions, and is not so prejudicial to characters attacked, as the whispered lye, the dark hint, and jesting story told with a sting at the end of it. I know a person, who has an admirable knack at defamation in this sly, oblique, insinuating manner; he has stabbed many a reputation with all the appearance of festivity *and good humour*; in the midst of gaiety, in the social hours of convivial mirth, malice preys inwardly on his soul; sometimes he is given to deal in the marvellous, to captivate the attention of his *admirers* — (generally fit tools for him to work with) and to leave on their minds a lively impression of his own consequence. Surrounded by a group of these creatures, he will now and then recount most wonderful wonders! *"speciosa miracula,"*[45] celebrate his own feats, prowess, and hair breadth scapes, in short forge such monstrous improbabilities, as would shock the faith of the most credulous jew.

They listening, gape applause.

Conticuere omnes, intentique ora tenebant.[46]

Answer 6. Rules or ordinances respecting the practice of the courts may be made without any danger of prejudging questions of law. "Judges have been called upon in council to advise their sovereign *on questions of law"* — true — and in consequence of their advice, pernicious measures have been frequently pursued by sovereigns — witness, the proclamation for levying ship-money, the dispensing power, and others equally unconstitutional. These examples should make judges very careful how they advise their sovereign; for bad advice they are amenable to parliament, and some of them have been punished, for giving extrajudicial and unconstitutional opinions. "Expedit reipublicae ut sit finis litium." "Misera est servitus ubi jus est vagum" — are sentiments truly liberal and useful; equally so, are these — *a free constitution will not endure discretionary powers, but in the cases of the most urgent necessity. The property of Englishmen is secured by the laws, not left to depend on the will of the sovereign, or of officers appointed by him.* There is an impropriety in advising measures tending to the immediate benefit of the *advisers.* Self-interest may warp the judgment of the most upright; hence, the maxim, "no man ought to be a judge in his own cause." The advisers of a measure as *legal* and *expedient* will probably remain of the same opinion when they come to determine on its legality in their judicial capacity. Should the question be brought before the court of appeals, ought the officers, who are deeply interested in its decision, to sit as judges? If it would be unjust in them to *judge* of

[45] Wonderful miracles!
[46] Vergil, *Aeneid* 2, 1. "All were hushed and held their gaze upon him, eagerly attentive."

the legality of the proclamation, there was surely some impropriety in *their advising* it. The chancellor in all causes of intricacy is advised by an assistant, whose opinion would not, I presume, be asked, if interested in the suit. Should a bill be filed against the usual assistant, for instance, by a Dutchman, could he be so insensible, as not to discover some anxiety at seeing his adversary in the capacity of an adviser, directing and guiding the opinion of the judge? Would not the impropriety strike even a Dutchman? Would he not have great reason to suspect an unfavourable decree? Had there been an open rupture, a declared enmity, which still subsisted between the assistant, and one of the parties to a chancery suit, and notwithstanding the assistant should discover an inclination to act in his usual capacity, would not his conduct raise indignation in every honest mind? Reader make the application.

Answer 7. "The governor was not to be directed by the votes of the majority of the advisers, they having no authoritative influence" — on a former occasion we were told — "there can be no difficulty in finding out his (the kings) ministers, the governor and council are answerable in this character." If the governor is not to be directed by the advice of his council, Why should they be answerable for their advice? He by adopting the measures advised makes it *his own* — because he uses his *own* manly judgment, the advice of the council can have no authoritative influence over him, and therefore according to Antilon's latter opinion, contradicted by his former, the governor must take the whole blame upon himself. Oh unsuspicious Eden! How long wilt thou suffer thyself to be imposed on by this deceiving man? "The fee for the seals was the same in all the proposed regulations"; and none of them have the least efficacy, wanting the sanction of law. To exact fees under the settlement of the new table, proposed by the lower-house, would be equally unlawful, though not so dangerous, as to exact them under the settlement by proclamation — "*the governor receives his fees now*" — and receives them instantly, and will not do the service without immediate payment. The practice may become general, and the good natured easy people of Maryland, will, I dare say — submit to it without reluctance or murmuring.

Answer 8. Antilon has admitted that he concurred with the rest of the council in advising the proclamation as *expedient* and

legal — he has since justified it — as *a necessary unavoidable act.*
It is not the first time that *"expediency* has covered itself under
the appearance of *necessity."*

From whence does Antilon infer this necessity? "The judgment,
or decree, says he, awarding the costs must *necessarily* be *precise"*
— but the judgment cannot be *precise,* unless the officers fees,
which constitute part of the costs be settled; if not settled by a law,
they must be settled by *some other authority* — and therefore he
concludes they must be settled by proclamation — "Why not by
the verdict of a jury? Endless litigation, it is answered, would
ensue from that method of settlement. A much greater mischief I
reply — would result from the other; charges would be set, and
levied on the people without, nay, against the consent of their
representatives. Between two such evils. What choice have we
left? The choice of the least. Hard indeed is the fate of the province to be reduced to such extremity, that *some officers* may enjoy
great incomes for doing little. The secretary's office is a mere
sinecure — yet has he had the assurance to ask a net income of
£ 600 sterling per annum to *support his dignity.*[47] To hear Antilon
talk in this strain is enough to rouse the indignation of apathy
itself, but indignation sinks into contempt, the moment we reflect
on the *farcical dignity* of the man.

Answer 9. The fees settled by proclamation have been proved
a charge upon the people; now the settling a charge upon the
people without the consent of their representatives, *is a measure
striking at the root of all liberty.* Antilon has endeavoured to justify the measure by precedents. The precedents he has produced
do not in the least apply. The settlements of fees made by the
judges appear to have been merely authentications of the *usual*
and *antient* fees. The long disuse of inquiries into the conduct of
officers gave them an opportunity of exacting *new* and *illegal* fees;
the grievance was suffered to run on so long, that at last it became
difficult to distinguish the *new* and *illegal,* from the *antient* and
legal fees. The fees so certified by the judges, were to be deemed
antient fees; to facilitate their scrutiny — "juries of officers and
clerks were impanelled to inquire, what fees had been usually

[47] See above in Antilon's fourth letter, note 46.

taken by the several officers, for the space of 30 years last past," on a supposition, I presume, that fees, which had been paid for so long a time, were probably *antient fees*.

The judges therefore, I conceive, did not settle in that instance the rates of fees, but certified what were the rates *heretofore settled*.

With us, the rates of fees were not settled: the delegates did not request the governor to issue a commission to the judges to fix the rates; they remonstrated against the apprehended exercise of the unconstitutional power of settling them by his sole authority. I hope it has been proved, that if the judges settled, that is, imposed fees, *not before settled*, they acted against law and consequently *wrong*, and therefore, *"if what has been done be wrong, it confers no right to repeat it."* To establish which axiom the considerations were cited. I have known you, Antilon, long enough to form a true judgment of your character, and I have exhibited a true picture of it to the publick; an intimacy I have cautiously avoided, as dangerous, and disreputable. The frequent repetition of the word *"Barber"* in all your papers, makes me suspect some concealed wit or joke; perhaps it may be founded on the production of *your fertile invention*; pray disclose it — I will add it to the catalogue; you understand me.

Answer 10. The fees allowed to the petitioning sheriffs by an order of council of the 15th of July, 1735 had, it seems, been omitted in the proclamation issued 1733,[48] and such fees only thus omitted as had been settled by *any act of* assembly or *established* by any former order of council were allowed: fees allowed by such orders of council, cannot, perhaps, with strictness, be called increased fees, unless the former rates were increased, but the reasons already assigned, demonstrate, they are *new fees*. Had these services, to which fees were annexed by a subsequent proclamation, been totally omitted in all former orders of council and temporary acts, would such allowance of fees have been lawful or not? If lawful, it is plain, fees would in that case have been increased, being annexed to services never before provided for — If unlawful, it should seem, that the power, which at the original

---

[48] See above in Antilon's fourth letter, note 32.

creation of constitutional offices, might have annexed a fee to every service then enumerated, would be concluded, and might not annex fees to services not then enumerated, though actually performed by the officers; so that, whether an officer may lawfully receive a fee, does not depend on his doing the service, but on that service having been enumerated, and having had a fee annexed to it in the first settlement, or table of fees; but if under a right to receive fees co-eval with the institution of constitutional offices, the king or his deputies may settle fees, that is, ascertain what fees an officer shall take for doing a service, not having a settled or known fee annexed to it, then may government increase *ab libitum*[49] the amount of officers fees. Ingenuity will point out many services performed by old officers, that have no *settled fees* annexed to them, and the right to receive *such fees* being old and constitutional; the settlement of *such*, cannot according to Antilon's doctrine, be deemed an annexation of *new fees* to old offices.

Answer 11. "When the governor in 1692 undertook to regulate fees, there was an act of assembly for that purpose." The delegates did not object to the governor's undertaking to regulate fees, *because they were already regulated by law*. If that had been the real cause of the objection they would have declared it, to have precluded at once all controversy; but they objected upon this general principle — "that it is the undoubted right of the freemen of this province, that no officers fees ought to be imposed on them but by the consent of the representatives in assembly" — To which general position the *governor agreed*. The delegates produced several acts of parliament to shew, that government could not settle the fees of officers by prerogative; but if they relied on the act of assembly then in force, why did they not cite it? Where was the necessity of citing acts of parliament to prove what was already most clearly decided in their favour by a positive and subsisting law of the province? — The instances mentioned by Antilon of fees settled by proclamation prove only the actual exercise of an unlawful prerogative. The dangerous use which has so often been made of bad, should caution us against the hasty admission of even good precedents, which should always be meas-

[49] At pleasure.

ured by the principles of the constitution, and if found the least at variance, or inconsistent therewith, ought to be speedily abolished. "For millions entertain no other idea of the *legality* of power, than that it is founded on the exercise of power" (G). "There is nothing saith Swift, hath perplexed me more than this doctrine of precedents; if a job is to be done" (for instance a provision to made for officers), "and upon searching records, you find it hath been done before, there will not want a lawyer (an Antilon) to justify the legality of it, by producing his precedents, without ever considering the motives and circumstances that first introduced them, the necessity, or turbulence, or iniquity of the times, *the corruption of ministers*, or the arbitrary disposition of the prince then reigning."[50]

Answer 12. "It is not probable the fees of some officers will in time exceed the governor's income." Such an event is most probable. The governor's fees as chancellor, fall far short of the register's fees for recording the proceedings of the court, copies of bills, &c. The register pays his deputy 40 or £ 50 a year, and pockets fees to the amount of 50,000 pounds of tobacco, discharged in money at 12s6 per hundred pounds. Except the marriage licenses, all the other branches of the governor's revenue will probably decrease, or continue in their present state. The secretary's and commissary's fees must increase with the increase of business, the trouble and expence do not increase in proportion. The secretary has no trouble; the expence of this office is a mere trifle compared to his profits.

Having, at length waded through the argumentative part of my adversary's last paper, I am now come to the passages more immediately addressed to myself; for, Antilon still insists that I

(G) *Vide Pen. Farmer's 11th letter.*[51] *I recommend an attentive perusal of that letter to my countrymen; it abounds with judicious observations, pertinent to the present subject, and expressed with the utmost elegance, perspicuity, and strength.*

---

[50] Jonathan Swift, *The Drapiers Letters*, reprinted in *Prose Works* (Oxford: Basil Blackwell, 1959), 10:40.

[51] John Dickinson, *Letters From a Farmer in Pennsylvania to the Inhabitants of the British Colonies* (Philadelphia, 1769), letter 11:88.

have assistants, and confederates; silly, as my productions are, he will not allow me the demerit of being single in my folly. Formerly I was accused of confidence, and self conceit, now I am represented as begging from others, the little sense contained in my last piece.

Antilon can reconcile contradictions, and expound knotty points of law, just as they may suit him. —

> Veniet hic de plebe togata
> Qui juris nodos, et legum ænigmato solvat.[52]

You see, Sir, I take every opportunity of complimenting your abilities, somewhat at the expence of your integrity, I confess, but not of truth. The observation, that, an unlimited confidence in a bad minister will be assuredly abused — *"besides the merit of being true,"* has this further merit, *the application of it to Antilon was just.* He denies in the most direct terms the pernicious influence ascribed to him. The most notorious criminals seldomest plead guilty; the assertions of *one*, who has long ago forfeited all title to veracity, cannot be credited. I repeat the questions put to you in my last paper. Was the proclamation thought of by the whole council at the same instant? Who first advised the measure? Did you not privately instigate some member of the board to open the scene of action, while you lay lurking behind the curtain, ready to promote mischief, though unwilling to be thought the *first mover?*

Matters of a public concern are the objects of publick disquisition. When the real advisers of a measure, from the secrecy of the transaction, are unknown, we must look to the *ostensible minister;* if the *known* character of the *man*, should perfectly correspond with the *imputed* conduct, an assurance of the truth of the accusation instantly arises in the mind, far superior to the evidence grounded solely on his denial of the fact, and his most positive asservations of innocence, or *confe[5]derated guilt. "Many members of the council have already avowed the part they took in the measure"* — and pray what part did they take? that is the very thing we all want to know. If they acted only a secondary part, if

---

[52] Juvenal, *Satires* 8, 50. "From the crowd will come one that can solve the knots of law and the enigmas of the statutes."

mislead by your artful misrepresentations, and sophistical reasons, they coincided with your opinion, not the least degree of blame can be imputed to them. "They have expressed their resentment at the indignity of the imputation" — what imputation? that they were imposed on by your artifices; Are they the first, will they be the last, whom you have deceived? If any gentleman of the council has taken offence at what I have said, it must be owing, either to misapprehension, or to *your crafty suggestions*: I meant not to offend, it would grieve me

To make *one honest man* my foe.[53]

You still carp at the maxim, "*The king can do no wrong*," or rather at the application of it to the governor; the publick, and you more than anyone see the propriety of the application; the governor perhaps, when too late, may be sensible of it also, and wish that he had not placed a confidence, which he will hereafter discover has been abused, and may possibly give him many hours uneasiness. "*The Citizen is a wretch*," (says Antilon) "*haunted by envy and malice*" — Antilon has been already called upon for his proofs; the truth of the accusation rests intirely on his *ipse dixit*, which is at least presumptive evidence, that the accusation is false. Why Antilon am I suspected of bearing you malice? Have you injured me? Your suspicion implies a consciousness of guilt. What should excite my envy? The splendor of your family, your riches, or your talents? I envy you none of these; even your talents upon which you value yourself most, and for which only you are valued by others, are so tarnished by your meannesses, that they always suggest to my mind, the idea of a jewel buried in a dunghill. As we agree in the essential point, that the revolution was both just and necessary, it is needless to say more on the collateral question, whether the abdication followed or proceeded that measure; the dispute at best, is almost as insignificant as that about the words *abdicated*, and *deserted*, which disgraced the house of lords.[54] That the national religion was in danger under James the 2d, from

[53] Alexander Pope, *An Epistle from Mr. Pope, to Dr. Arbuthnot* (London, 1734), line 284.
[54] See the discussion in the introduction.

his bigotry and despotic temper, the dispensing power assumed by him, and every other part of his conduct clearly evince.

The nation had a *right* to *resist*, and to secure its civil and religious liberties. I am as averse to having a religion crammed down peoples throats, as a proclamation. These are my political principles, in which I glory; principles not hastily taken up to serve a turn, but what I have always avowed since I became capable of reflection. I bear not the least dislike to the church of England, though I am not within her pale, nor indeed to any other church; knaves, and bigots of all sects and denominations I hate, and I despise.

> For modes of faith let zealous bigots fight,
> His can't be wrong, whose life is in the right.[55]
>
> POPE

"Papists are distrusted by the laws, and laid under disabilities" — They cannot, I know (ignorant as I am), enjoy any place of profit, or trust, while they continue papists; but do these disabilities extend so far, as to preclude them from thinking and writing on matters merely of a political nature? Antilon would make a most excellent inquisitor, he has given some striking specimens of an arbitrary temper; the first requisite.

He will not allow me freedom of thought or speech. The resolves of a former assembly against certain religionists have been compared to the resolves against the proclamation. I again repeat, the unprejudiced will discern a wide difference between those resolves, and the spirit which occasioned them; it would be no difficult task to shew the disparity, but I choose not to meddle with a subject, the discussion of which may rekindle extinguished animosities. The contemptible comment on the expression — "*We remember and we forgive*," scarcely deserves animadversion. "This," says Antilon, "is rather too much in the imperial stile." The Citizen did not deliver his sentiment only but likewise the sentiment of others, *we* catholicks, who think we were hardly treated on that occasion, *we* still remember the treatment, though our

---

[55] Alexander Pope, *Essay on Man*, 3:305–6, printed in Pope's *Works* (Edinburgh, 1767), 2:216.

resentment hath intirely subsided. It is not in the least surprizing that a man incapable of forming an exalted sentiment, should not really comprehend the force and beauty of one. My exposition of the document of Minucius, as applied by you,[56] is warranted by the whole tenor, and purport of your publications. To what purpose was the threat thrown out of enforcing the penal statutes by proclamation? Why am I told that my conduct is very inconsistent with the situation of one, who "owes even the *toleration* he enjoys to the favour of government?" — If by instilling prejudices into the governor, and by every mean and wicked artifice you can rouse the popular resentment against certain religionists, and thus bring on a persecution of them, it will then be known whether the toleration I enjoy, be due to the favour of government, or not. That you have talents admirably well adapted to the works of darkness, malice to attempt the blackest, and meanness to stoop to the basest, is too true. The following lines convey an imperfect idea of your character:

> Him, there they found,
> Squat like a toad, close at the ear of Eve;
> Assaying, by his dev'lish art, to reach
> The organs of her fancy, and with them
> Forge illusions, as he lists.[57]
>
> —MILTON.

Impudence carried to a certain degree, excites indignation — pushed beyond it, becomes ridiculous. The Citizen's *scandalous misrepresentation* of Petyt is again insisted on. "*The Citizen referred to the jus parliamentarium, he knew the book was in the hands of few.*" If in your hands it was sufficient; he knew you exceedingly well inclined to expose his misrepresentations, ever upon the catch, and ready to lay hold of even mistakes and inaccuracies, and when acknowledged, still to harp upon them. The crude notions of British polity, which Antilon in a former paper imputed to the Citizen, were quoted as the notions of Montes-

---

[56] See p. 152 above.
[57] John Milton, *Paradise Lost*, 4:800–803, printed in Milton's *Works* (New York: Columbia University Press, 1931), 2:135.

quieu, enlarged upon, and explained by the writer of a pamphlet
on the privileges of the lower house of assembly in Jamaica; he
was apprized thereof in my last paper, and he calls this exculpa-
tion a *tiny evasion*. The notions whether crude or not, were not
the Citizen's; but I presume to assert, that so far from being *crude*,
they are judicious, and discover a perfect knowledge of our constitution.

"Hume's history is a studied apology for the Stuarts, particularly of Charles the first." Has the historian suppressed any material
facts? If not, but has given an artificial colouring to some, softened
others, and suggested plausible motives for the conduct of Charles,
all this serves to confirm the observation, that an account may in
the main be true, but not *intirely impartial*; the principal facts may
be related, yet the suppression of some attendant circumstance will
greatly alter their character and complexion. I asserted that the
constitution was not so well improved, and so settled in Charles's
time, as at present. In answer to this, Antilon remarks, that the
constitution was clearly settled in the very point infringed, by the
levy of ship-money. To this I reply, that the petition of right was
only a confirmation of former statutes against the same unconstitutional power, which had been assumed by most preceding kings in
direct violation of those statutes. To the imputation *"That you have
always fathered your mischievous tricks on others"* — you reply —
"roundly asserted, but what proof have you?" — sufficient to support the charge — the mask of hypocrisy, which you have worn so
long, is now falling off; the peoples eyes are at length opened; they
know the real author of their grievances; all *his efforts* to regain
lost popularity will be ineffectual? once distrusted, he will ever
remain so. A particular detail of all your *mean and dirty tricks*
would swell this paper (already too long) to the size of a volume.
I may on some future occasion entertain the publick with Antilon's
cheats.

Flebit, & insignis tota cantabitur urbe.[58]

They would discredit even a Scapin, and therefore must not be
blended with a question of this serious and general importance.
You have said, *"You do not believe me to be a man of honour or*

[58] Horace, *Sermons*, 2, 1, 46.

veracity." It gives me singular satisfaction that you do not, for a man destitute of *one*, must be void of the *other*, and cannot be a judge of *either*. Your mode of expression, which in general is clear and precise, in this instance discovers a confusion of ideas, to which you are not often liable; but you have stumbled on a subject of which you have not the least conception.

Verbaque provisam rem non invita sequentur.[59]

If once the mind with clear conceptions glow,
The willing words in just expressions flow.

Honour, or *veracity*! Are they then distinct things? Do you imagine that they can exist separately? No, they are most intimately connected; who wants *veracity* wants *principle*, *honour* of course, and resembles Antilon.

FIRST CITIZEN

[59] Horace, *Ars Poetica*, line 311.

Index

THE JOHNS HOPKINS UNIVERSITY PRESS

This book was composed in Janson text and Bank Script display type by Maryland Linotype Composition Company, Inc., from a design by Victoria Dudley. It was printed on Warren's 60-lb. Sebago, regular finish, text color stock and bound in Columbia Mills Bayside Linen by The Maple Press Company.

Library of Congress Cataloging in Publication Data

Dulany, Daniel, 1722–1797.
  Maryland and the Empire, 1773.
  (Maryland bicentennial studies)
  Dulany's "Antilon" letters and Carroll's "First
citizen" replies first appeared in the Maryland
gazette, Jan.–July 1773.
    1. Maryland—Politics and government—Colonial
period, ca. 1600–1775—Sources. 2. Maryland—
Constitutional history—Sources. 3. Dulany, Daniel,
1722–1797. 4. Carroll, Charles, 1737–1832.
I. Carroll, Charles, 1737–1832. II. Maryland gazette.
III. Title. IV. Series.
F184.D825 1974   975.2′02′0922   73–8128
ISBN 0–8018–1547–9